MY LIFE AS A WIFE

Love, Liquor and What to Do About Other Women

ELISABETH LUARD

BLOOMSBURY

LONDON • NEW DELHI • NEW YORK • SYDNEY

First published by Timewell Press 2008
This paperback edition published 2013

Bloomsbury Publishing Plc
50 Bedford Square
London WC1B 3DP

Bloomsbury Publishing, London, New Delhi, New York and Sydney

www.bloomsbury.com

A CIP catalogue record for this book is available from the British Library

ISBN 978 1 4088 3125 0
10 9 8 7 6 5 4 3 2 1

Typeset by MPS Limited
Printed and Bound in Great Britain by CPI (UK) Ltd, Croydon CR0 4YY

www.bloomsbury.com/elisabethluard

In memory of my father
Wing Commander Richard Maitland Longmore,
MBE, DSO, DFC.
(1917–1943)

ACKNOWLEDGEMENTS

THANKS ARE DUE TO MAGNUS LINKLATER AND *THE TIMES* FOR permission to include Nicholas Luard's obituary. And for advice and support over the years to: my sister-in-law Priscilla White, sister Marianna Falconer, best friend Venetia Parkes, Christopher and Rosemary Logue, Michael and Victoria Hastings, Elspeth Vernon and Holly Rumbold (style-queens of Hollywood Road), Humphry and Katherine Wakefield, Richard and Virginia Storey, Milet Delme Radcliffe, Hugh Millais, Dominick Elwes, the great and unforgettable Miriam Rothschild, Denis and Jenny Mollison, Magnus and Veronica Linklater, David Grenfell and (late, lamented companions in the desert and elsewhere) David Towill and Bobby Hesketh. And most particularly to my good friend, broadcaster and writer Jen Skiff, recipient and saver of emails during the worst of times, for encouragement to share bad days as well as good. To cousin Sue Casacia for introducing me to the American branch of my mother's family. To my late aunt Janet Worth for stories of my father's family. To Drusilla

Beyfus for supplying me with a reason to write this book: a copy of her interview with Nicholas and myself published in *The English Marriage* in 1968. To my agent Abner Stein for far more than I could ever list. To publisher Gerard Noel for allowing me to write the book I wanted to write, and copy-editor Chris Parker for care and attention when undeniably needed. And above all, to my children and grandchildren for tolerance and unconditional love.

Contents

PREFACE

Obituary in *The Times*, 28 May 2004, by Magnus Linklater

NICHOLAS LUARD

Impeccable subversive who kicked against the establishment and then protected the environment

IT WAS CHARACTERISTIC OF THE EX-PUBLIC SCHOOL, OXBRIDGE-educated generation which launched the satire movement in Britain in the 1960s that Nicholas Luard, who was at the heart of it, should have been himself a Wykehamist, former Guards officer and Cambridge graduate. Behind these impeccable credentials lurked a fully paid-up subversive.

Satire in those days was daring in a way that is now hard to comprehend. The Establishment Club in Soho, which Luard co-founded with Peter Cook, mocked every convention of a very conventional period. As he himself said later: 'Authority was everything: you disobeyed any form of it, from a schoolmaster to a doctor, at your peril.'

Yet, on the stage of the tiny, smoke-filled former strip-club in Greek Street, no holds were barred. Lenny Bruce, the American comedian, poured out his corrosive lampoons. John Bird, John Fortune and Eleanor Bron dissected class, sex and religion. The cast of *Beyond the Fringe* – Cook himself, Jonathan Miller, Dudley Moore and Alan Bennett – experimented with ideas more daring than anything they could put on in a conventional theatre. The poet Christopher Logue wrote lyrics for the jazz singer Annie Ross. Upstairs, Gerald Scarfe exhibited merciless cartoons of political figures.

Luard was never a performer himself, but he could and did help to turn ideas into reality: during the brief satire boom, he funded and ran The Establishment, went on, with Cook, to buy *Private Eye*, published an arts magazine, invented poetry posters with Logue, opened another social club, and ran a production company which at one point employed 81 people in his cramped Soho premises. Richard Ingrams described him as 'the Brian Epstein of the satire boom ... the only satirist to wear a suit'.

But Luard was not much of a businessman. Members of The Establishment were offered £50 credit, and some fell into the habit of cashing cheques for £50 at each of the bars every night of the week. There were also demands for protection money from gangsters. When The Establishment closed, and after he had sold his interest in *Private Eye*, Luard continued to back causes. He helped refugees from the apartheid regime in South Africa; launched the first London Marathon with Christopher Brasher; campaigned, with Laurens van der Post, for the conservation of the Kalahari Desert; and founded the John Muir Trust which bought up threatened areas of Scottish wilderness. Passionate about Africa and Spain, he wrote extensively and well about both. 'He wanted to change things that needed changing,' said a friend. 'He was less bothered about how he got that done.'

A life that was often beset by financial problems, by family tragedy, and a long battle with alcoholism was nevertheless illuminated by courage, humour and an unquestionable sense of adventure.

Nicholas Lamert Luard was born in London, but was taken as a child to Teheran, where his father, Jock McVean Luard, a Scot from the island of Mull, was manager of BP's oil interests. His mother, Susan, was a Lamert, whose father's wealth stemmed from the de la Rue printing company. It was a legacy from him which Nicholas later used to back The Establishment. Both sides of his family were of Huguenot stock, a fact that Luard always regarded as important.

His parents split up during the war, and Nicholas and his sister were brought back to Britain by their mother, who stopped off for six months in Kenya, instilling in the young Nicholas his taste for Africa. Brought up by a succession of nannies, he was educated at Winchester, which he claimed to dislike but from where he won a place at Magdalene College, Cambridge. National Service with the Guards intervened, taking him to Krefeld in Germany in 1956, a tense time in Europe after the Hungarian uprising, when Luard took unofficial leave to help refugees crossing into Austria.

At Cambridge he read English under F. R. Leavis, was treasurer of the Footlights (where he got to know Peter Cook), became president of the Pitt Club, and boxed for the university as a light welterweight.

He spent a year in America, where he taught poetry at Philadelphia University, after which he and Cook decided to press ahead with what Cook called 'a shadowy fragment of an idea' for a satirical club based on cabarets they had seen in Germany. The early success of The Establishment coincided with *That Was the Week That Was* and the founding of *Private Eye*, which they bought in 1962.

But financial problems multiplied. A Lenny Bruce tour was cancelled when his entry to Britain was barred by the Home Office, and the *Eye* was sued by Randolph Churchill – its first writ. This was served while Luard was on honeymoon with his wife, Elisabeth Longmore, who worked on the paper's staff, and was the stepdaughter of the British Minister in Mexico. A hurried return managed to salvage the situation, but Luard decided to sell his share of *Private Eye* to Cook, before the company went into liquidation.

Luard now severed his links with satire, beginning a writing career and a peripatetic life which was to continue throughout his marriage to Elisabeth. They moved to Spain, where they built a house near Algeciras and stayed for nine years, bringing up their children there. For a year they lived in Auberon Waugh's house in the Languedoc, then London, the isle of Mull, and finally Wales. In all these places he wrote – first thrillers, then travel books and longer novels, while Elisabeth became a celebrated writer on cookery.

Luard based *The Warm and Golden War* on his experience in Hungary, *Andalucia* on his time in southern Spain, and, after a wildly ambitious and hazardous journey across the Kalahari with Elisabeth and several friends, he wrote his best travel book, *The Last Wilderness*, as well as two novels, the second of which, *Gondar*, enjoyed considerable commercial success. Later, a climbing trip to Nepal resulted in *Himalaya*.

Always athletic, he and his friend Chris Brasher ran the New York Marathon together in 1979, and two years later, Luard helped him to launch the London equivalent, and gave the commentary on the first race.

His growing interest in conservation issues led him, in 1981, to found the John Muir Trust, with Nigel Hawkins, a journalist and Professor Denis Mollison, an academic. The idea was to raise money to buy up and protect unspoilt areas of Scotland, safeguarding the livelihoods of those who lived there. Today it owns large parts of the Cuillin Hills, Ben Nevis, and other fragile places, and is the second largest landowner in Scotland. The trust's also active in Wales.

A confirmed romantic, Luard liked nothing more than embarking on adventurous and frequently perilous journeys. Witty, occasionally acerbic, curious about his fellow human beings, and serious about his religious faith, he had a wide and eclectic circle of friends. In 1991, tragedy struck when his daughter Francesca was found to be suffering from Aids. Luard dealt with the crisis by embarking on a pilgrimage to Santiago de Compostella, and writing a book about it, *The Field of the Star.* 'One expresses hope through prayer,' he said at the time. 'I knew God could not save Fran, no power could save her. At the same time one was left with hope. There is a conflict, but I believe the human mind can accommodate it.' Fran died 18 months later.

In 2000 Luard was found to be suffering from cancer and was given a liver transplant. His death followed a recurrence. His wife and three remaining children survive him. *Nicholas Luard, writer and environmentalist, was born on 26 June 1937, died 25 May 2004.*

INTRODUCTION

THIS IS THE STORY OF MY LIFE AS A WIFE. OR HOW TO STAY MARRIED for forty years without actually murdering your husband. A love story.

Marriage, after all, is nothing out of the ordinary. People do it all the time, some of us – in the hope that things will work out better next time or because we lose our partner for some other reason – more than once.

Forty years ago, I thought it'd all be worth it. And maybe it was. But we never did reach the sunlit uplands, my beloved and I. True love was never a match for the bottle. And Nicholas was never a man who did things by halves. For the record, he said, he'd never have made it as far as he had if he hadn't had me.

What more can anyone ask? Plenty, actually. Anger is the first thing most of us feel when someone we love dies before we're ready. And with reason. Abandonment, regret for what might have been and now will never be. Loneliness. But these things pass. Death comes to us all.

In *Family Life*, the other side of our story, I told a tale of a mother, a mostly absent father and four children who grew up in wild and beautiful places, one of whose number died of Aids, the disease of our time. My intention here is to tell the story of a long and sometimes turbulent marriage, longer than most but shorter than some, which survived till death did us part. A marriage which, like most marriages, was neither good nor bad but somewhere in between. I've tried to tell the truth – given that truth, along with laughter and sadness and all the things that make us who we are, is whatever we believe it to be at the time.

As a food writer by trade, I write recipes, though other things as well: sometimes travel, a couple of doorstopper novels, a pair of autobiographies. All include cooking. I can't help myself. My children say it's a control-thing. They may be right. I agree that I write about cooking because food does what I tell it to do. Nothing else in my life has ever done that. Give me a larder, a knife and a heat-source, and whatever it is, it'll work. Family – well, no one controls what happens in families. People are born, they live, and they die – and most of us hope that what we do in life will endure beyond our own mortality.

Cooking is my personal short-cut to happiness. Cooking, it seems to me, is a universal language, a way of sharing the good things of life with strangers as well as friends. In a household in Turkey or Morocco or anywhere on the southern shores of the Mediterranean, you will be offered a little spoonful of something sweet as soon as you step through the door – a mouthful of sweetness to sweeten the talk.

When I am asked what I do for a living, and I explain that I write about food and cookery, I know perfectly well that I am admitting to what many would consider a frivolous occupation. Not worth discussing in the same breath as art or literature or politics – ranking somewhere beneath sex as a proper subject for serious attention.

Usually I hold my peace. But sometimes I feel impelled to point out that food is the *only* serious subject. Everything else is mere frippery, the frills on the apron of life. It is to fill the breadbasket that men make war, foment revolution, seek to conquer new lands. I don't need to point out that Leif Ericsson was in pursuit of the cod shoals when he bumped into Newfoundland. Or that it was the urgent need to satisfy her people's craving for Eastern spices that prompted Isabella of Spain to fund Columbus's voyages. Or that one might argue that the Vietnam war was all about control of the rice bowl, the Mekong Delta. Or indeed, that the wars over oil supplies are all about cheap transport and petro-chemicals to fertilize the soil: with our food routes now trans-continental, low-priced fuel has become economically essential.

Trade route means food route, and with much of our food supplies now transported halfway across the world, this is as true today as it ever was. Cookery – home cooking and the traditions of the domestic hearth – lies at the heart of that which makes us different from our neighbours. We remain instinctively tribal, and often identify other 'tribes' by referring to what we perceive, usually impolitely, as their preferred diet. There is truth in this: we do indeed smell of what we eat, however much we muffle our olfactory nerves. And we all know what we mean when we use the expression 'it doesn't smell right'. Food taboos – voluntary abstentions and religious dietary laws – serve to reinforce this sense of belonging. This is not all bad news. Knowing who you are, taking pride in the traditions of the community, can make us kindly and hospitable, able to be generous to strangers.

The Chinese never discuss serious matters at table: you may talk of the state of the cherry blossom, but never the state of the nation. My sister, a year or two back at an official banquet in Beijing – she's a senior barrister herself and married to a former high-ranking member of the Labour government – found herself seated next to an important Chinese official. 'And how, in Your Excellency's esteemed opinion,' she enquired with diplomatic *politesse*, 'is the policy of one-child families proceeding in the rural regions?' Her host, who'd shown a remarkable mastery of English until that moment, suddenly lost his fluency and the rest of the meal, all twenty-two courses of it from bird's-nest soup to thousand-year-old eggs, was completed in silence.

Even when I'm alone, I cook to please myself. Actually, I do more than cook, I prepare miniature feasts, choosing serving-dishes with care, adding a spoonful of this, a sprinkle of that to finish the dish. Much as other women would not dream of leaving the house without lipstick, eyeliner and a touch of pink along the cheekbone, I won't sit down to a meal unless the table is well dressed. Nothing grand, mind you, but pretty enough to gladden the heart.

It came to me early in life, no more than six years on the planet, that the most valuable thing one person can do for another is cook. I can well understand why women in other cultures prefer to serve their men and retire to enjoy their meal elsewhere. In this I may well be a creature of my time – the post-war years, as it happens, since I was born in the 1940s. As the nation recovered from the shortages at the end of the hostilities (I was three years old at the end of the war, already fatherless), we, the war babies, were still taught, as generations of mothers had taught their daughters, that the way to a man's heart was through his stomach. And most of us still believed it.

Things never work out as they should. I acquired the necessary skills, then married a man who found his happiness in a bottle. Red wine mostly, though forays into the whisky were not unknown. Did liquor make Nicholas happy? Who can say? Sometimes, sometimes not. What's certain is that it killed him. The genes were good: both his parents lived well into their nineties. Nature was on his side: his body was strong; of average height (I topped him by an inch or two when wearing heels), wiry and tough throughout his life, with well-formed muscular limbs, broad chest, a weightlifter's shoulders, a prizefighter's stamina.

As a young National Serviceman, Nicholas boxed for his regiment well above his weight, at university he pulled an oar for his Cambridge college; by his forties he had made three crossings of the Kalahari Desert, in his fifties he ran three marathons and a double, the Cape Town Vets. But by his sixtieth birthday, the liver was shot to pieces and the body could take no more.

The story, of course, is that all writers fuel their work with drink. All their heroes did the same: Hemingway, Fitzgerald, Dylan Thomas, Kingsley Amis. Maybe Shakespeare was a drunk and he too dead before his time. Or blind Homer, spinning his tales of gods and men, perhaps he too drank too much of the blood-red wine by the wine-dark sea.

Writers' wives – those of us with families dependent on an author's earnings – never pass a typewriter without anxiety. Just hit those keys, I'd say. I don't care whether it's the alphabet or *War and Peace*, I need to hear the noise.

My own anxiety, in the early years of marriage, led to a return to gainful employment as soon as I was able. My secretarial skills – typing, shorthand, book-keeping – were of little use in the marketplace while my children still needed me at home. I could, of course, type up Nicholas's elegant hand-written manuscripts ready for submission to a publisher, but this was scarcely a money-spinner. And anyway, once we had taken up residence in a remote valley in the Andalusian hinterland, there wasn't an office for miles.

But I could draw. By which I mean I can transfer a three-dimensional image to a one-dimensional surface neatly and accurately in a form that appeals to those who like their pictures to match the wallpaper. My skill was marketable. There were people who'd buy botanically accurate watercolours of flowers and anatomically correct paintings of birds and who'd encourage their friends to commission something similar. In no time at all, I'd found a market. My happiest moment was the sale of a painting of a vulture to a buyer who mistook it for an eagle. I admire the vulture. It cleans up other people's messes. Eagles, well, they're the warrior class and I've always had trouble with war.

Nicholas admired the warrior trade. He'd been a warrior himself, running refugees out of Hungary in the bloody uprising of 1956. And though still a schoolgirl, I knew of the struggle. Later in life, as a trailblazing conservationist, he had no trouble shooting a stag. I, happily for our relationship, never had a problem cooking it. I'll even skin it and chop it if I have to, though I'd rather deal with a rabbit.

Roll back the years to 1968. A fashionable young couple, five years married, are interviewed among some twenty others for a national newspaper on the changing state of couplehood in what's by now considered a bit old hat: Swinging London.

As members of the permissive society, asked the journalist, how were we coping with the state of wedlock? Mick Jagger defines the age, Germaine Greer is teaching us how to liberate ourselves as women, Kinsey has just published his report, men and women are as bisexual as they please, and those of us who are married with children – or unmarried and with children nonetheless – are doing the best we can. Under the circumstances, that is. And under the circumstances, most of us have to admit that circumstance doesn't favour us right now.

But if wild is what we're doing, are we having fun?

Some of us are, some of us aren't.

Most of our identities are masked, names and addresses changed, though since many of us are known to each other and no doubt to others from the gossips, reading between the lines it's not very hard to work out which couple is which.

The journalist who asked the questions, Drusilla Beyfuss, published the edited transcripts in one of the first of the colour supplements, the *Telegraph*'s Saturday magazine. On publication day – our pseudonyms were Simon and Carey – I flipped through the interviews, his and hers, without much thought. I remember only that I'd felt a pang of irritation at the illustrator's idea of how I dressed, since twinset-and-pearls was never my style.

And then I forgot all about it. Until, not long widowed, walking in the garden of the farmhouse in Wales where Nicholas spent the last years of his life and I now live and work and enjoy the visits of my grandchildren, there floated into my head something chosen by the interviewer as a conclusion.

There were other things which must have been a bit of a disappointment: 'She has an income from a trust fund. One day

I guess she will be a very rich girl, she must be, I can't see how she can help it.'

Nicholas was wrong. My mother's money came from her great-grandfather, Bernard Baron, founder in the 1880s of the family fortune, and was held in trust for her children. My mother managed to break the trust in the early 1960s at a time when the family business was in turmoil and she needed to sell her shares. Permission was granted by the courts on condition that she handed over a certain proportion of the money to her heirs. 'It's not much now,' she said to me at the time. 'The rest will come later.' In the event, she left what remained of her fortune to the children of her second husband. What's done is done. Nothing creates more bitterness in families than quarrels over money.

I recognize much in the interviews that remained true to the end. Nicholas, when asked if he thought the marriage would last, replied, 'We'll stay together because we're stronger than most other people. It's as simple as that.'

The marriage was never simple. Marriages never are. There's compromise and accommodation and forgiveness and patience and the need not to apportion blame. Above all, there's patience. And in all the years I never doubted – well, not for long – that it would all come right in the end. Only a moment or two that I didn't believe with all my heart there'd come the day when we'd reach the land where dreams come true.

Some of us reach the sunlit uplands, some of us struggle to reach the foothills, some of us give up altogether. How was it for those who love each other all their lives with never a moment's regret, those gentle folk who go hand in hand into the sunset – was it as hard for them?

Nicholas was fourteen when Dylan Thomas bought him his first drink, though I never knew where or why or what it was that allowed such a thing to happen. The poet was a man for darkness of the soul: *Do not go gentle into that good night, / Old age should burn and rave at close of day; / Rage, rage, against the dying of the light.*

Old age escaped him, though not the rage. There were times when I knew the anger was there, though I never understood the cause. Unless it was mortality itself, the despair that comes to a man when he understands that all things must pass.

'I don't think,' he said in the interview with Dru Beyfuss, 'that Elisabeth would support me if I was in the wrong. Her moral judgements are based on a code of values she has worked out for herself. She is also,' he added, 'a very, very tough girl, in terms of being resilient and courageous.'

Perhaps that's true. I am indeed resilient. And I agree that very little frightens me. This, the story of my life as a wife, is no disaster movie. Give or take a train smash or two, I'm not complaining. I've had more than my share of happiness. Still do. If we're allotted three loves in our lives – first love, great love, last love – the last is the least expected. Grandchildren are, after all, my children's children, not really mine at all. And yet the connection is direct. Love is all it takes to bind a child, nothing else required.

This is the story of a lifetime. Two lifetimes, one of which ended long before it should. Nicholas, it's fair to say, was always ahead of his time. And we never did reach the sunshine on the hilltops, my sweetheart and I.

A love story is not the way I thought it would be when I first began to write. A little rough around the edges – imperfect, untidy – this is a love story like any other love story. Love given and love received; we shared a life.

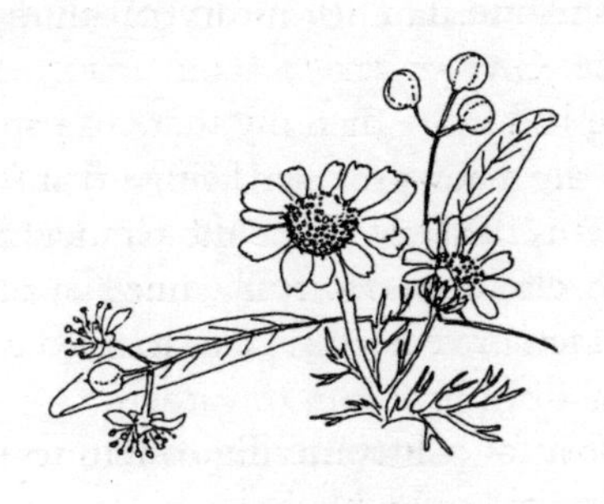

PART ONE

26 APRIL 2004 THERE'S A BIRTHDAY IN THE FAMILY. THE GRANDCHILDREN have planned a party in our little square of garden, a celebration.

Celebrations are hard to find these days.

We are in London for the time it takes. Wales is no longer possible. We cannot live too far from help. We have borrowed a basement flat in Fulham Road. The house itself belongs to friends. The place is only minutes from the hospital, and we're grateful.

Double doors give access to a square of lawn enclosed by walls. Sunlight falls on grass through trees. Across the wall is the Brompton Cemetery. On good days, when Nicholas is feeling strong, we walk among the gravestones, measuring the distance, calculating without words what the distance covered means, taking pleasure in the birds which crop the tangled seedheads on the grave plots.

We walk slowly, increasingly slowly.

For the birthday tea, I've baked a cake. It's iced in pink and stuck with little candles, one for each year past, an extra for the year to come. Life goes on. We're alive until we're dead. Nicholas's sixty-seventh birthday is still a month away. I fear – sometimes hope – he will not last that long.

Movement from room to room is hard. There's need of a wheelchair. Community Nursing refuses our request. Not yet.

Not yet?

I know what they mean. They mean that things have not yet gone far enough.

They're wrong.

We have, however, been provided with a commode.

The commode has wheels. Once the pan has been discreetly tucked inside the seat, it becomes a wheelchair. Slowly we go through the movements necessary to transfer a ruined body from bed to chair, from bedroom to garden.

We rest in the little courtyard, impossible to move up steps to grass.

Nicholas, my husband of more than forty years, marathon runner, ex-boxer, the most beautiful man I ever saw, is rake-thin, grey-skinned, sunken-shouldered, lacking muscle or even strength to lift his head.

This is what happens at the end.

And we are close now. I know we're close. Most days I think I'm the only one who knows how close.

We are moving into twilight. Not yet dark, but no longer daylight.

CHAPTER ONE

Long, Long Ago

> *'For my belief is ... that if we have £500 a year each of us and rooms of our own; if we have the habit of freedom and the courage to write exactly what we think; if we escape a little from the common sitting-room and see human beings not always in their relation to each other but in relation to reality; if we face the fact that there is no arm to cling to ... the dead poet who was Shakespeare's sister [and who never wrote a word] will put on the body which she has so often laid down. Drawing her life from the lives of the unknown who were her forerunners, as her brother did before her, she will be born.'*
>
> VIRGINIA WOOLF, *A Room of One's Own* (1929)

WE MET, MY BELOVED AND I, IN THE BACK-OFFICES OF *PRIVATE EYE* some time around Issue 11. He the proprietor, I the office typist. As soon as Nicholas walked in, I had no doubt whatsoever that this was the man of my dreams. Whether or not the object of my affection realized this at the time, I have no way of knowing. I made no secret of my intentions. Well – I was young and knew no better.

How did I court my beloved? I cooked for him, what else?

Private Eye was housed in a warehouse in Neal Street, on the edge of Soho. A brisk walk from the 19 bus took me through the Brewer Street Market and along Old Compton Street. On every corner and tucked away down every alleyway, was what I most missed in life, the flavours and scents of the Mediterranean. Soho was the busiest red-light district in town – still is – and perhaps because of this it was also one of the safest places in the city. The Soho manor was run by bent coppers and East End villains: the Krays and the Richardsons. Both coppers and villains respected a young woman's right to walk through the streets on legitimate business without molestation, provided she wasn't a professional. And anyone could tell a professional at first glance. Well, almost.

In Soho – the square mile bordered on one side by Oxford Street and on the other by Shaftesbury Avenue – you could find Italian pasta of every shape and size, and the pearly little round-grain rices which swelled in a broth and were just as perfect for paella as they were for a risotto, though the two, it seemed to me, were pretty much the same. The shelves were stacked with glistening bottles of greeny-golden olive oil and jewel-coloured wine vinegars. On the floor stood sacks of multi-coloured beans, dun-coloured chickpeas and dusty brown lentils. And for the price of a smile, a chunk of ham bone might be thrown in for free.

Fresh Mediterranean vegetables could be bought only in season, but all year round there were preserved tomatoes in jars, artichokes under oil, preserved fish from the barrel. There were, too, wonderful cheeses – parmesan and brie, camembert and roquefort, mozzarella for a home-made pizza.

Soho suited the way I'd always loved to eat. I cooked chicken with peppers, beans with chorizo, purées of aubergine flavoured with cumin – but only in private. In public, I took care to keep my foreign ways to myself.

Then Elizabeth David published *Mediterranean Food* and everyone started talking about garlic and olive oil and how good food tasted when cooked with wine instead of water. This came as a surprise to me. Certainly Mrs David's writing made you want to cook the dishes she described, but the recipes, it seemed to me, were so simple, so everyday and normal, they needed no instruction.

It wasn't just that Elizabeth David was a serious cook, she was a scholar. She was respectable. She had learned her craft from Norman Douglas, a writer much admired among the literary mafia. Until she published the books which made her name, only foreigners talked about food. And if you talked about food – or worse, confessed that you cooked foreign food – you couldn't really be English. School food had been truly terrible. Spam fritters were the worst, though Monday mince came close. The bread tasted of sawdust and came sliced in a packet. How on earth could a person mop a plate or use it as a scoop when the stuff fell to bits in your fingers? They didn't. No one used bread as a mopper or a scoop. They left it till it was stale and spread it with margarine and if you were lucky you might be allowed a knife blade of thick red stuff which was supposed to taste of strawberries but didn't.

Mrs David changed all that. At a stroke, I wasn't a foreigner at all. I was fashionable. So I cooked not just for me, but for everyone else I knew. Every week, always on the same day, I declared open house at eight o'clock – no need for invitations. And if I invited a young man who took my fancy, he joined the group without commitment. Girls who made the first move were considered bold little madams – unthinkable that a woman should pay her share in a restaurant, or worse, pay the bill herself. Dinner parties were the way our parents entertained their friends, social occasions, no commitment. And afterwards, we might go dancing at the Four Hundred in Leicester Square, or the Blue Room, the nightclub in the Berkeley Hotel where elegant young men with double-barrelled names played piano and sang medleys from *The Boy Friend*.

The plot bore fruit. I cooked the kind of dishes I loved to eat myself: Spanish chicken with lemon, French rabbit with mustard, Greek pork with cinnamon, Provençal beef with cloves, lamb with quince. And afterwards, the beautiful young man I was engaged in courting owned a nightclub, providing me with the perfect excuse for spending long hours in his company.

Meanwhile, at *Private Eye*, where I worked all day, contact between the new proprietor and the office secretary was strictly business as usual. Office romance was out. Office romance – boss and secretary jokes – were meat and drink to the *Eye* boys, the oldest cliché in the book.

*****

Many have told of the early years of *Private Eye*, how it was first published, a scrappy yellow rag, bastard offspring of *Parson's Pleasure*, a schoolboy jape. All I have to add is that I went to work there for five pounds a week in 1962, soon after the first issues appeared. The first proprietor, the man who offered me the job, was Andrew Osmond – handsome, charming man-about-town, every maiden's dream – not mine, I hasten to add, my interests lay elsewhere.

Andrew had been an officer in the Gurkhas, he was clever and sophisticated and all the things the young men of my acquaintance were not. Since he was shortly to take up far more respectable employment at the Foreign Office and the *Eye* was in need of working capital, he sold most of his shares to the co-proprietors of London's first (and only) satirical nightclub, The Establishment. Peter Cook didn't think much of the *Eye* at the time – and anyway, he was busy with other things – but Nicholas went ahead.

The editor in those days was Christopher Booker. Christopher wrote the serious stuff, the political stories no one else would print. Cartoons and a peculiar genius for spotting the absurd were supplied by Willie Rushton. Richard Ingrams wrote most of the irreverent stuff which caught the *Zeitgeist*. The print order hovered around ten thousand, not enough to pay the bills. Even so, even in the early days, everyone who was anyone read it.

The weakness of the magazine was distribution. Moore Harness, our distributors, were specialists in top-shelf magazines. Which was all very well in Soho, but meant that no respectable newsagent, offered a title which indicated keyhole-peeping by distributors best known for unclad ladies, would touch it.

Subscribers accounted for about half the print order. Other outlets were specialist bookshops in university towns and London's literary bookshops – all too few, then as now. Foyles was our only major outlet, with Bernard Stone at Turret Books in Notting Hill accounting for the majority of the rest. Literary and specialist bookshops paid their bills well after the due date, sometimes never – as I knew well enough, since it was I who collected the money. My duties were strictly secretarial. I wrote up the accounts, sent out invoices and paid bills whenever there was anything to pay them with, and typed up the copy for the printer. The other office girl, Mary Morgan – on her way to becoming Mrs Richard Ingrams – couldn't type at all.

As soon as the magazines came back from the printer, anyone foolish enough to volunteer took a bundle and sold them for cash on the street. My favourite beat was Cambridge Circus in the company of performance poet Irwin Corey, a skinny little fellow with shoulder-length grey hair who looked as if he slept under a railway bridge and called himself the Professor.

'University of Honolulu, grass skirt division,' he'd explain when challenged, waving a bony hand. The Prof had taken to arriving at the office first thing in the morning for a wash and brush-up.

The Prof's sales technique involved taking up a commanding position on the kerb and rolling up one trouser leg, exposing an unsavoury length of scarlet sock, yellow sock suspender and hairy shin. He would then jump out into the traffic in the path of an oncoming vehicle, waving his exposed extremity in much the same way as Long John Silver might wield a wooden leg.

'Stop, you bastards! Help!'

If the trick was successful, the anxious driver, fearing he'd inflicted injury, would wind down the window and come to a halt. As the Prof's accomplice, I had to leap forward and thrust the magazine through the open window while the Professor demanded the money.

Needless to say, the hit rate was low.

*****

I was born in London during the Blitz. A little mistake, said my mother, a product of the reproductive panic that grips women in wartime. Not much of a start, you might think. There were two of us, my brother and I, born at the wrong time to a mother with enough of a fortune to see her through a lifetime and a father dead for his country.

We, the daughters of wartime, reached adulthood at the end of the 1950s, a decade in which rationing was still in place, television was limited and in any event was in black and white, and the world was run by the survivors of two world wars. For all that we invented the Beatles, lusted after the Rolling Stones and marched to ban the bomb, we had no confidence in our power to change the way we lived our lives. Rich or poor, we were the second sex. Our future was mapped out from birth: marriage and babies constituted our destiny, and the sooner the better.

The generation that followed us found the answers to the questions we were asking. They were the ones who went to San Francisco and wore flowers in their hair. The ones who smoked wacky baccy and wrote the manuals on how to get lucky or happy or find the g-spot or whatever it was that got you where you wanted to be to do your own thing.

And if that's not clear, you were born too early or too late and can never expect to get there. Which doesn't mean that we were a generation of know-nothings saving ourselves for marriage. The very reverse. We had the pill, were canny enough to get hold of it, and knew enough to know that virginity got you nowhere.

Which was exactly what got me into the situation in which I found myself, married and pregnant, though not, I must admit, in the right order. Some seven months after marriage, I had a baby. A year after that I had another. Seven years passed, and finally there were four – a story told in an earlier tale of life and love and what it means to be a mother with no real idea of how to behave.

How could I have known? As a young woman with no father and a mother whose attention was concentrated elsewhere, I had no experience – still less a blueprint – of how a family should function.

Our mother was rich, we lacked for nothing that money could buy. In later years, when family friends would say that they had pitied us when we were children, I'd say we were the beneficiaries of benign neglect. Nothing wrong with neglect, provided it's benign.

My earliest memories have little to do with family and much to do with food. I remember the taste of blackberries from the hedge, a little dusty and warm from the sun, the sourness of sorrel, the oniony taste of hedge garlic, the salt in samphire picked from the sand dunes.

My father was a pilot in the RAF, Wing Commander Richard Maitland Longmore. He was the son of an airman himself – Air Chief Marshal Sir Arthur Longmore, a pioneer of the First World War. My early years were spent on the Norfolk Broads, near where my father's squadron was posted when war broke out. For my brother and me, my mother employed a young girl from the village to take us for walks in the countryside while the rest of the servants got on with the real business of the household: entertaining her husband's brother-officers to elegant dinner parties.

After our father was listed missing-in-action – a euphemism for gone-for-good – my mother moved the whole household (except the village girl, the first in a long line of abandoned nursemaids) back into her mother's house on the outskirts of London. Hedgerow gatherings were replaced by suet dumplings and Victory meatloaf.

There were occasional treats. I remember the gritty texture of real butter icing made with granulated sugar – I kept the leftovers wrapped in a screw of paper, squirrelled away inside the piano till the mice found them and that was that. I remember, too, the chewiness of dried bananas, the sugary crunch of pressed dates; the sweet oily scent that lingered under my fingernails after I had eaten my first orange.

In wartime, nothing was ever thrown away, a lesson I never forgot and which came in useful later in my life. There were times when my own children could recognize a leftover at forty paces – as a preliminary, it must be admitted, to taking evasive action.

Wartime menus had logic as well as predictability. The Sunday roast (rare, unless someone had been busy on the black market) meant cold-cuts on Monday, cottage pie on Tuesday. If Wednesday was bacon and cabbage, Thursday was bubble-and-squeak.

Skinning a chicken or trimming the fat on meat to reduce the calories would have been tantamount to treason. Still is, if you ask me. It's as plain as the nose on your face that the less you eat the thinner you get. A couple of weeks in a famine zone does the trick just fine. Refugee camps are full of very thin people – a point which would seem obvious from watching news bulletins showing overweight relief-agency officials flown in to inspect the misery.

I had many of my frugal habits from Nanny. Mary Agnes Davidson Pocock arrived in my life when my brother was six and I was five. She was known as Nanny Hildyard to the other nannies in the park, whose hierarchy was determined by their employers' surnames. Mary Agnes was auburn-haired, green-eyed and large-boned and came from Aberdeen, the granite city on the east coast of Scotland.

We lived at the time in a mock-Tudor bow-fronted town house in Sussex Square near Paddington Station in central London. My mother had chosen the place as convenient for the park and with sufficient space for a nursery floor, while the rest was large enough to accommodate cook, scullery-maid, housemaid and ladies' maid. Her intention, in the aftermath of the war, was to make a new life with her new husband, my stepfather, Toby Hildyard, ex-airman, good friend of my own father at Eton, and now a fledgling diplomat.

My brother and I were known as tearaways among the nannies who pushed Silver Cross perambulators in Hyde Park, several of whom had been engaged in turn to smack us into shape. Most of them didn't even wait to learn our names. They just locked us in the broom cupboard and waited till we had learned our manners.

Soon after Nanny's arrival, my brother, a skinny under-sized seven-year-old, was sent away to preparatory school. For all of my years and all but one of his we'd never been apart. For me, and no doubt for him in his cold shared dormitory among unknown people in an unfamiliar place, the world had ceased to turn.

Nanny Pocock arrived like a rescuing angel. She took the time to curl my hair in rags and make drop scones for tea. She didn't wear a uniform as all the other nannies did. She had taken employment as a nursemaid in a large household in the country and had moved to my mother's London household to improve her prospects. She had once had a suitor, a young man who had been her childhood sweetheart, but had died in the war. Her mother, like mine, had been widowed by the war, and she too came south with her daughter and moved into a little house on the outskirts of Aylesbury.

On her first day out – days out were once a month, with a weekend every three months – Nanny took me with her to visit her mother. At the bottom of her garden were snow-white ducks which laid pale blue eggs and foraged for worms in the kale patch. Nanny said kale was much like cabbage but tasted much nicer. Nanny also said Aylesbury ducks were so famous they were even sold in Harrods.

Nanny smelled of apricots and Dettol and sometimes just a little of whisky, her medicinal bedtime drink. She was plump and gentle and kind – three things my mother was not. She had soft freckled skin which turned bright red in the sun and had little gold hairs at the edges of her upper lip. She spoke softly with a lilt as they do in the Highlands, and called me 'wee hen' and 'pet lamb' and I loved her with the single-minded adoration only an unloved child can feel.

I didn't tell her how passionately I felt. Experience told me grown-ups, however much you thought you could trust them, were unpredictable. Nanny might take fright. Or worse, be sent away for ever.

Meanwhile Nanny taught me to eat porridge with cream and salt instead of sugar, and sandwiched marie biscuits together with a layer of sticky pink icing which hardened when kept for an hour or two before you ate it. She did all these things in the little kitchenette that led off the nursery, allowing her to prepare breakfast and tea without disturbing Cook in the basement. And she never ever threatened to lock me in the broom cupboard.

When my brother came home from boarding school for the Christmas holiday it was noticed he sometimes struggled for breath. A tendency to asthma was diagnosed and a burning-inhaler prescribed. Shortly after the burning-inhaler arrived, Nanny went to visit her mother for the weekend. My mother replaced her with a temporary nanny, one of the gorgon nannies who had previously locked us in the broom cupboard.

Not wishing to awaken the gorgon snoozing in an armchair by the fire, my brother decided that he and I should transfer his breathing-stove to our shared bedroom, allowing us to play together undisturbed.

The stove was on the top of a tall bureau. My brother fetched a chair and climbed upwards, instructing me to wait beneath with my arms upstretched, ready to receive. Grasping the stove in both arms, he lowered its chimney towards me. The stove was full of boiling oil. Happily I shut my eyes just before the burning liquid reached my upturned face.

Transferred to hospital, I drifted in and out of consciousness thereafter, unable to do anything but dream. The dreams remained so vivid in my memory that thirty years later, I still believed what happened in my dreams was true.

'Nonsense,' said my mother. 'You were unconscious for a month.'

My face was healed by Archie McIndoe, the surgeon who had patched together the pilots and airmen burned in the Battle of Britain – one of the few times in my life when my famous airforce surname worked to my advantage. When I returned home from hospital, Nanny cut out the mask which covered my face and had to be replaced daily along with the dressings. I have a narrow scar along my upper lip and a memory which responds to the scent of petroleum jelly mixed with something tarry, and the sight and feel of a certain brushed-cotton fabric printed with tiny flowers still sold for children's nightgowns.

Nanny held my hand when we crossed the road and took me to the park to teach me how to make daisychains and didn't mind waiting while I searched for ladybirds under the bark of plane trees. She taught me, too, to nibble the young buds of hawthorn when the trees came into leaf in spring and let me drink at the drinking-fountain with the other children when I was thirsty.

In later years, when my stepfather was posted to Mexico and the family had grown to include a younger sister, my mother suspected Nanny of carrying on – a euphemism which covered everything from my own bad behaviour to whatever the servants might get up to – with the Mexican houseboy, a handsome fellow with the burnished skin and high cheekbones of the Mayas. I sincerely hope she was, even though at home in the *barranca*, where the poor people lived, Felipe had a wife and children and several other ladies who took a keen interest in his small salary.

Like so many women of her time, Nanny, lacking money or qualifications of any kind, had had to resign herself to a life of looking after other people's children – a fate for which I had ample reason to be grateful, along with crumpets toasted on the nursery's little gas fire and spread with butter and honey for tea. Nanny had heather honey sent down from Aberdeen, and she had ways of acquiring more butter than ration books allowed.

'It's the auburn hair,' said Nanny, patting her curls. 'Where there's a will there's a way.'

Victory Meatloaf

My Edinburgh grandmother's wartime recipe speaks for itself – the restrictions of rationing mitigated by the presence of an egg. It's rather good, particularly if you include gooseberries.

SERVES 4

225g minced pork (sausage-meat, if you must)
Same weight wholemeal bread-crumbs soaked in cider
2 tablespoons chopped parsley
4 onions or leeks, skinned and finely chopped
1 egg
½ teaspoon ground pepper
½ teaspoon grated nutmeg
½ teaspoon powdered sage
¼ teaspoon powdered bayleaf
1 teaspoon salt

To finish
More cider for basting
(optional) gooseberry purée, no sugar

Mix all the ingredients thoroughly. Press the mixture into a greased loaf tin. Bake at 375° F/190° C/Gas 5 for an hour, basting with cider to keep the loaf moist. Good with gooseberry purée, unsweetened. Serve with baked potatoes and dripping, and home-made grain mustard mixed with cider or gooseberry juice.

CHAPTER TWO

The Way We Were

'To be Catholic or Jewish isn't chic. Chic is Episcopalian.'

FLORENCE NIGHTINGALE GRAHAM, AKA ELIZABETH ARDEN

MOST OF US HAVE SOMETHING IN OUR GENETIC INHERITANCE WE need to resolve, and my mother's Jewishness was mine.

To a girl such as I, raised as a stepchild in a family which disapproved of luxury, with paternal grandparents who spread their morning toast with marmalade or butter but never both, my mother's family, the Jewish side, was as glamorous as any Hollywood A-lister.

My Baron grandparents dressed in exquisite clothes and ate delicious food cooked by real French chefs. My grandfather, unfortunately for his descendants, worked his way through the family fortune on the racetrack at Epsom and Ascot, at bridge in Berkeley Square, on the tables at Deauville and in the Salle Privée in Monte Carlo.

As a child, I was aware of the joys, never the drawbacks, of a social life which included playing golf with the Duke of Windsor and entertaining everyone who was anyone at large, fully staffed houses in both town and country.

The founding-father of my mother's family's fortune, Bernard Baron, came to Britain in the 1880s barefoot and in rags, a refugee from the Polish–Russian border. The Poles didn't wait for Hitler, they did the job a little earlier all by themselves.

I knew little of the circumstances which had caused the family to flee, some to Baltimore, others to London. But by the time the old man hung up his top hat, he had not only endowed three generations with the wherewithal to see them through their natural lives, but had given more than half his fortune to the care of the poor and homeless, non-Jew as well as Jew, in the land of his adoption.

My maternal grandmother was the old man's granddaughter, a child of the American branch of the family. The Levys had done well in Baltimore in the cloth trade. My grandfather, his nephew and a Levy himself, was heir to the London-based tobacco business – but only if he married within the family and changed his name to Baron, continuing the patriarchal line on both sides of the family.

By the time my mother and her sister were born in the early 1920s, the Barons were well established in London society. The great Jewish names of the time – Rothschilds, Sieffs, Wolfsons, Isaacs – were welcome in all the right circles, royalty included. If the Prince of Wales – darling of the nation before he vanished into the shadows for love of Wallis Simpson – could invite Jews to his weekend retreat at Windsor and encourage them to entertain his mistress, so could everyone else.

My grandmother had her salon decorated by Syrie Maugham and my grandfather shot pheasant with the Duke of Norfolk. As a racing man he owned at least two rather famous horses and Lester Piggott wore his colours. Meanwhile, his daughters were introduced to society by the only acceptable route, presentation at Court. My grandfather, just to make sure, bought himself a knighthood for thirty thousand guineas, a considerable sum at the time. My grandmother celebrated by having her linen monogrammed with intertwining initials and set about marrying off her daughters, both possessed of considerable dowries, into the aristocracy. Her daughters had other concerns – not least the sudden eruption of war – and neither of them bagged a title.

'I don't know exactly how much was there,' said my mother in later years. 'But I can tell you it was more than Hannah Marks had.'

Since Hannah was the daughter of the founder of Marks and Spencer's, this was very rich indeed.

My mother, had it not been for the war and her own determination to marry whom she wanted, could have taken her pick of the young men about town looking for an heiress to pay off the death duties. The great landowners, for the first time ever, had to pay taxes on what they passed on to their descendants. Land had to be sold, belts tightened. And even when they'd paid them, the owners of grand houses enlarged during the days of Empire could no longer afford the servants to run them.

The aristocracy had always solved their problems by marrying heiresses. Never mind where the money came from – slave trade, investment in colonial India, Australia, the Americas, coal, steel, the railways. No difference if the money was Jewish, since the children, naturally, would be brought up in their father's faith. And after a couple of generations, no one would be able to tell the difference.

The Barons were certainly upwardly mobile. Great-grandfather Bernard had been content with a modest house in Brighton and drove himself to London in a four-in-hand. His descendants, however, wanted something more in keeping with their station.

The family fortune, scarcely dented by the Great Depression, was enthusiastically deployed to maintain his descendants in the style to which they soon became accustomed. In the 1930s they bought the family home where I was born – well, give or take a night or two in the London Clinic – a vast mock-Tudor pile on the outskirts of the capital large enough to serve as a convalescent home for East End mothers and their newborns when war broke out. In town they lived in one of the last of the private houses in Belgrave Square, where my grandmother entertained rather less lavishly in wartime, but still managed to run a salon.

Miriam Rothschild, a contemporary of my mother's, remembers my grandmother and her two daughters as very chic, very glamorous women holding court at one of the coveted corner tables in the grill-room at Claridges.

'The Barons were very *fashionable.* Not like us,' Miriam told me when I worked for her many years later as a botanical artist. Fashionable was not a word Miriam attached to anyone she admired. 'The English Rothschilds were not like the Barons. We were a dull lot compared to them.' Which was something of an understatement considering her formidable intellect and the extent of her fortune. 'Your mother was a beauty and a flirt, like all the Baron women. Our tastes were more serious.'

My grandmother's unserious tastes made little impression on my father's family. My Aunt Jan, sole survivor into the new millennium of my father's generation, was the source of most of my information about the days when my mother and my father were married. Not for long – four years from start to finish.

I had often wondered, as I grew older and had a chance to consider such things, how they met at all. The two families lived very different lives. My paternal grandfather, an Air Chief Marshal by the time I was born, was one of the hundred or so young men who flew string-and-balsawood flying-machines over the trenches in the First World War. The Longmores lived in service accommodation, comfortable but by no means rich, and were neither society folk nor London-based.

It seemed not only unlikely that my mother and father's paths would cross but equally unlikely they'd have had much in common if they did.

My aunt remembered their meeting very well. 'It was in 1939 at a weekend party at the Sitwells' in Northamptonshire, not far from Grantham where we lived. The boys – your father and the

Sitwell sons – had been at school together and Millicent had been invited by one of the others. Dickie said your mother was very pretty and very bold and he wasn't used to that kind of thing.'

What kind of thing?

'Girls who knew what they wanted and weren't afraid to go and get it.'

I recognize that.

'Dickie already had a girlfriend and your mother got rid of her. I think my brother rather admired that in a girl. In no time at all they were engaged.'

And how, I enquired, did my father's family take to their eldest son's choice of bride?

'It was unexpected,' said my aunt thoughtfully. 'We knew Millicent was Jewish, but no one really minded that. My mother was a Maitland, non-conformist, Earl of Lauderdale and all that. The one thing she couldn't stand was the Pope. Marrying a Jew was a great deal better than marrying a Catholic. And Dickie was very determined. Our father was in Cairo at the time, so he was out of the picture. In any event my father was not particularly reliable where women were concerned – rather too fond of the ladies of Cairo, a little hard to contact. So, things being as they were, my mother was the one who went to meet the Barons.'

My aunt hesitated, then continued, smiling: 'Don't misunderstand me, my dear, but the way my mother told it was a little naughty. You wouldn't have known it at the time but your grandmother could be rather wicked.'

My aunt paused again: 'My mother knew about the Barons, but she didn't expect them to be quite so – *grand*.' Grandness, I knew, was not something of which Aunt Jan approved. 'War was coming and it wasn't easy to get around. So Dickie borrowed a plane and flew my mother down to meet the in-laws.

'Bertha was a stickler for lateness and luncheon was strictly at one. They arrived on time, but at first my mother thought Dickie must have mistaken the number. The house in Belgrave Square was enormous. And then the butler opened the door and there they were, all in a row, three tiny black-clad crows perched on identical chairs. One was your mother, one was your aunt and the other was your grandmother, but my mother said she couldn't tell which one was which.'

I found the scene hard to imagine and even harder to forget. I do indeed remember a portrait of the three Baron women wearing exquisite though undeniably identical Molyneux dresses – black silk crêpe with soft white collars. But three black crows, surely not?

'We all thought the story wonderfully funny,' continued my aunt. 'We teased your father, of course. But Dickie took it all in his stride. He always did. I don't remember him ever being discouraged or disappointed by anything or anyone. He always saw the cheerful side of things.'

I recognize his cheerfulness. I have it myself.

After the war my mother married again. Her choice was a friend of my father's from his schooldays, David Henry Thoroton Hildyard, known as Toby, second son of a vast Victorian mansion, Flintham Hall, set four-square in Nottinghamshire mud, with cowsheds and piggery and a man-made lake with punt and several acres of roof which needed mending. The decision seemed very right and proper. The Longmores and Hildyards were friends and neighbours and my father had been an instructor at Cranwell, where he'd taught both Hildyard brothers to fly.

At the wedding in the Savoy Chapel in London, the best man, Toby's elder brother Miles, heir to the pile, professed himself delighted that his brother would have a hand in the upbringing of his best friend's children, said my Aunt Jan.

My mother took Christian baptism so the pair could marry in church. She did not, however, take her new religion far enough to have herself confirmed. Superstitious nonsense, she said, and held her line to the end.

My own father had made no such demands on his bride. The marriage ceremony was conducted in the bride's parents' home in the presence of a rabbi under a Jewish wedding-canopy.

'Which was *not* what we expected,' said my aunt.

The Longmores, however, managed to have religious balance restored by the Chaplain to the Royal Air Force, who delivered a Christian blessing.

'And that,' said my aunt, 'was as far as it went.'

Second time around took the bride up the aisle in full-length gold lamé with the children of the previous marriage, my brother and myself, as bridesmaid and pageboy. At the time, said my aunt, there was much talk of changing our name from Longmore to Hildyard.

And had it not been for my Longmore grandmother's objections, said Aunt Jan, this might well have happened.

'My mother wouldn't have it,' said my aunt. 'She knew her own mind.'

*****

As a child, I never cried. Not even when my stepfather beat me as correction for wrongdoings – although, since I was no more than seven or eight at the time and we were all in Montevideo, my stepfather's first posting in South America, my transgressions were certainly minor.

One year, lacking the wherewithal to provide my family with Christmas presents – my pocket money was regularly forfeit after transgressions – I emptied out the insides of the Christmas crackers imported by my mother from London through the diplomatic bag. I disposed of the hats and mottoes and wrapped the little presents to put under the Christmas tree. This was the second batch of crackers. The first lot had arrived bearing the words 'contains explosives' on the package and had been taken out to a small island in the middle of the River Plate and blown sky-high by the Uruguayan navy. Nothing so entertaining had happened since the German battleship, the *Graf Spey*, had been deep-sixed by British destroyers during the Battle of the River Plate in 1943.

Justice for my misdeeds was always administered by my stepfather some days after the event at my mother's request, allowing me time to reconsider my position and come up with a convincing apology. This was never my choice. The caning – a certain number of strokes – was followed by an hour's silence in church to consider what I'd done.

If I didn't cry, the assumption was I wasn't sorry. True enough. I preferred to sulk. A caning didn't change my mind. I'd shut myself in my room and wedge my bottom against the door, sometimes for days at a time, emerging for meals, which I refused to take anywhere but in the kitchen. Looking back on my childhood, I can't say I felt I was badly treated. That was just the way things were.

It was something of a relief when my mother's and stepfather's attention switched elsewhere, to a baby brother born in 1952, soon after Toby took up his post in Montevideo. This liberating turn of events left me relatively free from supervision, and I took to going home at weekends with the maids whose families lived in the *barrio.*

The *barrio*, a sprawling tin-roofed shanty town behind the docks, serviced the harbour port, which existed for the benefit of the cattle ranchers of the interior. Nights in the *barrio* were spent curled in a pair of tattered armchairs pushed together in a corner of the one-room shack, where I slept happily through the comings and goings of the evening. Language was never a problem since I spoke the colonial Spanish learned in the school playground rather more easily than I did English.

In the *barrio*, I acquired my own maté gourd, a container about the size of a goose egg, out of which a mildly hallucinogenic tea was sucked with a metal straw. The brew was very hot and you had to be careful not to burn your mouth. The gourd had a silver rim as well as a silver straw, and my name was written on it in poker-work, which meant that when I sat on the stoop, passers-by would greet me by name.

People, I noticed, didn't think children listen to gossip. I loved the gossip and took care not to draw attention to myself when interesting things were being discussed.

One of the more interesting *barrio* topics concerned the off-duty habits of His Britannic Majesty's Ambassador, Douglas Howard.

Ambassador Howard, it was well known in the *barrio*, was accustomed to leave the residence on a Friday evening wearing full ambassadorial finery – Savile Row pinstripes, Jermyn Street shirting – carrying a small suitcase. On Sunday evening he was returned to the residence in an unmarked police van wearing seamed stockings, high heels and a skirt. And when, halfway through his tenure, the British sent a cruiser and two destroyers to celebrate the hundredth anniversary of Uruguay's liberation from the colonial power – Spain, as it happens – Ambassador Howard disappeared into the innards of the cruiser as soon as it docked and didn't reappear till it left.

Unsure of what this strange behaviour might mean, I passed the information on to Nanny, who retired to whisper in a corner with Miss Murray, my mother's ladies' maid.

'Least said, soonest mended, pet lamb,' said Nanny. 'Don't tell your mother.'

As if I would. Sir Douglas – retired ambassadors always got their knighthoods – was redeployed to the consulate in Florence, where he reigned in queenly fashion from Sir Harold Acton's villa in Fiesole.

My mother probably knew all about it anyway. However, when Mrs Thatcher ordered the navy to set sail for the Falklands – islands I had always understood to be the Malvinas – it occured to me that in the light of Ambassador Howard's habits, news of which must surely have reached the junta in Buenos Aires, it was no wonder the Argentinians thought the British unlikely to do more than make irritated noises through the usual diplomatic channels.

After his tour of duty in Uruguay and a spell back at the Foreign Office in London, Toby was posted to a consular position at the British Embassy in Madrid.

Meanwhile my mother, with a toddler in the nursery and hopes of another to come, decided that something had to be done about the leftovers from the previous marriage. By this time, my brother and I spoke Spanish unless requested to do otherwise, and didn't know how to find Britain on a map.

'Here it is,' said Nanny, breaking off from ironing baby garments to find an atlas and put her finger on a smudge of pink. 'At least it's not abroad.'

Nanny, seasoned traveller as she already was, didn't approve of abroad.

My mother picked a boarding school in the Malvern Hills sight unseen, and popped me on the train with my school trunk stuffed with hairy brown clothes and viyella blouses which had to be worn with a tie.

My brother, recovering from a bout of coeliac disease – a dietary intolerance, life-threatening if untreated – accompanied the rest of the family to Madrid. When he recovered, he was despatched for the sake of his health to Le Rosey, an international school in Switzerland for the sons of the rich and over-privileged.

This, said Nanny, was a mistake since it would certainly leave him with a taste for marrying foreign women. As usual she was right.

The school I attended in the Malvern Hills, Lawnside, specialized in problem girls, those who for one reason or another had been thrown out elsewhere or those who, by reason of spending time in foreign parts, were educationally disadvantaged. I fell into the latter category – or possibly the former, since my brother and I had long since acquired a reputation for intractable behaviour.

'Never mind,' said Nanny as she packed my trunk and tucked in a bottle of syrup of figs – lovely stuff, laced with heroin. Regulate the bowels, said Nanny, and everything else would follow.

Beyond this kindly precaution, Nanny's advice was to speak English at all times and not tell anyone where I'd been.

It wasn't only Nanny who disapproved of all things foreign. So did my schoolmates. I followed Nanny's advice and kept quiet about the things that set me apart – the ability to read and write in both French and Spanish and reel off the capital cities, rivers and mountain ranges of the Americas without recourse to a map.

Those things I couldn't do at all well, reading and writing in English, led me to devour the contents of the school library with a passion other girls reserved for fantasies about boys. Not that there was much of that around: the headmistress had gone through all the books with a razorblade and removed everything that might be of interest to young girls, the naughty bits. Which led, as soon as I left the place, to an appetite for proscribed reading-matter such as *Lady Chatterley's Lover* – at the time available only under plain cover in editions printed abroad.

There was still, for my mother, the problem of what to do with me in the holidays. School offered seven months' incarceration and five months' liberty. Madrid, my mother decided, was suitable for Christmas and the second month of the summer break, when General Franco's entire government and the diplomats posted to the Spanish capital moved to San Sebastian, as a demonstration of power in the hotbed of dissent that was troublesome north.

We all moved to the seaside town of Zarauz, where my brother and I netted the shallows for shrimp and searched the tide pools for greeny-blue swimmer crabs to take home to the cook. The cook, a sturdy lady from the Basque country, taught us to eat everything we found, shell and all, salty and crunchy and still warm from the boiling-pot. In the evening we ate spoonfuls of golden apple jam with eggy-bread dusted with cinnamon, and drank mugs of hot milk sweetened with honey to which the cook, unbeknownst to our mother, had added a few drops of apple brandy.

At other times – Easter holidays and the first six weeks of the long summer break – were spent with my Baron grandparents wherever they found themselves. If Sir Eddie and Lady B. were in Paris, I'd catch the overnight boat train from Victoria Station, arriving the following morning at the Ritz still wearing my school uniform – brown tweed overcoat, clumpy lace-ups and thick woollen knee socks.

My Baron grandmother didn't understand school holidays. Her entire life was a holiday. January took her to St Moritz for the snow. March was spent in Marienbad to take the waters. April was taken in Montecatini for the cure and May transferred them to Eugénie-les-Bains for the diet, where the *chef-de-cuisine*, predecessor to Michel Guérard, was working on a new lighter way of cooking, *cuisine minceur.* We didn't leave Eugénie until my grandfather had lost his paunch and I had shed enough puppy fat to wear a swimsuit on the beach at Cannes.

The main amusement among the rich, then as now, was spending their money eating, drinking and moving restlessly from place to place. The places that attracted the rich drew ambitious young chefs keen to make their name and earn their stars. And body-conscious clients such as my grandmother and Wallis Simpson – two socially ambitious young women who had both grown up in Baltimore – were dressed by the fashionable Paris couturiers who demanded high standards of the women to whom they consented to sell their clothes. Bottoms and bellies were vulgar and curves heavily corseted. In the evening, when a décolletée was in order, the merry widow, a rather fetching whale-boned waist-clincher and bosom-lifter, ensured that everything stayed put.

'At least I'm thin,' my mother was fond of saying whenever she was feeling sensitive about her role on the planet.

Easter found my grandparents in Venice at the Gritti Palace or the newly built Cipriani in the lagoon. Depending on the weather, I spent my days in the museums and galleries, or watching the gondoliers poling their way down the canals, or winding my way past crumbling palazzos down narrow alleyways which always somehow seemed to lead me back to the Bridge of Sighs. Juliet was fourteen when she met Romeo, and I was old enough to dream.

Shopping was a full-time occupation for my grandmother. Venice was a source of exquisite lace and linen and Florence, a day trip out of the city, yielded Pucci clothes and Ferragamo shoes. Meanwhile my grandfather played bridge with his cronies. At lunchtime I'd join one or other or both of them at Harry's Bar. The menu never varied: peach bellinis and poached fish for my grandmother, whisky on the rocks and grilled steak for my grandfather, fresh orange juice with buttery little croque-monsieurs for me.

'That's enough, darling,' said my grandmother, as I helped myself to a third.

Sir Eddie and Lady B. spent their summers in Monte Carlo, where they kept a suite at the Hôtel de Paris. The hotel was alerted to my arrival in advance and sent a taxi to fetch me from the airport at Cannes. If my grandparents hadn't yet arrived, I'd buy a baguette for my supper and eat it dipped into a tumblerful of chilled sweet wine – a taste I've never lost – sitting on the balcony watching the comings and goings in the square below. And since they never travelled without sending their personal servants in advance, babysitting the granddaughter was never a problem.

As soon as my grandparents appeared, the pattern changed. Evenings were spent in the casino and mornings in the sunshine at the Lido. If the Greeks were in town, there'd be lunch on one of the yachts. The Greek boats lay at anchor in the roads just outside the harbour walls, and guests were ferried out by tender, fast little motor boats which followed the yachts around like greyhounds on a leash.

'Wear your new Pucci slacks, darling,' said my grandmother. 'And don't speak unless you're spoken to.'

The owners of the yachts were heavy-set, dark-skinned men, short of stature but with broad working-men's shoulders, who wore peaked captain's hats, smoked cigars and stood sailor-style with one hand in the pockets of their nautical jackets, rocking back and forth on their rope-soled yachting-shoes.

Their names were hard to pronounce – Onassis, Niarchos, Goulandris, Mavroleon – but easy to remember from reports of their doings in the papers. Their wives, if that indeed was what they were, were young and pretty and very sophisticated and had no time for children like me.

They wore beautiful clothes in swirling rainbow colours – turquoise blue, lipstick pink, sunshine yellow – and their names were even more familiar: Ava Gardner, Maria Callas, Rita Hayworth. What I envied most were their wonderful breasts. Nanny said I was a late developer and all good things come to those who wait. This was not much consolation for a twelve-year-old schoolgirl, even less so as I turned thirteen and then fourteen, and finally, still lamentably flat-chested, left school at fifteen.

'Never mind,' said Nanny. 'All in good time.'

Meanwhile, as reward for polite behaviour and wearing my Pucci slacks, I was allowed below decks to the galley to watch the cooking. Greek food, I concluded, was somehow more primitive than the fancy confections of French cuisine. It lacked, too, the rice and pasta dished up by Italian cooks in Venice and Florence.

Bread came with everything, but it was bread which tasted like proper bread – chewy and sturdy and a little sour and perfect for mopping up the oily juices that came with everything. The Greek chefs spoke very little English and shouted at each other in no language I could understand, but they sat me on a stool and fed me as they cooked.

I ate octopus tentacles, purple and white with the fine violet veil left on the skin, sea urchins split to show the five little slivers of orange flesh scooped from the prickly carapace with a sharp-edged spoon, salty slivers of browny-red fish roe over which one needed a thread of greeny-gold olive oil.

'It is good. You must eat,' announced the chef as he placed another delicious morsel in front of me.

If Greek cooking was not at all like French or Italian, it was even less like English cooking. Greek cooking was scarcely cooking at all, since you added or subtracted as you pleased when the food was set on the table. Fish soups came with a garlicky sauce which could be stirred in or eaten with the bread. There were, too, aubergine fritters hot from the frying-oil, tender white beans, fat and floury and as big as a penny, stirred with parsley and garlic, pastries layered with toasted almonds and drenched with honey.

On the yachts, lunch went on till the sun went down and the motor boats returned for the guests in time to change for dinner. Everyone changed for dinner. And for lunch and tea and sometimes even for breakfast.

The dress code in the Salle Privée was just as strict as it was on the yachts. The Greeks had a preference for cream cashmere dinner jackets and hand-tied bow ties in crimson or navy velvet, beautiful cream silk shirts fastened with tiny jewelled studs, navy-blue trousers with a stripe up the side and shiny black patent slip-on shoes with gros-grain bows. And they all smelled of cigar smoke and aniseed brandy. The women were splendid in even more glamorous silks, their throats and ears ablaze with rubies and sapphires and emeralds.

My own evening outfits – I had a choice of two – were round-necked pink silk with black polka dots which dropped unflatteringly just below the knee, and full-skirted green taffeta with a cross-over neck fastened with a jade butterfly brooch bought for me when my grandfather had had a win at the tables in Singapore. My jewel box also contained a charm bracelet from Nanny with little tokens added every year at Christmas, and a wing pin in cut steel, as worn by RAF wives and daughters, given to me by my Longmore grandmother in memory of my father. I wasn't allowed to wear the pin at home in case it upset my mother.

Sophisticated I was not. And in such company, sophistication was what I longed for. Even if I borrowed a pair of my grandmother's elbow-length black kid gloves – the ones which fastened at the wrist with tiny pearl buttons and could be slipped off the wrist so you could use your fingers to scoop up an oyster, a demonstration of sophistication if ever there was one – there was very little I could do to look older than I was. And I longed to be grown-up and gorgeous and wear beautiful clothes and have a good time on a yacht. The only thing I didn't want to do was marry one of the men who provided these things.

The private gaming-rooms, the salles privées, were guarded by a doorkeeper, a man who never forgot a face and knew exactly who was allowed to enter.

Once inside, no one minded who you were or what you did as long as you didn't interrupt the gamblers. The champagne was free and there were all sorts of delicious things to eat. There were oysters of course, warm and juicy under little hats of crisp breadcrumbs. And smoked salmon rolled round white asparagus tips, bite-sized vol-au-vents filled with scraps of lobster in cream, tins of caviar set in crushed ice to eat by the spoonful with hot melba toast. Everyone picked at the food, even the men. I, however, more than managed to make up for anyone else's lack of appetite.

The evening's entertainment ended abruptly shortly before midnight, when the high rollers arrived and the evening's business began in earnest. My grandmother beckoned me to her side and tipped an attendant to see me safely across the square and up to the suite.

My grandmother never lost her American accent, a Baltimore drawl, soft when she was happy but which rose an octave when she was cross.

She was seldom cross with me – which was more than could be said of my mother. But she was quite often cross with my grandfather – mostly, it seemed, because he'd lost at roulette, or put too much on the nose of his own horse on the racetrack, or had stayed up too late playing chemin-de-fer at the casino and gone down to the Greeks.

It was very easy to lose to the Greeks. The syndicate was run by professional gamblers rather than the men who owned the yachts. The shipowners might well have done the bankrolling, but they were much too smart to take a hand.

When my grandfather won, my grandmother didn't mind the gambling at all. On days when he'd won, he'd take her to Boucheron or Cartier and all would be sweetness and light. Until, that is, the run of luck came to an end and he was back in the dog house. On nights when his luck was with him, my grandmother would wake me just before dawn, the time when a gambler's luck changes, and send me across to the casino to fetch him home.

Her perfume is still the way I remember her best. She matched her scent to the time of day: crisp and fresh in the morning, light and floral at midday, musky and heavy in the evening. At night, if she had already prepared herself for bed, she smelled of lemon zest and peppermint.

Her nightclothes were crêpe-de-chine, rustling as she moved, a long slip of soft pink silk covered by a slender overgarment which fasted up to her neck with tiny buttons, leaving room for her pearls. Even at night, she never took off her pearls.

The pearls clicked on the nights when she came to wake me, bringing me out of my dreams.

'Darling –' she'd whisper, no further instruction needed.

Rubbing the sleep from my eyes, I would dress myself in my green dress – superstitiously, for such an errand, I never chose the pink – and took the elevator down to the basement. After midnight I didn't need to cross the square. Late-night visitors to the casino from the hotel could make their way underground through a long tunnel which gave direct access to the Salle Privée.

I never was a gambler. The house always wins, said my grandfather in a rare moment of clarity, and the double zero ruins the odds at roulette. All serious gamblers know this, my grandfather told me, but none of them believes it. My grandfather was a serious gambler and he didn't believe it either.

Serious gamblers don't take kindly to interruptions. So I would settle myself patiently on one of the little gilt chairs and wait till I caught his eye. This never happened until he was ready to leave. And then, meek as a lamb, he'd follow me back through the tunnel.

My grandfather cashed in his chips soon after his sixtieth birthday, a few weeks before I was married. Probate was declared at seven thousand pounds, all that remained of his fortune. My grandmother bit the bullet, sold the pearls, moved to a smaller apartment and reduced her ten-strong entourage to what she considered the bare minimum: chauffeur, ladies' maid and cook.

It was fun while it lasted.

Octopodi ladolemono

Octopus in oil and lemon juice, as prepared by the Greeks, is a sailor's dish best prepared by sailors and fishermen since the octopus must be very fresh. Octopus, one of the most intelligent creatures in the sea, takes shelter from Mediterranean storms in rocky outcrops beneath cliffs. To catch your octopus, you will need a boat, flippers, a mask and a spear. This is the easy part. Now comes the work. Once you have gathered your octopus, you must pick it up without fear and swing it forty times against a rock. Thirty times if it's small, fifty if it's large. First the flesh is hard, but slowly it softens. Now you must rinse it in seawater so that it foams. Unless you do this, it will never soften. You'll know when it's ready because the tentacles will curl onto themselves like the tendrils of a vine. Do not remove the freckled veil which tells you the octopus is perfectly fresh. No Greek would eat a white octopus. The veil turns red during cooking and it's this that tells you that the octopus was still alive when it went into the pot. Seawater is the best cooking medium. Octopus needs very little liquid and yields a great deal of juice as it cooks. Dress it with the oil pressed from the fruit of your own olives, juice from the lemons which grow on the tree in your own garden, and sprinkle it with oregano gathered from your own hillside. If these things are not possible, you will never understand why octopodi ladolemono is a feast for the gods.

SERVES 6 TO 8

1 kg octopus, prepared as above
150ml water
1 level tablespoon salt

To dress
6 tablespoons extra virgin olive oil
Juice 2 lemons
A handful of oregano, leaves only
Salt and pepper

Cook the prepared octopus in the water with the salt until tender: 30–40 minutes. Keep the water just trembling – don't let it boil. Leave to cool and slice it carefully into pieces – all of it is good. Dress with oil, lemon juice, oregano leaves, salt and pepper and provide toothpicks so that your guests don't need to use forks. Metal spoils the flavour. All is ready. Set out the glasses with the ouzo and fetch water from the well, since you will also need to quench your thirst. Now you may call all your friends to share the feast.

CHAPTER THREE

On Being a Debutante

> *'The fault of our society has been to emancipate women but to refuse to furnish (to train them for) their freedom. They are to be equal to us; but the only equality offered them is ours, the male definition (in social and career terms) of the concept. So the only ones who gain are the masculine type, the ones who can copy them. All that has happened to the true women is that they have been turned out, like so many caged birds, into a world where they cannot fend for themselves.'*
>
> JOHN FOWLES, *The Journals*: 5 November 1966 (Cape, 2006)

IT'S 1959 AND I'M TO BE A DEBUTANTE AND FIND MYSELF A HUSBAND.

Last year's debutantes wore ostrich feathers on their heads and curtseyed to the Queen. This year's debutantes are to curtsey to a cake. The cake is a copy of the one cut by Queen Charlotte whose royal husband, Hanover George, tried to ban her from his coronation. Not much of a recommendation for the matter in hand, it seemed to me.

The palace business, it was rumoured, was removed from the social calendar by Princess Margaret – spoilt little madam said Nanny, who had all the dirt from Crawfie, the royal nursemaid – who complained of all the common people running around the palace and giving themselves airs.

My grandmother had been presented to Old Queen Mary – no one ever referred to George V's widow as anything but Old – an event recorded in a framed photograph given pride of place on my grandmother's dressing-table. The photo showed my grandmother in full-length Vionnet with pearls as big as quails' eggs, and my grandfather in tights, frock coat with sash and the insignia of whatever order had handed him his expensive knighthood. Beside them stands my mother's younger sister Berenice looking plump and sulky in bias-cut white satin with what looks like a dead cockerel on her head.

I am relieved I don't have to wear the cockerel but would rather not do the Season.

There are reasons for my reluctance. I have already had a glimpse of the world outside and it seems to me that doing the Season is likely to close more avenues than it opens.

Nor am I certain I want to be married. Ever.

Six months earlier, as a prelude to launching me on the marriage market, my mother had decided I must be finished. Finishing – polishing the rough edges left by incarceration at boarding-school – took place either in Florence for the art or in Paris for the French. I was treated to both.

In Florence I learned that painters liked nothing better than to paint or sculpt the human body in a state of complete undress. I provided myself with pencil and paper and set about finding space in a studio which offered life-drawing classes. While the female models were entirely unclothed, the male models wore little black bags over their bits-and-pieces, adding to the fascination.

Within the week, my mother found out and had me smartly removed. Stopping me doing things was my mother's way of ensuring I didn't get above myself, a sort of intellectual foot-binding designed to keep me safe for marriage.

My mother could see there was already a problem. There were signs I was beginning to know my own mind.

'Takes one to know one,' said Nanny. 'The sooner you've been finished the better.'

Everyone who went to Paris to be finished attended Mademoiselle Anita's. The nuns at Mademoiselle Anita's taught sophistication, poise, charm and how to please a man. Which was a tall order for a three-month stint, and made doubly unlikely since the nuns were by definition celibate.

I shared my thoughts with Nanny.

The nuns, said Nanny, Catholic and convent-educated herself, knew a lot more about pleasing people in that kind of way than men would ever know. And no, she wasn't going to tell me what she meant. I'd find out all about it when the time came.

Paris, I thought, might well be the time to learn.

Opportunities for learning were hard to come by. At night, I was safely locked away in a dormitory with three other young English girls in a third-floor apartment with brown walls and rattling plumbing under the stern eye of an iron-haired war widow. None of us dared enquire which of the wars was meant.

By day, in theory, I was to learn French at Mademoiselle Anita's with the other English girls. In practice, I could already speak the language perfectly well since I had to learn the language, the lingua franca of diplomats, as a child. After a week of boredom in class, I managed to persuade the nuns that I'd be better off in the French side of the convent.

Having removed myself from the rota among the English, I never registered among the French. Instead, I hopped on the back of a Vespa – since you ask, the owner's name was Gilles and he'd been at school in Switzerland with my brother – and headed off for the Sorbonne to listen to Simone de Beauvoir telling us all the things I secretly thought might be true but never knew how to express.

Encouraged by what I was hearing, I set about discovering what it meant to be a woman. A command of anatomically correct French expletives learned from my brother went down well in the Deux Magots and the Brasserie Lipp, where the artists gathered. Liberation, however, took no more dangerous a form than ordering pig's trotters and tripe sausages just to show that I could.

Paris at that time was all things it should be: rough and thrilling and beautiful. On every street corner there were cafés where people were arguing over politics and philosophy and poetry. Simone de Beauvoir was right: we were free and equal and life was wonderful and everything was there for the taking.

Simone de Beauvoir had an uphill struggle. Many years later, when I was driving down the Autoroute du Soleil from Paris to Provence with a trunkful of nappies and babies quarrelling in the back, I turned on the radio and heard a familiar voice. Simone de Beauvoir, a very old lady by now, was in discussion with Bernard-Henri Lévy, a philosopher admired as much for his youthful good looks as the depth of his thinking. Under philosophical scrutiny was the meaning of Mademoiselle de Beauvoir's most celebrated aphorism, 'One is not born a woman, one becomes one.'

'*Je trouve*,' said Bernard-Henri, concluding the argument with typical French elegance, '*une femme qui ne se maquille pas un peu vulgaire*.' Bernard-Henri's statement – that he found a woman who didn't paint her face a little vulgar – might be considered ample provocation for a sharp retort. Mademoiselle de B. replied with gentle courtesy, 'Precisely my point, Monsieur Lévy. We have only ourselves to blame.'

If a woman who doesn't wear make-up is a little vulgar, what I learned in Paris was how to ring my eyes with kohl, apply false eyelashes, wear very pale lipstick and dress in black from head to foot.

Not very creative, you might think, but you'd be wrong. I was a woman with a future – even if I hadn't yet acquired a past. I had read Colette and listened to Edith Piaf. At the movies,

I watched Jeanne Moreau flirting with both her lovers in *Jules et Jim*. In the cafés I learned to smoke Gitanes and drink very small cups of very bitter coffee very fast and wave my hands around to emphasize my words.

But words was all it ever was. I returned dutifully to my billet every night and only rarely stayed out until midnight. And the Vespa-owning Gilles, as it happened, posed no threat to any young woman's virtue. So I returned to London with my virtue intact, wearing black toreador pants, a high-necked black sweater, flat ballet pumps and what might easily have been a pair of dead tarantulas stuck to my eyelids.

'Take it all off,' said my mother. 'You look absurd.'

I was still a virgin. There was no doubt of that. Even though there had been talk at boarding-school that you couldn't even be sure you really were a virgin, said those who went to Pony Club in the holidays, since riding made things stretch.

Some of us thought you could get pregnant by sitting on a warm lavatory seat. Or if you swam in a public swimming-pool frequented by boys. Some of the older girls had crushes on some of the younger girls. Some of the girls had a crush on the English mistress, the boarding-school equivalent of Nanny's nuns, an angular woman with yellow teeth and nicotine-stained fingers who wore a hairy tweed suit, had a deep voice like a man, and invited her favourites to visit her in her attic bedroom after supper. Since I was never a favourite, rumour was all there was. Not least because for one whole year, immediately after two girls were sent home in the middle of term, we were not allowed to walk on the hills in pairs.

Small pockets of social and political dissent emerged among the older girls. Mostly these took the form of talking to boys from the Malvern Boys' College who came to watch us on the hockey pitch. Some of our parents were senior Conservative politicians, which encouraged many of us to decide we'd vote Labour as soon as we could. And when Rose Dugdale, two years older than I, fell in love with an IRA gunman and went to jail for armed robbery, I knew exactly why she had done it.

The big question, however, was how far could you go before you were gone?

There was, said Nanny, a price for Going All the Way.

The price involved the rabbit test, which everyone knew about and no one discussed. There were rumours that if the rabbit died, you were in trouble. No one would ever marry a girl who'd had to take the rabbit test and paid the price. But since bad girls, as far as I could tell, enjoyed the kind of popularity that led to proposals of marriage, rabbit testing or not, the story just didn't add up.

Although Paris had provided a degree of enlightenment, the French did not appear to have the same view of the relationship between men and women as the English did. By the time I left school, my knowledge of the reproductive process had been limited to the sex life of the Amazonian tree frog as outlined by the Reverend Bruce Parsons, the vicar.

Reverend Bruce had a red face and a bull neck and a habit of mopping his forehead with a large red spotted hankie into which he sometimes blew his nose. These minor drawbacks counted little when weighed in the balance by impressionable schoolgirls keen for any experience offered by someone who wore trousers, even if he was the vicar.

The vicar's lecture was eagerly awaited, not least because biology was not an option on the school curriculum. In the event, the lecture was something of a let-down. If the church expected young women entering the holy state of matrimony to take their lead from tree frogs, then the church was missing the point.

Anatomical differences were discussed with interest. Some of us had kissed and cuddled with boys at Pony Club sleepovers during the holidays. I, on the other hand, had earned myself a small stash of pocket money by selling sight of my brother's willy, visible through a carefully widened hole in the bathroom partition, to two of my schoolmates when we were on holiday in the backwoods of Uruguay. But that didn't really count.

Since then my own holidays had been spent in a thick woolly swimsuit on the beach with Nanny. That is, if I wasn't up till all hours in the casino in Monte Carlo with my gambling grandfather. And as for what I'd learned in Paris, I was canny enough not to admit anything learned from Brigitte Bardot in *And God Created Woman*. Which wasn't much, since the censors demanded that all participants in scenes involving bedrooms keep one foot on the floor and there was a lot of suggestion and very little detail.

I consulted Nanny.

'Wait and see,' said Nanny.

*****

And now I am to be a debutante and marry well.

Never mind if marrying well doesn't fit my own agenda, or if I find the young men not to my taste or me to theirs. I have no means of earning my own living – apart, that is, from my qualifications as housemaid or mass caterer – so, as Nanny points out, I don't have a choice.

My mother, undeterred by the absence of royal patronage, is working up a head of social steam. She plans a ball at the Savoy.

A ball is a powerful card. A dinner-dance at a grand London hotel is the social equivalent of trumps in spades. Many of my fellow debutantes have to share a dance between two or three. And while a ball in a London hotel is not quite as grand as a ball in a stately pile of which your father is the last in a line of titled incumbents, on a social scale of one to ten, it rates a nine.

The subtext, of course, was that your parents were rich enough to supply you with a dowry. Money was never talked about directly, but the story could be read elsewhere – in jewels and clothes and chauffeur-driven cars. No matter if these were borrowed finery. Not so very different, it seemed to me, from the transactions conducted by those other ladies of the night, the ones who stood beneath red lights in doorways.

Ballgowns are ordered. As are knee-length cocktail dresses for the early evening, calf-length dresses suitable for dinner-dances, day dresses to be worn to Wimbledon for the tennis (last day,

Centre Court only), Henley for the boat race (Leander colours if your brother or cousin's at Eton), the Fourth of June (nothing posh), Ladies' Day at Ascot (single flower on top of head, no hat brims).

Debs-of-the-year never wear the same outfit twice.

Debs-of-the-year in my year were Henrietta Tiarks and Lindy Guinness. Neither was a classic beauty, both had loads of Daddy's money. Henrietta scooped the future Duke of Bedford, Lindy made an arrangement with the Marquess of Dufferin and Ava.

Meanwhile, my days are filling up with fittings. These are not pleasant. Quite apart from the boredom of the sessions – everything had to be cut out in calico first and pinned and tacked directly on to the body – there are endless discussions of my physical shortcomings. Too plump, too broad, too narrow, too flat. I still seem to be a late developer in all the places that matter.

My mother does the choosing. Norman Hartnell is to be full-skirted off-the-shoulder pink tulle with pearl embroidery; also lipstick-pink duchesse satin, strapless, with waist-cinching belt (my favourite). Hardy Amies supplies yellow-flowered chiffon with flounces (not nearly sophisticated enough, in my view), and navy slub-silk with net underskirts and bustle. All have court shoes and evening bags dyed to match.

The Season begins with tea parties. These are organized, we're told, so that we can get to know the other debutantes. Some of us were already at school together. We form cliques. Most of us don't want to get to know anyone we don't already know.

The real business of the day is conducted by our mothers. Fixing the dates for dances is a competitive business. Everyone holds her cards close to her chest and shows her hand only when somebody calls her bluff. Full-scale white-tie ball in private house (say, the Londonderrys) trumps black-tie dinner-dance in a catered venue in Pavilion Road.

All very informal, says my mother, emerging from the scrum with the air of a rug salesman who has just done a particularly good deal in a camel market in Marrakesh.

'Life,' says Nanny when I complain of the boredom of having to write people's names in little address books and make diary dates for six months ahead, 'is not all beer and skittles.'

My mother decides to explain the form. The form, it transpires, is the importance of saving myself for the wedding night.

First things first.

Do I know how babies are made?

Absolutely.

This is not entirely true. I have a general grasp of the parameters, not much of the mechanics.

My mother, meanwhile, has mixed herself a stiff martini.

'So what exactly do you know?'

'I know about sperm,' I offer. 'And eggs,' I add, though with only the most general idea of how the two might be linked.

My mother takes a sip of the gin – she liked her martini very dry, no olive – and studies me. 'All I can tell you is that the night before I married your father, my mother told me that sex is something which happens on Friday and isn't very pleasant.'

I consider this.

'Does it hurt?'

'Of course,' says my mother. 'When your brother was born,' she continues, 'I thought he'd pop out through my navel. While you,' she added severely, 'were the result of too much Christmas pudding.'

Shortly afterwards I found myself cautioned for disreputable behaviour in a public place by the duty policeman outside Winston Churchill's town house while engaged in an unrewarding entanglement with a young man in an E-type Jaguar who, unlike Gilles, had shown willing.

Lack of reward was inevitable since the design of the vehicle and restrictions imposed by my undergarments were such that any young man attempting to scale the foothills of desire was bound to arrive at his destination, so to speak, all passion spent.

'I'll let the pair of you off this time, miss,' said the long arm of the law. 'And don't let me catch you at it again.'

At what?

As far as I was concerned, we'd not even arrived at first base. And anyway, the owner and the E-type had vanished down the street as fast as snow in summer.

I report back to Nanny. What's the matter with me? Still more important, what's the matter with them?

'Given half a chance,' says Nanny, by way of reassurance, 'men will take liberties.'

What liberties?

I'd know when the time came, said Nanny, patting her auburn hair into its victory roll, a sausage-shaped curl which curved round the back of the head and needed nightly attention from heated rollers.

'When you've been Through the War,' added Nanny, capitalizing the important bits for emphasis, 'you Find Out More than is Good for You.'

This was more like it. The war, I knew, had led to a lot of people finding out more than was good for them. Including my mother. And on more than one occasion.

I remembered a pair of red woollen socks last seen on the feet of a blond blue-eyed six-foot Swede but which were found folded neatly at the end of the sofa of a morning.

And then there was a gorgeous Italian – I knew he was gorgeous even though I was only a toddler – with deep dark eyes and shining curly hair who smelled exquisitely of lemons and called me *'bella ragazza'* and showed me how to greet a lady by bowing low over her hand and kissing her fingertips without quite touching. It felt like having your fingers brushed with thistledown. And at the time (and long afterwards) I nourished the hope that he might marry my mother and we could all be happy smelling of lemons and brushing fingertips for ever.

Which might explain why, soon after my debutante year, as a young woman of just eighteen summers, I learned a great deal more than was good for me from another handsome Italian just as adept at brushing fingertips, and much else besides.

After the incident outside Sir Winston's residence, opportunities to indulge in badness rarely came my way. And when they did, the source was never any of the young men I briefly fancied. And at seventeen, my fancies flew all over the place. A female such as I – of breeding age, deprived of any opportunity to express what nature was telling her – might very well head off into the sunset with the first personable male of twenty-something who crosses her path. Discrimination comes later. That's just how it is.

'Make sure you wear clean underwear,' said Nanny, then spoilt it by adding, 'you might be knocked over by a bus.'

And even if opportunities for taking chances did actually arise, hand-stitched ballgowns were complicated affairs: Dior's New Look required full skirts, tight bodies and more frilly underpinnings than a Degas dancer.

Let me explain about ballgowns.

Ballgowns of the time come in two halves. The upper part, the bodice, is strapless and held in place by heavy whale-boning gripped at the waist by tightly hooked petersham ribbons. Suspended from the waistband are three to four or even five layers of stiff net petticoat which scratches the legs, snags the nylons and acts as a deterrent to all exploratory fumblings, even if the wearer permits.

Beneath all this lies full body armour: roll-on corset, suspenders, stockings, cami-knickers with buttoned gusset. However, since the bosom is free of any constraints apart from the whale-boned bodice, any strenuous movement of the upper body, as is usual when doing the Twist, leaves the bodice facing in a different direction from the contents, rendering the energetic dancer briefly freed from all constraint from waist to neck.

There was, in other words, room for manoeuvre for any young man who knew his way around. While the young men seemed not to be aware of this, their fathers certainly were. Hand-creep was a major hazard when dancing with the older generation. Bored fathers, unlike their sons, are amused by sassy young girls who answer back. I was flattered by the attention, but other people's fathers were not what I had in mind. I learned my lesson, avoided the dancefloor and hid a paperback under the roll-on.

Thereafter I spent most of each evening in the ladies' cloakroom with my nose buried in a book. If I wasn't going to get the experience I was after first-hand, second-hand would do. This meant that during my debutante year, I read my way through Henry Miller's *Tropic of Capricorn, Lady Chatterley's Lover* and Lawrence Durrell's *Black Book*. In fact, I read my way through most of the volumes published by Maurice Girodias's Olympia Press, which were banned in Britain but obtainable from the English Bookshop in Paris.

The books arrived under plain cover, care of Nanny.

Nanny didn't read books. But she did have a Scotswoman's reverence for literature and could be relied on not to tell my mother. However, since most of the erotic goings-on between the distinctive green covers were very weird indeed, I didn't see in what way the information gleaned could be put to practical use.

Going all the way seemed a lot more complicated.

For now, however, my virtue is in no immediate danger since my mother has employed a chaperone – a service offered by a dowager duchess fallen on hard times – to keep an eye on me at dances when she's busy elsewhere. Which mostly she is.

On the days my mother isn't elsewhere, she awaits my return in the drawing-room, her personal sanctuary, a room I'm not allowed to enter without asking permission.

This gives me a good excuse to avoid detection when I return home too early by removing my shoes and tiptoeing straight to my room.

Not tonight. Tonight my mother is waiting.

'Is that you, darling?'

I can tell by her tone that she isn't pleased.

It's me. Darling it is.

'Did you have fun?'

I agree I had fun. We both know this is a lie or I wouldn't be back before midnight.

'Did you dance with any nice young men?'

Absolutely. I reeled off a list of nice young men – mostly lies.

'Anyone special?'

Ah. 'Not really.'

Wrong reply.

I know and so does my mother that I'm not a success.

A successful debutante is one who gets herself engaged by the end of the Season to the heir to a few thousand acres of arable within a couple of hours of London, or at the very least a young man headed for Lloyds.

If Simone de Beauvoir had taught me how to think for myself, the other thing I had learned in Paris was that I wanted to be an artist. To this end, on my return from France I had applied for a place at art school, the Byam Shaw in Notting Hill. The place was there for the taking, though I hadn't yet worked out how to pay the fees.

In my bedroom, small and cosy under the eaves and with the all-important lock on the door and an enormous cupboard specially installed for the frocks, behind the satin and silk was everything I needed to embark on my chosen career: easel, canvas and paints. The turpentine and oil used to mix the pigments left a faint perfume on the clothes, releasing discreet little puffs into my nostrils as I danced.

At night, if I left the curtains open, I could work by the light of the street lamps without detection. My chosen subject, since I knew the human form was the proper study for any artist, was myself without my clothes.

Painting self-portraits, naked or clothed, is of limited interest to an artist such as I proposed to be. I needed variety of the kind which might be observed in Soho's strip-clubs. Clearly not even I could wander around such dangerous places alone, so I persuaded an amiable young man with a double-barrelled surname and prospects which would certainly be attractive to my mother to take me to Raymond's Revue Bar.

I had no very clear idea of what to expect of a strip-club. I simply imagined that whoever was prepared to take her clothes off in public must be someone who thought as I did, as Simone de Beauvoir did, that women who had no reason to be ashamed of their bodies weren't afraid to show them.

I did, however, have the good sense to wear the clothes I'd come home with from Paris – androgynous black from head to foot.

The expedition was more than worth the trouble. Very beautiful, very tall young women no prettier or older than I, were wearing fishnet tights and whale-boned bodices clinched into waists of astonishing smallness and kicking their legs in the air without the slightest sign of embarrassment. And then they removed what little they wore and the lights went off and that was that.

This was the life for me. I didn't want to be a wife. I didn't even want to be an artist. I wanted to be a showgirl and join the famous Bluebell Girls and do the can-can at the Folies-Bergère and live in Paris and collect admirers.

The Bluebell Girls, said Nanny, were the cream of the cream.

After the show, I shared this view with the nice young man, who hastily took me home and thereafter dropped me like a hot potato. Quite right too. No respectable young man should be seen around with a girl like me.

'Men are like that,' said Nanny.

Actually, I explained to Nanny, I didn't want to be a debutante at all, I wanted to be a showgirl and appear nightly to an admiring audience who wanted nothing more than to tuck money in my stocking-tops. I had the qualifications. I could do the splits and stand on my head. And my elbows were double-jointed. Furthermore, I could dance. I had played the nominate role in *The Boy with the Wand of Youth* at the Elgar Festival in Malvern Winter Gardens and received favourable mention in *Tatler.*

Nanny considered the proposition.

'You have to be six feet tall,' said Nanny, who always knew about such things.

At five feet seven in my stockinged-feet, I'd never make the grade.

Worse, approaching the end of my year of optimum marriage-ability, I am still in full possession of my virtue.

Something has to be done.

Now for the Italian.

Coronation Chicken

Constance Spry, a woman of modest beginnings, invented this dish to mark the Queen's coronation and it was served at every debs' dance thereafter. Good for the cook-hostess, says Mrs Spry, since it can be prepared in advance and served from the sideboard.

SERVES 6 TO 8

1 medium-sized roasting chicken or boiling fowl
Carrot, onion, celery-top, bayleaf, thyme, parsley
1 glass white wine
6 peppercorns
Sea salt

For the sauce

1 tablespoon butter
1 slice onion, finely chopped
1 dessertspoon curry powder
1 teaspoon tomato purée
1 glass red wine
Bayleaf

For the mayonnaise

3 egg yolks
500ml mild olive oil
1 tablespoon French mustard
Juice 1 lemon
Salt and pepper

To finish

3–4 tablespoons whipped cream
2 tablespoons apricot jam
Salt and pepper

To decorate

Toasted almonds
Small white grapes

Put the chicken, vegetables, herbs, peppercorns and salt in a roomy saucepan, add the wine and just enough water to submerge the bird completely. Bring to the boil, turn down the heat, lid and leave to simmer until tender – allow 60 minutes for a roaster, about 2 hours for a boiler. Leave the chicken to cool in the broth, then skin, de-bone and cut the meat into bite-sized pieces, reserving the rest of the broth.

Make the sauce. Melt the butter in a small saucepan and fry the onion until soft. Stir in the curry powder and let it fry for a moment. Add the tomato purée, bayleaf, wine and 300ml of the chicken broth, and let it bubble uncovered until reduced by half. Strain and leave to cool.

Meanwhile prepare the mayonnaise. Start with the eggs and oil at room temperature. Fork the yolks in a bowl with the mustard. Using a wooden spoon, work in the oil, drop by drop at first, more freely as the sauce emulsifies. Finish with a spoonful of lemon juice. Season with salt and pepper and reserve.

To finish, stir the cooled sauce and the apricot jam into the mayonnaise, and fold in the whipped cream. Fold all but a third of the mixture into the chicken, and pile it on a pretty serving dish. Spoon over the remaining sauce, and decorate with toasted almonds and peeled de-seeded grapes. Serve with your favourite rice salad. Very retro-chic.

CHAPTER FOUR

Girl about London and Mexico

> *'Annette had never been in love, although she was not without experience. She had been deflowered at seventeen by a friend of her brother on the suggestion of the latter. He would have arranged it when she was sixteen, only he needed her just then for a black mass.'*
>
> IRIS MURDOCH, *The Flight from the Enchanter*

I LOST MY VIRGINITY IN A ROCKPOOL IN ACAPULCO ON VALENTINE'S Day just before my eighteenth birthday to a handsome Italian, quoter of the love poems of Catullus, a diplomat more than twice my age, the perfect lover.

He broke a date at the film festival with Françoise Dorléac, Catherine Deneuve's even more beautiful sister, to meet me at midnight by the ocean beneath the cliffs where slender brown-skinned boys dive in the dusk from a height for money.

The moment of truth, well, it wasn't much, truth be told. And no, the earth had yet to move. No one's perfect, and water's fine for fish.

Just the same, I'd done it. At last I was no longer a girl but a woman. Surely everyone would notice? No one noticed a thing.

Afterwards we met discreetly once a week all through the winter after working hours in Mexico City in the residence of the Italian Ambassador. Which was indeed who my lover was. Ambassadors, particularly those who lacked a wife, were not usually so young, however elderly he seemed to me.

So I entertained happy thoughts of *signora la ambasadora* and learned, among other things, how to prepare a fiery *pasta putanesca* (a dish prepared by all Italian lotharios to induce passion in a mistress), that the salt must be dissolved in the vinegar before you dress a salad, and how to pass a sip of fennel-flavoured liqueur – *strega*, the witch – from mouth to mouth without spilling a drop.

*****

Back in London after my month's holiday, I put my experience to good use. I wasn't exactly a bad girl, but I certainly made the most of my freedom to choose.

And choose is exactly what I did. Those were the days of dates with different young men every night of the week – if you were lucky and the young men were amenable – with time out for good behaviour on Sunday. Not that I slept with everyone I dated. Not at all. There were plenty of practical obstacles in the path of true love, not all of them mine.

And then I fell in love, and that was that. I had no interest in anything that had gone before; my beloved was all I wanted.

Nicholas, to be sure, had both beauty and brains – he'd taken a First at Cambridge and boxed for his regiment and every girl in London wanted to date the man the newspapers called the King of Satire – but the real attraction was more subtle.

Nicholas loved women. He understood the point of women. And there were not many of his generation and upbringing who could do that, who could actually *see* women. Most men look at us – at least when we're young and pretty and sure of our attraction – but they never really see us. Nicholas did. He saw women for all the reasons we want to be seen – not because we're alike but because we're different. And he understood what makes women different from men, what makes us valuable.

The drawback – let's not over-egg the pudding – is that such men see similar value in all the women they meet, old or young. There has to be a spark, but men like Nicholas can find most women attractive, given a chance, and they him. Which makes them great companions but terrible husbands. Not that all men blessed with this unusual attribute are necessarily unfaithful, just that their perceptions work to their advantage.

'Ask no questions, tell no lies,' said Nanny when I appealed to her for guidance. The path of true love, she explained, never ran smooth. However, she added, always remember to keep the money for the gasman in the teapot. Excellent advice which I'd have done well to follow but never did.

We were a little short of role models in those days, before Ms Greer got the bit between her teeth and we finally got the message.

The Establishment was run by men. *Beyond the Fringe* was an all-male gang cracking all-male jokes. And the lads at *Private Eye* were precisely that: a bunch of lads turning out a grown-up version of a boys' own mag. *That Was the Week That Was* employed Millie Martin as resident songbird, but the serious stuff was delivered by the men. And in the basement at the club where the jazz musicians came to play, singer Annie Ross delivered the subversive songs of poet Christopher Logue.

There was no doubt that we, the young women of those times, were secondary to our men. When we married, we changed our names.

Wendy Cook, Peter's first wife and the mother of his children, put her finger on the problem when interviewing their mutual friends for her biography of her ex-husband. Gay Gottlieb, wife of Sidney Gottlieb, Wendy's psychiatrist at a time when her marriage was running into trouble, had been looking at an old photograph of everyone sitting round the kitchen table at the Cooks' house in Hampstead.

Wendy entertained in style and her dinner parties, as I well remember since both Nicholas and I were often included, were remarkable for the excellence of the hostess's cooking, Peter's moody firework brilliance, and a guest list which included John Lennon, Ken and Kathleen Tynan, Paul McCartney and Jane Asher, Barry Humphries, Peter Ustinov, John Bird, Christopher Logue, Jonathan Miller, Dudley Moore, Richard Ingrams, David Frost and Bill Oddie.

A starry line-up, looking back on it, though none of us, Wendy points out, was overawed at the time. Gay and Wendy decided that the women round the table all looked depressed. "'I think this was because they were the wives of famous husbands," said Gay. "We were struggling with that, although we were all very capable people, many of whom eventually got very good jobs. We were just an accessory then, though. We had to look good, of course, but the women were only there because they were wives or girlfriends.'"

*****

Wind back the clock to 1961. After my debutante year, you will remember, I had enrolled at art school, first at the fee-paying Byam Shaw, and then, when I realized I couldn't afford the fees, at City & Guilds in Kennington. State-funded, the teachers were relaxed in their view of what was required of their students. We punched the clock in the morning, but not in the afternoon.

My rent was covered by my mother but for the rest, I was on my own.

I needed to earn a living. The job at the *Eye* was undemanding, paid just enough to cover the groceries (even then I had exacting tastes), and no one questioned my working hours as long as things got done. So I never confessed to a double life, arrived at work after the morning session at art school and no one complained since my wage was low and I was perceived, not inaccurately, as the kind of girl who danced all night and got up late.

Of an evening, I would persuade whichever young man had claimed a place in my diary to take me to The Establishment. There I would wait, heart pounding, for the appearance of the co-proprietor. Shameless hussy or liberated woman? Whatever it was, it worked. My chances improved considerably when Nicholas moved the offices of *Private Eye* into the green-room at the back of the club. As book-keeper as well as general dogsbody and office typist, I was given a desk under the eye of Mr Platman, The Establishment's accountant, and free run of the club.

Nicholas had no wish for anyone else to know of the attraction between us. Nights were spent together at my little flat in Pimlico, never at Nicholas's bachelor flat north of the park in Hyde Park Square – which, in any event, seemed to be somewhat overcrowded with the pretty young women who did odd jobs around the club or were to be found at the bar of an evening.

I was in love. Who was I to question my loved one's lifestyle?

Until I took employment at the *Eye*, I had kept my wage-earning strictly nine-to-five. Secretaries in offices were considered fair game for the boss, and since I had no interest in attracting the attentions of middle-aged married men looking for extra-curricular activities, I took temporary work in the basement typing-pools of estate agents and moved to a new job as soon as anyone tried to promote me. Promotion to the upper offices meant I'd be expected to accompany the boss for cocktails with clients, and I had better things to do with my evenings.

At the *Eye*, the young men who employed me were little older than myself, and while the usual stereotypes applied – standard fare was jokes about politicians and their secretaries, elderly gents in pursuit of busty blondes with no brains – I had no objection to making the tea as well as typing up the copy.

The crew at The Establishment, lacking the preponderance of public schoolboys, took itself more seriously than the lads at the *Eye*. The subjects tackled by the resident company were mostly political, sometimes social, but the view had very little to do with women.

And then came Lenny.

Lenny Bruce was different. He talked about the things which interested Simone de Beauvoir, but he talked about them as a man – and a man who loved women and wasn't afraid to talk about what men and women did together and why. Paris was nothing compared to this.

Lenny filled the spot left vacant by the resident company when Peter moved the cast to New York.

By now I was a regular at the club. The proprietor's high-class tottie, said Frankie Howerd, who headlined briefly when Dame Edna Everidge failed to please the crowd.

Lenny was older than the rest of us by some ten years. He was pale and thin and dressed in black and he always had a fag-end hanging off his lower lip. But what he really did was drugs. Serious drugs, the kind for which you need to pay a great deal of money, or which might be obtained by declaring yourself a junkie and getting your supplies free if you were prepared to register with a doctor and stand in the queue at midnight in a chemist in Piccadilly Circus.

Lenny talked about heroin and other drugs most of us had never heard of and what they did to you. He talked about cancer, impotence, orgasm, abortion, syphilis and sex. Mostly he talked about sex.

What Lenny was saying was that love and sex were part of the same deal. That sex was an act of procreation as well as love, and that men and women should respect it for what it was. Night after night, discarding any pretence of an escort, I crouched on a stool in the stage manager's box, marvelling at a man who could so readily express what I hadn't even known I felt.

Sometimes he said nothing at all, rerunning tapes of something that had interested him on the radio, punctuated at intervals by shouted comments or barks of laughter. These were not the best nights, and the audience left in droves, cutting down on bar takings and scaring off the punters. You never knew whether Lenny would be heroined-up and flying, or miserable and down – whatever it was, it showed in the takings.

When things became increasingly troubled at the club, I thought it wise to take a month or two out of the firing-line. Not that I'd given up on romance. It was simply that I thought it better that my beloved should sort himself out without a lovelorn girlfriend waiting for commitments he might not be willing to make. Nor was I anxious for marriage. I simply knew that this was the man with whom I intended to spend the rest of my life.

Meanwhile, my mother's house in Mexico could still provide a safe haven, so I gave in my notice at the *Eye* and booked myself on a plane. There was employment available at the embassy and I would be able to pay my own way.

*****

My mother's house was on the outskirts of the city in a residential suburb, a modern building entered at roof level with another three floors running down the ravine to the servants' quarters below.

As was my mother's habit, there were servants in plenty. Chief among these, Felipe the houseboy and Esperanza the cook. Between stairs, ruling the roost and offering a running commentary on the moods and peculiarities of her employer, was Nanny.

'Your mother,' said Nanny, 'doesn't think much of your young man.'

The assessment was not unreasonable, I had to admit, since after a week or two of silence, Nicholas felt the need to talk. Telephone calls came through between two and three in the morning and the only telephone in the house was by my mother's bedside.

After we'd established this was a cause of anxiety, my beloved took to sending telegrams. These were delivered at hourly intervals through the day and always in the wrong order – page 4 was incomprehensible until pages 1, 2 and 3 arrived.

'Fancy that,' said Nanny.

My embassy duties were not particularly taxing. I checked in at nine and left at five, with weekends free. The rest of my time was spent, as was my habit, wandering round the local markets or in my mother's kitchen.

When entertaining other diplomats or members of the government, my mother liked French cuisine with plenty of butter and cream. Sunday lunch, the one day of the week when the family ate together, was roast chicken with all the trimmings. Trimmings had to include bread sauce. Bread sauce, my mother declared, was a Hildyard thing. Since I was a Longmore, bread sauce was not something I was expected to like.

Hildyard characteristics as possessed by my younger brother and sister were beauty, brains and breeding. Longmore characteristics attributed to my elder brother and myself were none of these things. Which, I imagine, was why I was always happier keeping company with the servants in the kitchen.

Esperanza provided plain English cooking for the dining-room upstairs: steak and chips, grilled fish, shepherd's pie, macaroni cheese, nothing to set my heart racing. But in the kitchen there were wonderful chilli-laced stews to scoop up with freshly baked tortillas, soft and chewy and a little gritty. And crisp hunks of pig skin, *chicharrones*, to dip into avocado mashed with lime juice.

On high days and holidays there were maize-flour dumplings, *tamales*, steamed at the back of the stove and eaten with fiery pickled chillies, pearly little ant eggs and bee grubs to scrape from their little octagonal beds in the wild honeycomb.

Esperanza's family was Maya from the badlands of the south, the mountainous region which bordered Guatemala, guerrilla territory, a no-man's land for the politicians from the big city. The living was hard in the mountains, and Esperanza had brought her family – grandmother and children – to the city, installing them in one of the shanty towns which clung to the sides of the *barrancas*, steep-sided ravines which dried out in summer but turned, in the rainy season, into foaming torrents.

The living was still hard, but the money my mother paid was good and Esperanza was able to save. Most years, the huts had to be rebuilt with debris rescued as the waters receded, and Esperanza was hoping to build a house that would withstand the floods. The *barrancas*, deep fissures in the volcanic mud of the central plateau, were formed from the original marshland that protected the Aztec capital from invaders. The marshes, too, provided breeding-grounds for edible tadpoles, large-bodied and succulent, which Esperanza cooked on special days when her family came to visit, and she could, on occasion, be persuaded to cook for me.

The meat for a stew was pork. Pigs were everywhere. Try not to run over a pig, said Esperanza, because the fat made you skid all over the road. By the roadside, small boys offered iguana and snake and the scrawny little wild turkeys which roosted high in the pepper trees that rimmed the ravines.

Esperanza did things in the old way. Everything was bought by weight. Beans, lentils, rice, chickpeas, the pork-belly melted down for frying-fat. Nothing was paid for unless there was no alternative. You didn't, for instance, need to buy *epasote*, the defining flavour of the Mexican kitchen, a weed that flourishes on every rubbish heap.

Her special dish, prepared for important occasions such as weddings and funerals, was a seven-day *molé*, a sauce that called for at least thirty different chillies to be pounded with raw chocolate in a huge stone mortar with a pestle as long as a man's arm. Once the paste had been prepared, water was added and the whole preparation transferred to a copper pan and left to bubble away on the back of the stove for a week.

Although a *molé* could be eaten with meat, Esperanza considered this wasteful and preferred to use her delicious dark sauce as a stuffing for *tamales*, steamed maize-flour dumplings, prepared in vast quantities to take to the churchyard on the Day of the Dead.

My job at the embassy was to type up reports to London for the Cultural Attaché, top copy only and free of typing-errors.

Typewriters at the time had no facility for altering what you'd written, so I kept going till the result was perfect, scrunched up the discards and tossed them into the wastepaper basket. Admittedly I was nervous and there were rather a lot, but since the baskets were emptied every evening by the official basket-emptier, the evidence vanished overnight.

Three days later I was summoned to Toby's office.

'And what,' said my stepfather, peering at me over a pyramid of scrunched-up paper, 'are these?'

On his desk were piled my crumpled rejects, smoothed to readability and clearly marked For Your Eyes Only.

'Those?' I replied gaily. 'Butterfingers, I'm afraid. Got it right in the end, though. Why?'

Toby frowned. 'I assume you read the Official Secrets Act before you signed it?'

Indeed I had.

'Then you're aware of your obligations.'

Obligations? The letters, I protested, were all about the Cultural Attaché's false teeth.

'So?' Toby looked at me thoughtfully, raised his eyebrows, picked up a fountain pen and tapped his molars.

And then the penny dropped – how could it not? John le Carré had just published the first of the Smiley thrillers. False teeth was – had to be – a secret code. I shivered. This was thrilling.

'Do I get the sack?'

'Considering your credentials –' Toby paused, then shook his head. 'Next time use the shredder.'

*****

Meanwhile, Nicholas, in my absence from London, had found his own safe-house out of the way of the troubles at the club.

He had fallen into the habit of visiting my Baron grandmother in Eaton Square on Sunday evenings when she held open house – smoked salmon and champagne, what else? – not exactly a salon, but a place where people could gather and talk. And people did just that. Politicans and bankers, shipowners and newspaper editors, industrialists and businessmen – to a young man engaged in undermining all those things the establishment holds most dear, the opportunity was too good to miss.

One such Sunday, a couple of months after I had left for Mexico, Nicholas decided to take Dominick Elwes, young man about town and a regular at the club, to one of my grandmother's gatherings. Dominick happened to be my grandmother's godson. His father was portrait-painter Simon Elwes, who'd painted young Bertha in the 1930s in full-length Hartnell with white fox stole, pearls and a diamond as large as a pigeon's egg on her finger.

Rumour had it that Simon, handsome and charming, had slept with every woman he ever painted, including royalty. His son was equally handsome and charming, though his talent lay in a ready wit, an appetite for gossip and a genius for storytelling which made him much in demand at smart dinner parties.

Since Dom had just eloped to Gretna Green with Tessa Kennedy – an heiress young enough to require parental permission to marry in England but able to marry once over the border in Scotland – Dominick found himself out of favour in polite society. Which might have accounted for Dominick's need to spend his evenings in Nicholas's company at The Establishment, where society was by no means polite, the company was amusing, and members could cash £50 cheques at the bar. Since there were three bars at the club, the canny punter could cash three cheques a night and bounce them all, a facility which contributed in no small measure to liquidity problems at the club.

My grandmother considered Nicholas's request to bring Dominick to one of her evenings. 'I don't think so, darling. Such a bore having to hide one's little boxes.' She considered, not without reason, heiress-napping as a prelude to the thieving of Fabergé eggs.

Then she relented. 'All right, darling, if you must. But make sure you empty his pockets before you leave.'

Polite society as gathered on that particular evening in my grandmother's drawing-room included Lord Beaverbrook, proprietor of the *Daily Express*.

Dominick never could resist spinning a good story to an appreciative audience.

The following day an announcement of impending engagement appeared in the gossip column of Beaverbrook's newspaper, which also happened to be my mother's favourite bedtime reading.

'Soho nightclub owner to marry heiress daughter of Our Man in Mexico' was the headline. Nicholas, contacted in his office at the club for comment, denied the story with a vigour which seemed to indicate he'd never even met me.

London newspapers took three days to arrive in the diplomatic bag.

*****

In Mexico, I too had found myself a safe-house – the equivalent of the wedged-shut bedroom door which provided me with sanctuary as a child – in Cuernavaca, a town some thirty miles out of the city below the lip of the high plateau, where the climate was, in colonial times, considered more suited to Europeans.

In the Casa Azul, the formidable Fanny Vernon, doyenne of the Franco-English fraternity in Mexico, kept open house. Just as long as you interested her, or were talented in some way she admired, or had otherwise earned her respect, you were welcome.

The place was awash with poets and painters – some of them famous, most impoverished. Leonora Carrington and (before my time) Diego Rivera. Fanny's equally formidable daughters had married into Mexico's ex-colonial high society and were friends of my mother's, but Fanny was the queen. If she approved, no one disagreed.

As with other visitors, I had free access to her library – all the latest from Europe – and could stake my claim to a quiet corner of her shady garden shaded by an ancient jacaranda tree. And although rooms sometimes had to be shared, there was always a bed.

So I took to spending my weekends at the Casa Azul, keeping out of my mother's way. The journey by public transport took three hours. Immediately after work on Friday evening, I caught the bus in the Plaza Mayor in the middle of the city and rattled down the pot-holed highway, crushed into a corner along with cackling hens, semi-tame turkeys of the native breed whose beaks could give you a nasty nip, and crated-up piglets which were either roped on top of the bus or tucked under the seat by their tattered owners.

Everyone carried a supply of tortillas wrapped in a cloth, and a plastic container with refried beans, pickled chillies and unidentifiable titbits of insect origin – the makings of a taco, the Mexican sandwich. Iguana meat was also popular, though this looked and tasted so much like stringy bits of chicken I never could tell the difference. As a foreigner – my accent was Uruguayan, lacking the sing-song lilt of Mexican Spanish – food was pressed into my hands throughout the journey. Although the lingua franca was Spanish, family groups would chatter together in Quiché or one of the thousand other indigenous languages of the villages.

As soon as I arrived in Cuernavaca, I'd make my way from the bus station across the busy marketplace and find my way through the narrow door in the long white wall which gave access to the garden from the street.

Once within, the beauty and tranquillity of the blue-tiled whitewashed mansion settled round me like a cloud. Outside the walls all was noise and bustle of street vendors selling pig-crackling from vats of boiling oil, cauldrons puffing out scented steam. Inside, there were always visitors and the talk was of the latest novels and who was exhibiting what and where.

In the cool of the garden, flame trees dropped their scarlet trumpets in the pool. Uneven in shape, the interior had been painted black to reflect the sky.

'Blue is so vulgar, don't you think?' said Fanny. 'Black is so becoming on the young. I never wore anything else when I was your age.'

Fanny loved the young – particularly the beautiful young – and her house was always filled with the children of her own children and the children of her friends.

'Old age is such a bore. There are so many things one can't do. One must take one's pleasures second-hand.'

Among Fanny's second-hand pleasures were the newspapers from Paris and London. 'One must keep up with the goings-on of one's friends.'

On Sunday afternoon, I had fallen into the habit of reading the bits I thought would interest her before I caught the bus back to the city.

That particular Sunday was drowsy and hot and lunch had finished late.

I was halfway through the society column before I realized what I was reading. The story seemed to have come from my grandmother. She was pleased with her granddaughter's choice. She enjoyed the young man's company and would be happy if things worked out.

Back in the city, my mother awaited an explanation. I protested my innocence. Whatever the truth of the story, it was certainly news to me. The latest batch of telegrams – delivered, as usual, out of order – had started with Andrew Marvell bewailing the inconstancy of women and ended with Dylan Thomas raging against the dying of the light. Not much there to indicate thoughts of happy-ever-after.

Whatever next?' said Nanny, scissoring out the cutting.

*****

Three days later – the time it took to arrive from London – Nicholas rang me from the airport.

Fortunately my mother was out.

'Just as I thought,' said Nanny as she handed me the telephone.

Should I fetch him and bring him home?

Absolutely not.

I protested that the guest bedroom was unoccupied and I was sure my mother wouldn't mind.

Not that either.

So I booked my beloved into a hotel in the centre of town with a view of the cathedral, gave him the address, and assured him I'd join him first thing in the morning.

'Quite right,' said Nanny. 'Your mother would have a fit.'

I arrived as promised, late in the morning. No sense in disturbing the traveller too early. The hotel was famous for the excellence of its cooking. Breakfast could be taken discreetly in the courtyard under the jacaranda trees, a romantic enough setting for our first encounter after the months apart.

In the midday sunshine, the trees were busy with bright-winged humming-birds.

My beloved would be tired. There had been a stopover in New York, another in Houston, and the traveller would need something substantial to restore his spirits.

I ordered coffee, fresh orange juice and a Mexican breakfast, *huevos rancheros*, fried eggs with black beans and chilli.

As soon as the coffee arrived, I rang Nicholas in his room.

When he finally appeared, his greeting seemed a little lacking in affection. Jetlag, I told myself. Or the height. At a thousand metres above sea-level, Mexico City takes a little getting used to.

I poured the coffee. Breakfast arrived.

Nicholas prodded his plateful thoughtfully, then pushed it aside.

'I've been thinking.'

He reached into his pocket, pulled out a little package done up with ribbons and pushed it across the table.

'Open it.'

My heart in my mouth, I did as he asked, untied the ribbons and flipped up the lid. There in the box, nesting on a velvet cushion, was a Dunhill cigarette lighter. Rolled gold, classic design, a space left for initials.

I said, 'It's lovely.'

He laughed. 'It's a token. You can have it engraved. You wouldn't need to change the initials.'

Our names both begin with an L – just the same, unwise to jump to conclusions.

I waited. Then he said, 'If I asked you to marry me, what would you say?'

I choked on a mouthful of scalding coffee.

'Yes,' I said. 'But are you sure?' Then added, foolishly, 'You should think about it carefully, you know. You've only just arrived.'

'I'm sure.'

'Really really sure?'

'Of course.'

Nicholas rose to his feet and held out his hand. Thoughts rushed through my head – happy, silly thoughts, nothing beyond the moment itself.

'That's settled then,' said the man of my dreams. 'We'd better tell your mother before we change our minds.'

My mother was not pleased. Nicholas spoke to my mother in the drawing-room alone. His intention, he told me, was to make a formal request for the hand of her daughter in marriage.

'I suppose I should congratulate you,' said my mother when I joined them in the garden. 'I'll have to talk to Toby.'

Toby was in Cuba. On a secret mission, said Nanny. She knew this because when she'd packed his luggage she'd spotted a miniature camera.

Cuba was in the news rather a lot. President Kennedy had sanctioned a pre-emptive strike at the Bay of Pigs and things were a little tense.

Toby's political leanings were never declared. He was a diplomat. He could argue anything both ways. He'd been sent to Berlin when the war ended to write the official history of the conflict from the German point of view. If he ever ventured an opinion it was that the German war machine had been very efficient and the world would be better off without the communists.

Not yet twenty-one, the law said I couldn't marry without parental permission. And my mother wouldn't give permission without consulting Toby.

Toby was in Cuba, we'd have to wait.

Time for a holiday, said Nanny.

Nicholas's pockets were empty, as were mine.

'Least said, soonest mended,' said Nanny, and raided her savings to send us on our way.

*****

'Of course, my dear,' said Fanny when I rang her to propose a visit. 'You'll both be more than welcome.'

Fanny loved good-looking young men, particularly if, like Nicholas, they promised news and entertainment. Nicholas slept most of the way on the bus. He'd travelled in Mexico before, a few years earlier when he was teaching at the University of Pennsylvania, in the company of a young woman who later reappeared in his life as yet another rescuing angel. Rescuing angels were always a feature in his life, though I was yet to discover this.

Meanwhile, I was blissfully happy and glad to take Nicholas to a place I loved and knew that he would too.

Fanny greeted us with a wave of her hand. It was the middle of the week and there were no other visitors at the house.

'There you are, my dear. So glad you've brought your young man. I gather your mother doesn't approve. Don't worry. I shall make up my own mind. Leonora has already told me all I need to know.'

Leonora meant Leonora Carrington, surrealist painter, one-time mistress of Max Ernst, and my mother's closest friend in Mexico.

'So this is the famous fiancé? Come here and let me look at you.'

Nicholas obeyed.

'Excellent. Just as I supposed. Attractive, good-looking and no doubt clever as a monkey. Sit here beside me and tell me all about what's happening in London and why Millicent doesn't want you to marry her daughter.'

Fanny listened while Nicholas talked. He told her all about his life in Paris – things I never knew – of days spent in the ateliers of painters, of wandering along the Seine and dreaming of fame and fortune as an artist.

It was Fanny who introduced my mother to Leonora and Leonora who encouraged my mother to paint. It didn't last. The messy paraphernalia of canvas and oils were soon replaced with the neat, controllable art of needlepoint. Perhaps she was right. Leonora's world was risky, full of unreliable lovers, careless of gender at a time such things were never talked of. Furthermore, the dreams which fuelled the artists' waking hours came from forbidden fruit, the magic mushrooms on sale in every Mexican market. 'Of course I knew what they were,' said my mother in later years. 'I never took them myself.' Then added, a little wistfully, 'But I rather wondered what it might be like.'

Many of the designs my mother stitched with painstaking precision – particularly as her eyesight failed her in later years and she was alone with her memories in her London flat – were a homage to Leonora, reproducing in minutest detail the nightmare creatures from someone else's dreams.

In Fanny's house, sooner or later, you met everyone who was anyone.

The excitement of the time were the archaeological discoveries in the jungles of the south, treasures uncovered and flooding into the cellars of the newly established Museum of Anthropology by archaeologists from the great North American universities. Chichen Itza and Palenque, the great Maya temple in the Chiapas, was in the early stages of restoration and there were stories of more wonders to come.

Fanny's daughter Florence was organizing an expedition to the southern jungles on behalf of a photographer for the *National Geographic.* Florence planned to accompany him herself, and she had persuaded the Museum of Anthropology to send along one of their trainees – so much easier to organize official permissions. The trip was in the final stages of planning, guides had already been arranged, and the group was looking for others to share the cost.

'I thought it might amuse you both, so I've booked you on the trip,' said Fanny. 'Before I told you I wanted to make sure your mother was wrong about your young man. You'll be happy to hear I approve.'

*****

A week or so later we were in a single-engined plane high above the southern jungles, with the rain beating against the windows, looking for somewhere to land.

Below us lay the broad green-gold ribbon of the river Uxumacintla. One bank marked the border of Mexico and the other of Guatemala, no-man's land for the expedition, since the two countries were not the best of friends.

Nevertheless, since the river provided both highway and food source for our guides, the forest dwellers, we'd be unlucky to be discovered if we did land.

The pilot circled uneasily, watching the ground for our destination, a narrow clearing in the forest where he could land his plane in safety and we were to meet our guides.

The plane bumped to a muddy halt, the pilot dumped his passengers and their belongings in an untidy heap on the ground, taxied away and was gone.

Five of us sat disconsolately on a huge pile of camera equipment, small amounts of luggage, no food, one borrowed shotgun, sufficient ammunition to provide the expedition with meat, and a two-way radio which wasn't likely to be of much use since there was no one around to listen.

'Up the creek without a paddle,' said Nicholas cheerfully, inspecting the gun and ammunition with a practised eye. 'Where's the boys?'

Our guides appeared just before sundown, three small brown men in baggy trousers held in place by hand-loomed serapes – the long stripe-patterned scarf which serves as everything from sleeping-blanket to baby-cradle. Between them, slung casually across poles balanced on their shoulders, was a dug-out canoe.

The youngest and tallest stepped forward and introduced himself in halting Spanish, while the others squatted on their haunches, chattering in Quiché, the bird-like language of the Mayas.

Chiapas Indios are short and stocky with broad flat faces, slanting eyes, jet-black hair and a reputation for settling a quarrel with a machete, a broad-bladed, razor-edged chopping-knife that looks like a Roman short-sword and is carried in much the same way, thrust into the serape worn as a belt round the waist. Under the current circumstances, the knives seemed reassuring.

'*Bienvenido a mi país*,' said the tall young man, smiling. 'Welcome to my country. My name is Juan Miguel.'

When he smiled, his teeth were very white and had been sharpened to points by something other than nature. It was still raining. Not a gentle rain but a tropical downpour, the kind of rain that produces impenetrable undergrowth and a river rising steadily to overflow its banks.

Juan Miguel unslung the canoe, packed in everything that needed carrying, and set off through the undergrowth at a brisk trot, his machete flashing through the tangled vines, clearing a path. We followed as best we could, a bedraggled line tramping through the mud.

Five hours later we came to a halt in a clearing by the river. The rain had ceased and the moon shed its silvery light through the jungle canopy, creating deep shadows and brilliant pools of moonlight among the trees.

The canoe was set down and emptied piece by piece on to a tarpaulin. Hammocks were unrolled and slung from branch to branch. A fire was lit and a pot of river water set over the flames to heat.

Juan Miguel squatted on his haunches, pulled the machete from his belt, and began to stir something white and powdery into the simmering pot. After a moment the liquid began to thicken and belch.

'Grits,' I said to Nicholas, by way of explanation. 'A bit like mealy-porridge.'

Nicholas grimaced. As a Scot – his father was born and bred in the Hebrides – he would never refuse a bowl of oatmeal porridge. But mealy was another matter. I knew from his tales what he had to eat as a boy in the wilds of Kenya; there was little he wouldn't do to avoid a bowl of mealy.

Juan Miguel smiled at the grimace. 'Your man prefers to eat meat?'

Indeed he does.

'I also prefer meat.' Our guide rose to his feet. 'Tell your man to bring the gun.'

Turning, Juan Miguel beckoned to one of his companions.

We followed them down the river. The moon had dipped below the trees, but the sky was bright with stars. The canoe, a scooped-out tree trunk, sturdy and broad, bobbed on the end of a rope, buoyant in the water.

We settled ourselves in place. Nicholas in front, me behind, the guides at prow and stern. No one spoke. The canoe held steady as we moved up-river against the current, slipping silently beneath the overhanging branches. The two oarsmen worked their paddles beneath the surface like the fins of a fish, first one and then the other, parting the water without leaving a wake.

When we were well clear of the camp, Juan Miguel steadied the boat with a hand on a branch and shone torchlight into the trees.

Little pinpricks of light were everywhere, some green, some yellow, some red. We weren't alone in the darkness. We drifted along on the current, slow-moving, the pinpricks held by the torchlight dancing like fireflies.

Juan Miguel leaned towards me. '*Son ojos* – eyes. Tell your man.'

'Which is which?' asked Nicholas, calmly shouldering the rifle.

I translated the reply.

The red is monkey, the yellow is lizard, the green is snake.

The beam of light switched from bank to bank as the paddles moved the boat through the water and the pinpricks came and went.

And then, with a quick flick of the paddles, we were nose-first into the bank.

'*Lo vea?* Do you see it?'

'See what?'

Nicholas clicked the safety catch.

The pinpricks had vanished, but caught in the torchlight's beam were two glittering shards of bright white ice.

One word hissed through the darkness, '*Tigre.*'

Tigre needs no translation. But the word, I knew, meant jaguar, a spotted jungle cat half the size of a tiger and twice as fierce, prized among the Mayas not only for the bravery called from the hunter, the beauty of its pelt, and its ability, said by those who knew the secrets of the universe, to change its shape at will.

Again came the whisper, '*Tigre.*' Then, with added urgency, 'Aim right between the eyes. Tell your man he must not miss.'

The beam held steady.

'Got it!'

My man had shouldered the gun.

The shot rang clear, the hunter's aim was true.

What was never explained was how a creature so clearly identified by the hunters had turned out to be nothing more dangerous than a snowy-feathered saffron-crested parrot.

Neither one of our guides expressed surprise or even disappointment. The very reverse.

'Parrot,' said Juan Miguel with happy anticipation. 'Makes excellent soup.'

Caldo con Chilaquiles

A *caldo*, bone-broth, can be made with whatever stringy bird or beast comes to hand in the jungle (or anywhere else, for that matter). An element of crispness is appreciated: this can be supplied by *chilaquiles*, crisp strips of fried leftover tortilla, or deep-fried strips of pig skin, *chicharrones.* All other ingredients are variable and are served separately from the broth to be added at will.

SERVES 4

1 litre strong beef or chicken broth
1 skinned, boneless chicken breast
8-day-old cornmeal tortillas, sliced into narrow strips
Oil for shallow-frying

Extras (choose among:)
2–3 large ripe tomatoes, skinned, de-seeded and diced
1 mild onion or 3–4 spring onions, finely chopped
1–2 avocadoes, stoned, skinned and diced
Few sprigs cilantro *or* epasote *or mint leaves, roughly chopped*
Quartered limes for squeezing
*Puffy pork cracklings (*chicharrones*)*
*Grated cheddar-type cheese (*queso añejo*)*
Pickled chillies – chipotles *or* moras

Bring the broth to the boil. Add the chicken breast and simmer for about 10 minutes till the meat is perfectly firm. Remove with a draining-spoon and shred.

Meanwhile heat a finger's width of oil in a frying-pan and fry the tortilla strips, a few at a time, till puffed and crisp. Transfer to kitchen paper to drain.

Provide everyone with a bowl and a spoon, and set the extras out on the table, along with the shredded chicken and the crisp tortilla strips, *chilaquiles.* Return the broth to the boil while people fill their bowls. If you've managed to find freshly prepared *chicharrones* (pork cracklings), add them later – they drink up the broth and become exquisitely spongey.

Ladle the broth into the bowls, warning people not to burn their tongues at the first sip. Some people like a squeeze of lime juice and a nibble of pickled chilli.

CHAPTER FIVE

Wedding Bells

> *'Those who talk most about the blessings of marriage and the constancy of its vows are the very people who declare that if the chain were broken and the prisoners left free to choose, the whole social fabric would fly asunder. You cannot have the argument both ways. If the prisoner is happy, why lock him in? If he is not, why pretend that he is?'*
>
> GEORGE BERNARD SHAW, *Man and Superman* (1903)

ON OUR RETURN TO LONDON, WE SET THE WEDDING DATE.

Nicholas refused an announcement in *The Times*, accepted my mother's offer of a reception at Claridges and agreed the ceremony should take place at St Margaret's Westminster, sister-church to the Abbey itself and for which he expressed a preference had it not been reserved for the royals.

My mother, still in Mexico but directing operations by telephone, was, not to put too fine a point on it, breathing fire.

The run-up to the wedding was a little tense. With Nicholas busy elsewhere, it fell to me to make the practical arrangements and meet the in-laws.

Nicholas's mother and father had divorced shortly after the war. Both had remarried and both had second families. Their marriage had lasted through the war years in Teheran, where Jock was responsible for keeping the oil lines open. Nicholas's earliest memories were of desert gallops on snow-white ponies delivered to the door by servants from the palace. The Shah, it was said, admired his mother's beauty enough to court her through her son.

Jock, I knew from Nicholas's stories of his childhood, had never paid much attention to the children of his first marriage once the divorce had been finalized.

Nicholas took his time in telling his father of his marriage plans, and the wedding was only four weeks away when Jock rang me to arrange lunch at the Savoy.

'Twelve o'clock in the grill-room, my dear. Bring my son. You may have more luck at finding him than I.'

I arrived on time. Nicholas was late. No matter. I knew the place well enough to make straight for the bar. At first glance, there was no one there – midday is too soon for city folk – and then I spotted a single figure, slender and bony, neat as a pin in his country tweeds, pipe in hand, reading the *Telegraph* and looking exactly as my beloved would look in thirty years' time.

I paused for a moment, happy to have a few seconds to prepare myself to meet the man who was shortly to become so important in my life. Lacking a father myself, I had high hopes of building a good relationship with my husband's father. My future mother-in-law had confirmed what Nicholas had already told me, that Jock was not a man who gave affection easily.

'I suspect,' said Susan, 'Jock never forgave me for divorcing him.'

But surely, I reasoned, a daughter-in-law would be welcome.

Jock glanced up as I approached, tapped the pipe carefully on the ashtray, folded the newspaper and placed it on the table, then rose to his feet.

I held out my hand, smiling. 'You must be Nicholas's father.' The statement seemed unnecessary, the likeness was so strong.

Jock looked at me carefully. 'What a clever girl you are. How did you guess?'

I laughed and shook my head, thinking the question ironic. It wasn't. My father-in-law, I was later to discover, found little in life to laugh at.

'So good of you to come.' He paused, then added, 'Where's my son?'

'He's on his way.' I had no idea where my beloved was. No doubt he'd arrive.

'In that case, shall we go through?'

The *maître d'hôtel* in the restaurant greeted me by name.

'Something tells me you know the place,' said Jock.

Indeed I did. The grill-room, I explained, was a favourite with my mother's family, my Baron grandparents. It was one of the few places open on a Sunday evening and Nicholas and I had often dined with them there. I added that I hoped the families would be able to meet each other before the wedding. I was sure they would have much to talk about.

'Indeed,' said Jock.

Ah. A man of few words. Gaining time, I busied myself with the menu. Actually, I didn't need to read it at all: I always had the same thing, *poulet sous cloche*, with smoked salmon to start. My father-in-law ordered tomato soup and the roast from the trolley.

'Since my son is not yet here and I have a train to catch, it might be wise to start without him.'

The first course arrived.

'Tell me, my dear,' said my soon-to-be father-in-law, inspecting the smoked salmon on my plate. 'Did you have much trouble at school, being Jewish?'

Smoked salmon, I was suddenly aware, is about as Jewish as it gets.

'No trouble at all,' I replied quickly, feeling the blood rush to my cheeks. 'I was brought up in my father's faith.' I could hear my voice rising to an anxious squeak.

Nicholas arrived.

No need to see the menu. 'I'll have whatever you're having, sweetheart.'

'Sweetheart' – bless him. Smoked salmon and chicken it was. 'I'll have whatever you're having' seemed to me exactly the right reply, given the way the conversation was heading.

'We were talking about my Jewishness,' I said.

'Really?' said Nicholas. He put his head on one side. 'But now you come to mention it – '

I kicked him on the shins. Nicholas was not a man to pour oil on troubled waters. The very reverse. His instinct was to trust that I was more than capable of dealing with trouble myself.

Not that Jewishness was trouble. The very reverse, since in the company kept by my betrothed, I was considered something of a duchess – a bit of posh.

Jock, meanwhile, had got the bit between his teeth.

'It must have been lonely for you – correct me if I'm wrong – not going to church with the other girls on Sunday?'

'Not at all,' I replied, my smile a little less bright. And then, just so there should be no misunderstanding, 'I was brought up in the Church of England, my father's faith.'

Jock leaned back in his chair and smiled. 'My dear – I have nothing against the Jews. Many of them, I've no doubt, fine people with excellent qualities. I wouldn't want you to misunderstand me.'

My cheeks were no longer red but white.

'On the contrary,' I said as sweetly as I could manage. 'I understand you perfectly. You mean that all Jews have curly hair, hooked noses and are greedy with money.'

This was it. The colour rushed back to my cheeks. I had surprised even myself by the strength of what I felt.

I glanced at Nicholas. His face was inscrutable. Had it not been for the faint crinkle at the corner of each eye – *yeux de tigre*, an admiring lady journalist from *Paris Match* had called them – I'd have thought he hadn't heard.

Jock placed his knife and fork neatly together in the middle of the plate and rearranged the napkin on his lap.

All three of us knew exactly what he'd meant. His son's betrothed might not worship like a Jew, might not even look like a Jew, but as sure as God made little green apples, a Jew was what she was.

My mother-in-law, Susan Spencer, was as warm and welcoming as Jock had been chilly.

'Pay no attention to my ex, darling – *I* never did. I divorced him for his dullness.' Then added, more thoughtfully, 'But I think you should know he's already met your mother.'

Really? He never mentioned it.

'He wouldn't of course. He wanted to know how much you were worth. The answer, I presume, was satisfactory or he wouldn't have invited you to lunch.' She paused. 'The Luards have a habit of marrying money. If you marry an heiress, the heiress pays.'

But I'm not an heiress, I protested. Never was. Never likely to be.

My mother-in-law smiled. 'Perhaps you should ask your mother.'

My mother, when asked, revealed she had indeed lunched with the father of the groom and had agreed to provide her daughter with enough to buy a modest family house in an up-and-coming part of the city, with the same amount in the bank to be released at the discretion of three trustees.

I was grateful, of course I was. But confused. The news was as much of a surprise to me as I was sure it was to Nicholas.

That evening, I joined Nicholas at his favourite nighttime bolt-hole.

The Colony Club – otherwise known as Muriel's after the beak-nosed proprietor – was the principal out-of-hours watering-hole for Soho regulars such as Nicholas. There were others – the French Pub and the Coach and Horses – but Muriel's was for serious drinkers.

The main draw at the club was Muriel herself. To some she was a foul-mouthed harridan, to others a port in a storm. Muriel liked to call a spade a spade, a queer a queer and a cunt – well – anything but a cunt.

Muriel's preference was strictly for her own sex. I remember the lovely Mona, a tall black beauty with a whiplash tongue. Nevertheless, she was surprisingly kind to the girlfriends of her regulars, maybe because she knew what their boyfriends were up to when they weren't there.

On the rare occasions I appeared in the narrow doorway at the top of the stairs in Nicholas's wake, Muriel would greet me with a warm 'Hello, lovely,' patting the stool alongside her own with a sharp 'Off you go, cunty,' if the seat was occupied by an alien bottom.

Most of Muriel's regulars were writers or artists or their hangers-on. Any evening you'd be likely to find Johnny Minton, Robert Colquhoun, Francis Bacon, Anthony Blond. Most were male, and most were what Muriel liked to describe as screaming queens, an accolade in such company.

Straights were spoken for by Lucien Freud and Jeff Bernard, though heterosexuality was not seen as excluding same-sex entanglements. Women who were there on their own account rather than, as I was, heterosexual arm-candy – Annie Ross, Sandy Fawkes, Diana Melly, Henrietta Moraes – were treated as roughly as the men.

The Colony also served as an informal exchange-and-mart for writers in search of publishers and artists in search of punters. Nicholas purchased three paintings from Lucien Freud when Lucien, already famous enough to show at the Marlborough (a gallery which didn't much like artists who moonlighted elsewhere), found himself pressed for the readies to pay off his bookie. And when Jeff Bernard mounted a posthumous clear-out of both Minton and Colquhoun's studios, Jeff signed the drawings himself and sold them to Nicholas. The Mintons and Colquhouns stayed on our walls, while the Freuds, recycled into the family bank account for small amounts of money when Nicholas himself ran out of cash, now hang in the Tate.

The room was small and dingy where daylight hit it, which was rare. The bar was alongside the entrance, with a loop-curtained window at the far end and an upright piano somewhere in the middle. The decor, if anything so haphazard could be described as such, was Edwardian brothel meets Manhattan speakeasy.

Someone was always thumping away at the piano and everyone talked at the same time, but the main purpose of the place was alcoholic oblivion.

The only excuse not to drink till falling-down drunk was pregnancy.

Muriel drew her own conclusions.

'Tie a knot in it, cunty,' she said to Nicholas.

Muriel held the view that since men didn't have to pay the price, at least they should be careful.

'If you don't want it, darlin',' she added to me, 'you'll need an address.'

'An address' is Soho-speak for backstreet abortionist.

'I don't even know ... I mean I haven't ...' I stammered.

Muriel showed her large yellow teeth, narrowed her boot-button eyes and patted my midriff knowingly.

'Believe me, darlin',' she said.

'But if I was, I'd – ' I stuttered. 'I'm sure we'd both be very happy.'

'Just a suggestion, darlin'.'

Actually it was a warning. Muriel knew a great deal more about the young man's lifestyle than did his bride.

I thought no more about it until the second fitting for the wedding dress.

Alarmed, I took the rabbit test.

Elated by the result, I carried the news to my beloved.

'Hang on a moment, sweetheart,' he said, putting his hand over the telephone to screen the caller. 'Be with you when I can.'

That evening I had my first bout of morning sickness. This was unfair. Morning sickness should happen in the morning. And this, no question, was not the right time to be sick.

Nicholas returned earlier than usual, bearing roses.
'How are you feeling, sweetheart?'
'Fine,' I said, and threw up in the sink.

*****

On the night before our wedding, I had no intention of letting the bridegroom out of my sight.

Bad company beckoned and things could go wrong.

My grandmother persuaded me otherwise. So much more sensible for the bride to get a good night's sleep in her warm, comfortable Eaton Square apartment.

Naturally I slept not a wink. Nor indeed did the bridegroom, but for rather different reasons. Nicholas kept a diary throughout his life and was reworking it for publication as his illness worsened, a task well suited to a man whose days were numbered. His account of the night before our wedding, buried among other notes of lesser interest to me, had indeed been spent at Muriel's:

> It was late, just after midnight, the first hour of the day I was to be married. The room was warm and dark and filled with smoke. Most of the Colony regulars had been in at one time or another. Frank Norman, Sandy Fawkes, George Melly, Lucien Freud – the usual crowd.
>
> Now, on a cold February night, almost everyone had gone.
>
> Muriel was still on her stool. Francis Bacon was still there and so was Jeff Bernard. Francis was sleepy and rumpled and happy that evening – and there were plenty when he could be morose and angry. He had bought champagne to celebrate my last night of freedom and he wouldn't hear of either of us leaving. Francis always hoped Jeff might be persuaded to change sides. Jeff was slender and young and handsome, fine-featured, with a lazy smiling mouth, nothing like he became in later years. He'd been a professional prizefighter for a year or two around the time

I was boxing for the army. We'd both been lucky enough to emerge unmarked. Tonight Jeff was drunk enough to flatter Francis but not yet drunk enough to fight.

'Luard,' said Francis thoughtfully. 'Must be French.'

I agreed that we were French. But, I explained, we were Huguenot French, refugees from the revocation of the Edict of Nantes, Protestant non-conformists.

'Good,' said Francis, refilling my glass.

Most of us were craftsmen, I continued, workers in metal and leather. Most of us arrived penniless but within fifty years we'd made our fortunes. In fact, I added, my earliest recorded ancestor is a certain Abraham Luard, merchant of the city of Caen. He's buried with his wife round the corner in St Anne's churchyard in Soho Square.

Francis listened thoughtfully. 'Ever been to see their graves?'

I shook my head.

Muriel was outraged. 'Never visited your ancestors? That's unforgivable! And you to be married tomorrow. You must find them immediately. You'll need their permission.'

Muriel reached under the counter and found the torch she used when she locked up the bar. She gave the torch to Jeff and pushed the three of us out into the darkness.

'Out! And don't come back before you've found 'em.'

It was bitterly cold in the churchyard. We were shivering and plumes of steam rose from our nostrils as we tramped round the gravestones, peering at the faint inscriptions in the torch's narrow beam, feeling with icy fingers at fragments of engraving. If Abraham and his wife were there, we were not the ones to find them.

We'll come back in daylight,' said Francis.

Tell em anyway,' said Jeff.

And so I did.

Afterwards, we breakfasted at Wheeler's on freshly opened oysters and cold Chablis. Francis talked of Titian's portrait of Pope Pius, of the sureness and elegance of the way the painter had handled the fall of the scarlet cape. Jeff wondered wistfully if I could put a word in for him with the editor of *Sporting Life* where he was hoping to write a column. We never went back to the churchyard.

And that was the day, with or without my ancestors' permission, that I was married.

*****

Our wedding day dawned bright with snow.

A February bride can expect snow on her wedding day.

That morning, I had been up at first light, hoping a brisk walk around the square might calm a severe case of bridal panic.

When in trouble, I eat breakfast. So I joined the early workmen at Victoria Station for the full English fry-up: eggs, bacon, tomato and sausage, three refills from the tea urn and two slabs of thick white toast with marmalade and margarine.

Reassured, I headed for Vidal Sassoon's smart new salon in Sloane Street to keep my appointment for the wedding hairdo.

There's something soothing about a salon hairdo – an inevitability about the process from wash to set to dry to would-madame-like-a-coffee – which acts like a cold compress on bridal nerves,

Calm returned. Safely back in Eaton Square, a young woman from Elizabeth Arden arrived to do the bridal make-up. Shortly afterwards, my mother turned up.

'I hope you're happy,' said my mother. Because if you're not, she needn't have added, you've only yourself to blame.

Rouge on the cheekbones, not too much – my colour was high enough already. Now for the eyelids, a cat's-eyes flick at the outer edge. There. That's done. Now for the dress.

My wedding dress was a concession to my mother – I saw myself in Mary Quant, or maybe a slip of dress from Biba – a formal bridal gown of silk organza with a high turned-over neck, long sleeves fastened at the wrist by tiny covered buttons, more buttons down the back reaching downwards till the skirt extended into a short fishtail. The veil was held in place by a coronet of winter-flowering blooms to match the bridal bouquet, a posy of Christmas roses, pale green hellebores with ivy trails.

The buttons of the dress took patience to fasten. Once they were done, there was no going back.

Eaton Square to Westminster takes twenty minutes. We circled Parliament Square under the watchful eye of the bobbies guarding the House of Commons, checking Big Ben till the hands were at ten past the hour, the proper delay for a bride.

The crowd milling around outside the church was mostly blue-helmeted bobbies and men with cameras.

At the sight of the cameras, my heart jumped into my mouth. My mother hated the press. Never mind. My stepfather was in Mexico, safe from the attentions of journalists and the kind of people whose names were on file at Scotland Yard. Which happened, I suspected, to be a fair proportion of the congregation assembled to see us married.

My brother escorted me up the aisle.

Today, as I approached my beloved at the altar on our wedding day, I was in no doubt that marriage would be, as Nanny put it, anything but a piece of cake.

The bridegroom was not in the best of moods. This I could tell by the set of the shoulders and the short delay to the bride's arrival while the best man, cartoonist Nick Garland, had to retrieve the bridegroom from his contemplation of inscriptions on gravestones in the churchyard.

I concluded that my bridegroom was either badly hungover or had forgotten why he was there. Possibly both. No matter, he's wearing the rented outfit, there's a carnation in his buttonhole and his best man is by his side. And never mind if the two are swaying gently in what surely cannot be a breeze.

The wedding guests were exactly as might be expected, those encountered by my beloved the night before the wedding.

I tucked my arm more firmly into my brother's elbow. At least there was one of the Longmore clan here present to see me married. Glancing around as we made our way towards the altar, I noted that the wedding guests, apart from members of our immediate families, were a motley crew.

Most of *Private Eye* was there, a draw for the press. Halfway up the groom's side were Ag and Bet, The Establishment's cleaning ladies, exchanging cheerful East End insults with Frank Norman. Beside him was Jeff Bernard looking much the worse for wear.

'Wotcha, darlin',' said Aggie as we passed, prodding an exploratory finger into my brother's buttock.

Further up the church, already making himself agreeable to my mother-in-law across the pews, was Kim Waterfield, one of The Establishment's regulars and a man whose company I much enjoyed, not least because he was one of the few who actually talked to me. Kim had just done time in Marseilles jail for a misdemeanour he strenuously denied but which had something to do with finance and a particularly glamorous girlfriend.

Behind them was Nicholas's one-time flatmate, a young actress, Anneke Wills, show-stoppingly pretty in a low-cut dress, holding in her arms an adorable baby girl whose father Nicholas swore he wasn't.

The reception at Claridges remains something of a blur in my mind, in spite of the wedding photographs taken by the press. There was no official photographer and as far as I remember, no one made a speech. There was, however, unlimited champagne and cake.

Anthony Haden-Guest, one of Nicholas's closest friends, spent the reception asleep under the wedding-cake table and later swore blind he wasn't present at all – which in a sense he wasn't.

As the guests left the reception, Frank Norman and Jeff Bernard were observed staggering down Mount Street with a crate of champagne apiece.

It was, as was only to be expected, not exactly a conventional wedding. The *Evening Standard* dumped the Duchess of Argyll and her messy divorce in favour of 'Red Headed Heiress Weds King of Satire'. The *Daily Sketch* published a photograph of

Nicholas with the gorgeous actress and her infant over the caption 'Guest Brings the Baby'.

My grandmother much enjoyed the fuss, though my mother, thankfully, returned to Mexico on the next plane out.

The honeymoon at the Ritz in Paris, a gift from my Baron grandmother, was cut short by the news that Randolph Churchill had slapped a writ on the *Eye* for defaming his father in a Rushton cartoon – an intervention which was more than welcome, what with Nicholas's hangover and the morning sickness and the general feeling that marriage – any marriage – might well be a mistake.

On our return to London, Nicholas and Willie Rushton, bearing Willie's irreverent cartoon of Randolph's least favourite politician, Rab Butler, made their way down to Churchill's country retreat to reason with the great man.

Randolph, Nicholas felt, was amenable to reason, not least because he'd returned a bunch of papers lost by *Private Eye* and relevant to the case. And since Randolph had taken the precaution of hiring every halfway competent libel lawyer in the land, reason was the *Eye's* last best hope.

Randolph, Nicholas later told *Eye* biographer Patrick Marnham, wouldn't let anyone have a drink until a deal had been struck.

Since Randolph was famously fond of the drink and the time was already approaching midday, Nicholas reckoned it wouldn't take long before the great man cracked. The room was full of unidentified 'assistants', witnesses to the proceedings. The sticking-point was not so much that there had to be a withdrawal of the allegations against Randolph's father Winston – a matter of the horsedealing which took place at Yalta – but the form the withdrawal should take.

'As the hours passed, Randolph started to sweat,' Nicholas told Marnham. 'He was clearly in poor shape and needed refreshment. "Get to your feet," he would say to some moderately distinguished scholar in his entourage. "Read from the lectern what I have written in the *News of the World*." He would then correct their emphasis.'

It was five hours before agreement was reached. A withdrawal was to be printed as a full page in the *Evening Standard*, though not in *The Times* – a considerable saving of money that the *Eye*, and Nicholas, would have been unable to find. No apology would be necessary.

The whisky was brought out and the entourage was introduced. 'Finally, Randolph asked us if we wanted to see the garden. It was pitch dark and pouring with rain but he found a torch and led us outside. There we stood in the mud looking at a rosebed in the torchlight.'

*****

Things, meanwhile, were not improving at the club, and Nicholas's other business interests were running into trouble.

Scene, his lavishly produced arts magazine, was struggling. His proprietorship of *Private Eye* was under threat and there was no more money in the kitty. The capital that came his way from a trust fund set up by his industrialist grandfather had already melted away; £20,000, a tidy sum at the time, had proved to be not nearly enough to launch a glossy magazine and keep other enterprises afloat when things went wrong.

Nicholas was an insider by birth and education, an outsider by conviction. A choice like that takes courage. By the time The Establishment opened and Nicholas took on the proprietorship of *Private Eye*, he was already on file with the Special Branch, Scotland Yard's counter-terrorist watchdog, as a danger to national security.

What the press had dubbed the empire of satire had begun to crumble. And Nicholas, forewarned that the creditors at *Private Eye* were getting jumpy, slipped the publication over to Cook for safekeeping. Nightclubs are a dodgy business at the best of times, particularly in Soho. And a theatre club which encourages dissent in the sons and daughters of the rich and powerful – well, it would be soothing to imagine that someone with the power to make things happen simply decided the whole thing had to be stopped before it got out of hand.

Meatballs in Tomato and Red Wine Sauce

Meatballs are the frugal housewife's standby. Cheap, easy to divide into small enough portions to fit in a toddler's fist, and the proportion of breadcrumbs to meat can be varied to suit your purse. Spanish housewives can buy ready-prepared meatball mince, but most prefer to pick their own combinations of meat and get the butcher to put it through the mincer twice.

SERVES 4 TO 6

The sauce

1kg ripe tomatoes
4 tablespoons olive oil
2 garlic cloves, skinned and finely chopped
1 glass red wine
(optional) ½ teaspoon dried chillis
1 short stick cinnamon
1 bayleaf
Salt

The meatballs

500g minced meat (pork and beef is the classic combination)
1 egg, forked to blend
6–8 tablespoons fresh breadcrumbs
½ large Spanish onion, very finely chopped
2 tablespoons chopped flat-leaf parsley
1 teaspoon cumin seeds, crushed
Salt and black pepper

To finish

2–3 tablespoons flour for dusting
2–3 tablespoons olive oil for frying

Start the sauce first. Scald, skin and chop the tomatoes. Heat the oil and fry the garlic until it softens – don't let it brown. Add the tomatoes, wine and chillies (if using), bayleaf, salt and cinnamon, bubble up for a moment, turn down the heat, mash to help the melting process, and leave to simmer and reduce while you make the meatballs.

Work all the meatball ingredients together thoroughly – the more you work it, the better. Spread the flour on a large plate. With wet hands (keep a bowl of warm water handy for rinsing your fingers), form the meat mixture into little bite-sized balls, roll them through a plateful of seasoned flour to dry the exterior.

Heat the oil in a roomy frying-pan, slip in the meatballs and fry, turning carefully to brown all sides, until firm and lightly browned. Add the tomato sauce, bubble up and simmer gently until the meatballs are tender – about 20 minutes. Serve with crisp chips fried in olive oil, as they like them in Andalusia, and a side salad of cos lettuce and mild raw onion.

CHAPTER SIX

Of Babies, Wine and Roses

'Some circumstantial evidence is very strong, as when you find a trout in the milk.'

HENRY DAVID THOREAU, Biographical Sketch (1918)

PLANS THAT INVOLVED ANTHONY HADEN-GUEST WERE, IT SEEMED TO me, even more likely to end in trouble than plots cooked up by Dominick Elwes.

So when, soon after we were married, Nicholas announced a quick trip to New York together to check out a proposition of Anthony's, I was unconvinced. And then it occurred to me that opportunities to travel together would be few and far between after the baby was born, and that a week or two in the Big Apple, whatever Nicholas got up to with Haden-Guest, might be too good to miss.

Nicholas made arrangements for us to stay in a bachelor apartment on the Upper East Side, property of a certain Nathan T. Bartlett, onetime mayor of New York, a man with a habit of befriending promising young men such as Nicholas. I did not enquire too closely as to the nature of Nathan's interest in young men, but from the framed photographs of handsome youths striking heroic poses in their swimming-trunks in poolside settings in the Hamptons, I could hazard a guess.

Gilbert Rodway – a friend from Cambridge, then a young barrister with a talent for connections – had arranged an invitation to spend the weekend in Washington as the guests of General Earl Wheeler at his official residence in Arlington.

Gilbert had presented Nicholas as a sometime officer in the British Army's Special Forces – forerunner of the SAS – who would be able to brief the assembled heads of NATO, also in residence for the weekend, on what was going on behind the Iron Curtain in the light of his experiences running dissidents out of Budapest during the uprising in Hungary. This particular story happened to be true. It was also true that Nicholas had been confined to barracks for much of his stint in the army owing to what was perceived as general insubordination – picking a fist fight with a senior officer over his duties on the Luneberg Heath. He had managed to evade ignominious dismissal only by saving a local child from drowning – an event that made him a hero in the local press and resulted in a mention in dispatches for heroism. Presumably, also, no one had bothered to check Nicholas's record with the Special Branch at Scotland Yard.

Mrs Wheeler entertained in stupendous grandeur in the elegant Georgian mansion which, somewhat poignantly, overlooks Arlington Cemetery.

The interior of the mansion had been recently redecorated in the English country-house style then in vogue on the East Coast: Blenheim grandeur with velvet drapes, rather than shabby-chic and a warning not to sit down till you've brushed off the dog hair.

Soldier servants in white gloves stood to attention by every doorway and the place was awash with feather-stuffed chintz, french-polished occasional tables, glistening chandeliers and flower arrangements balanced on marble pedestals.

'We like to make the place look homely,' said Mrs Wheeler.

We had arrived on Saturday afternoon, in good time for the grand dinner that evening, allowing, as suggested by the invitation, enough time for a little sightseeing.

The White House was not open for visitors – the First Family was entertaining that evening – so a swing round the war-room at the Pentagon was proposed. The Pentagon was silent and deserted. Everyone had gone elsewhere for the weekend, it being Saturday with a public holiday on the Monday.

The war-room was deep underground, reached through gigantic safe-doors which could be opened only by two people remembering the right ten-figure code and punching it in at exactly the same time. I was impressed. Pregnant as I was, I had no chance of remembering anything – including my own name.

The war-room, as empty and deserted as the rest of the Pentagon, was as sparsely furnished as the mansion was over-stuffed. In the middle of a vast expanse of thick carpet was an enormous mahogany table on which rested a bank of telephones, surrounded by a great many leather-upholstered wing chairs. On one wall hung a large map of the world flanked by the American flag. It was possible to imagine what the place looked like on a war day, filled with powerful men smoking large cigars and drinking brandy while deciding whether or not to bomb Hanoi.

I had had experience of men smoking cigars and drinking brandy under similar circumstances. On the day Kennedy set up the blockade of Cuba, I was staying with my Baron grandparents and my grandmother had arranged a dinner party at which I was expected to make up the numbers.

One of the guests was a Greek shipping magnate who owned one of the tankers heading for the blockade, another was the British head of Eagle Star, the company that insured the Greek tanker, a third was a South African financier who bankrolled the shipowner.

The radio, as the evening wore on, was tuned to an American news channel and dinner was punctuated by a running commentary on the crisis.

By midnight, everyone was drinking brandy, smoking cigars and arguing over whether the tanker should be ordered to turn back, thus landing the insurance company, the shipowner and the financier with the bill for an aborted voyage, or whether the tanker should continue on its way with a good chance of precipitating the Third World War.

Around four o'clock in the morning, the call was made and the tanker turned back. Which led me to conclude that the decisions that send men to war are made at four in the morning by men who smoke large cigars and drink too much brandy.

At dinner that evening in Arlington, the conversation between men who smoke cigars and drink brandy turned to the rate at which mothers could replace the twelve-year-olds being slaughtered in the jungles of Vietnam.

The CIA had done the calculations and come up with figures that proved there was no way the existing number of Vietnamese women could breed quickly enough to make up the shortfall.

They'd done the graphs.

All Uncle Sam had to do to win the war was keep right on bombing everyone down below to kingdom come. Demographically speaking, the cigar-smoking brandy-drinkers agreed, it was a no-brainer.

*****

'I'm off to Cannes,' said Nicholas, walking into the kitchen just in time for breakfast one morning soon after the birth of our son.

I had become accustomed to my husband's absences into the small hours of the morning, telling myself that whatever Nicholas was doing was what he had to do. After all, that was the price of marriage to a nightclub owner. And at least one of us was not being woken every hour by a fractious six-month-old with teething troubles.

The Establishment had been replaced by a new venture, Wips, a club for dining and dancing. The walls were lined with carpet in a tasteful shade of gun-metal grey and there was a tank with piranha fish, nasty little brutes which could strip a finger to the bone in seconds.

Collaborator in the enterprise was Timothy Willoughby d'Eresby, heir to the Earl of Ancaster. Tim was show-stoppingly good-looking, very rich indeed, totally unprincipled and did exactly as he pleased. He was, inevitably, a friend of Dominick's.

Tim was not likely to be a good influence on any woman's husband. But he was always kind to me on the rare occasions when I turned up at the club. He also had a glorious collection of Aubrey Beardsley's erotic drawings and another of George Grosz's political cartoons – impeccable taste, it seemed to me. And anyway, I reasoned, even if Tim did lead my husband into places I'd rather he didn't go, there wasn't much I could do about my husband if I wasn't there.

The nightclub, successor to The Establishment, was supposed to make back the money the satire business had lost. Nicholas's business interests had a way of merging into one another, like Russian dolls.

The hat-check girl was a very tall, very glamorous ex-Bluebell Girl called Candy Seymour-Smith. We had been at school together and her career had inspired my own desire to become a chorus girl. Regulars at the club included April Ashley, fresh from a sex-change operation in Tangier, Ken Tynan and his new and very beautiful girlfriend Kathleen.

Not surprisingly, considering the company available at the club, if Nicholas hadn't returned by dawn, I'd start to worry.

At the mention of Cannes, alarm bells began to ring. Cannes, as far as I knew, was of interest only to serious gamblers and elderly folk who liked to take the air in their wheelchairs under the palm trees. I sincerely hoped that Nicholas was not shaping up as a serious gambler, and he was certainly not yet ready for a wheelchair.

'Whatever for?'

'For the Film Festival,' said Nicholas. 'I've always been interested in making movies.'

Really? This was news to me. But there was a lot I didn't know about my husband's life before I met him.

I carried on mashing a soft-boiled egg into bread and butter for the baby's breakfast. When you're up all night with a teething infant, ideas come and go.

'What movie?'

Nicholas hesitated. 'We're still at the planning stage.'

At the mention of 'we', I stopped mashing.

'We' meant Dominick Elwes. Dominick, as always, spelled trouble.

'What are you up to?'

'Research,' said Nicholas, waving his hand vaguely.

'Research?'

'No trouble, I promise.'

Dominick's schemes were brilliant and wild and sometimes hilarious – but never not trouble.

Dominick and his wife Tessa lived in a large family house just down the street from Nicholas's bachelor flat in Hyde Park Square.

The Hyde Park flat was home to all three of us until our family house in Battersea, bought with my marriage money, was habitable.

Other temporary residents came and went from the back bedroom.

The flat was overcrowded, what with Nicholas's need to sleep late and the new baby, adorable as he was, taking up more space than a fashion victim with shopping-addiction, what with the nappies and the tiny garments and the crib and the pram and the high chair and all the other accoutrements essential to his survival.

Tessa's family trust, larger by far than mine, had bought her a whole house on three floors, with room enough for the couple's three young sons. There was a small garden at the rear where children could play.

On sunny days, rather than take the baby for a walk in the park on my own, I was in the habit of dropping in to Tessa's for coffee and advice. Tessa gave good advice on the problems we shared: lack of disposable income, small babies, unreliable husbands. We were the same age, but she had been married longer than I and seemed to know more than I did about how to handle a husband.

Tessa had a genius for making things work, which was just as well under the circumstances. Dominick's contribution to the household's prosperity was a collection of small ornamental objects covered in tartan, mostly obelisks. When the marriage broke up and the house was sold, Tessa removed everything including the lightbulbs (a detail I rather admired) but left the tartan obelisks neatly piled in a heap by the door.

At the time of the visit to Cannes, Tessa was moving into the I-don't-believe-a-word-of-it stage in her marriage, while I was more inclined to accept whatever I was told.

Whatever our separate reasons, neither she nor I had much faith in the scams Nicholas and Dominick cooked up together, all of which seemed to require a great of time spent elsewhere and certainly didn't include nappy-changing and potty-training or mashing soft-boiled egg into the breakfast toast.

Some of the scams were truly memorable, even considering that I was not in a position to remember the details.

One, a hush-hush deal involving man-made Russian diamonds, required regular attendance by everyone involved at the Playboy Club in Park Lane in the company of Victor Lowndes and assorted Playboy Bunnies.

Unfortunately, when you hit the diamonds with a hammer to demonstrate authenticity, they shattered into little bits, not unlike a car windscreen when hit by a stone. The Russian was not best pleased by the destruction of his assets, and Nicholas, somewhat unwisely, found himself obliged to call for assistance from some unpleasant men from Soho to reason with the Russian.

Nicholas's Soho contacts, a hangover from The Establishment, were not the kind of men who did favours for nothing. They did, on the other hand, like a bit of socializing. And whatever else Nicholas and Dom got up to, socializing was what they did best.

Dinner with Princess Margaret did the trick as a payoff for the Soho heavies, though it's possible that HRH was not entirely up to speed on the meaning of East End entrepreneurship.

There was, as I remember, another scheme involving the sale of a string of sandwich shops. The shops were apparently owned by Eric Hattry, a friend of Dominick, and the intended purchaser was impresario Willie Donaldson, a friend of Nicholas. Fame and fortune as the author of *The Henry Root Letters* came to Willie later, but for now he was simply the rich man who became even richer as a result of having the good sense to bankroll *Beyond the Fringe* when it transferred from Edinburgh to London.

The sandwich shop sale came to naught when it was discovered just before Willie signed the cheque that the seller didn't actually own the shops. Dom should have known better. Eric, a dapper gentleman-around-town well into his seventies, knew everyone who was anyone, including my Baron grandparents. He made no secret of his profession. Never a thief, he would say proudly, always a conman.

As a wedding present, he gave me a krugerrand to wear on a chain round my neck in case I ever found myself short of funds in distant places.

'You can change it anywhere for ready money, my dear,' said Eric. 'Something tells me you may need it as time goes on.' Eric was right; there was indeed a moment when ready money was exactly what was needed.

Shortly after the episode of the sandwich shops, Eric spent time at Her Majesty's expense for removing a silver teapot – Georgian, very classic – from a dealer's window in Berkeley Square, a charge he strenuously denied. Never a thief, he told the judge indignantly, he was only taking the teapot home for safekeeping.

Willie was used to losing money when Nicholas was around, though this did not, however, appear to injure their friendship. Neither was a man to hold rancour. Willie had already dropped a few thousand on *Scene*, Nicholas's ambitious arts magazine. And the two men had collaborated on a couple of disastrous theatrical enterprises. One of these starred Miss Fenella Fielding in a musical revue at the Vaudeville Theatre which attracted truly terrible reviews and ran for two weeks only. The other involved Agnes Bernell, a glass-shattering belter who had appeared on stage at The Establishment.

Willie booked her on Nicholas's recommendation to appear in cabaret at the Berkeley Hotel in Mayfair. However, as soon as she opened her mouth, a family of baby crocodiles, proceeding quietly about their reptilian business in an ornamental pool in the foyer, started to climb the walls, squeaking piteously.

'Take her off! Take her off! She's killing the crocodiles,' screamed the management, and offered to double Miss Bernell's wages if she agreed to leave the premises and never come back.

There was, too, Dominick's plan to fix the backgammon tournament at the Clermont by shipping a professional over from Vegas. Nicholas and Dom had just suffered a run of bad luck at the poker table – down a monkey, as Nicholas put it when he rolled home – and were hoping to make good the losses. Five hundred pounds was rather a lot of money at the time – enough to purchase a brand-new Mini.

Unfortunately the professional – though recommended as a first-class player by Black Jack Dellal, another Clermont regular – was a washed-up has-been, leaving the scheming pair to pick up the bill.

I rarely accompanied the two men to the Clermont, and nor did Tessa. There had been too much gambling in my life already, and Tessa had better things to do with her evenings.

I had never been a gambler and was never likely to turn into one, even when I was playing with someone else's money, not even my gambling grandfather's, who would sometimes slip a large rectangular chip into my hand as a bribe to buy him time when I appeared to fetch him from the Monte Carlo casino.

I had no idea how much the chip was worth, so I walked over to the nearest roulette table and put it all on number thirteen, my unconventional choice of lucky number. The wheel spun, the croupier raked in the chip, and the whole business took no more than a minute. Next time I changed the big and square into small and round and went out into the public area, the Kitchen, where smaller bets were placed. This time the business took half an hour. The third time I took the big chip straight to the cashier and exchanged it for ready money. Lots.

Dominick, a brilliant raconteur who could always hold an audience, had managed to sweet talk himself onto the house player's list at the Clermont, which meant that he could wine and dine there every night of the week for free.

Dom amused John Aspinall, owner of the club, and had had the good sense to strike up a friendship with Aspinall's mother, Lady Osborne, the woman who really ran the place.

Dominick's presence was a draw for the big hitters at the club. Titles were everywhere. Johnny Lucan, Nicholas's business pal Tim Willoughby, Spenny Compton, John Derby. Commoners were Aspinall himself, Mark Birley who ran Annabel's downstairs and financier Jimmy Goldsmith. Particularly Jimmy Goldsmith.

While the Monte Carlo casino had seemed a friendly enough place to the child that I was, the Clermont seemed to me, on the nights when for one reason or another I accompanied Nicholas on his gambling forays, a more dangerous place. There was coldness there, an indifference to what made people who they were, an honour code which had an undertow of menace.

Where, I countered crossly, was the honour in losing money at cards?

Women who appeared at the club, unless they were gamblers themselves – whether wives or mistresses or professionals who charged by the hour – were fair game for the men. No one made a fuss if you borrowed someone else's woman for the evening. There were plenty around; you could always find another.

John Derby, coming across me late one evening while I was watching Nicholas take a hand at poker, invited me with an unusual degree of persistence to be his lucky penny upstairs at the chemmy table.

Chemin-de-fer held no appeal. And lucky penny was certainly not the way I saw myself. Nor did I wish to go upstairs with anyone. Upstairs, in my experience, always led to trouble. When I explained the problem to Nicholas, he waved his hand and told me to have fun.

Outraged, I searched for Dominick. Lucky penny indeed. I was a married woman with a baby and a husband. Dominick, to my relief, decided that I was right, my honour had been called into question and that it was clear that Nicholas should challenge the offending Earl of Derby to pistols at dawn in the park.

The following morning, back at the flat in Hyde Park Square, there was much discussion over coffee and croissants as to whether or not the Luards – or indeed the Lamerts, as the distaff side of the family – were sufficiently armigerous to bear arms against an earl.

Armigerous, Dominick explained, had to do with the number of quarters on your family's coat-of-arms. Each quarter could be divided into another lot of quarters till, at some point, armigerousness cracked in.

Right.

Sir Ian Moncrieff of that Ilk, a man who knew a unicorn pursuivant from a lion rampant, was called upon to adjudicate by telephone.

'Don't be ridiculous,' I said. 'An apology will do.'

'What kind of apology?'

A dozen roses, I suggested, would do just fine.

Dominick, when he wasn't keeping company with Nicholas, kept company with the royals. That is, if Princess Margaret could be called truly royal, slumming it up as she was with photographer Tony Armstrong Jones – Inigo Jones, out 'e come Snowdon – who, everyone around London knew, rightly or wrongly, batted for the other side.

In the not-infrequent absences of the Princess's husband, Dominick was called upon to escort Her Royal Highness on nights when she needed amusement. The Princess had a penchant for good-looking young men, including Nicholas, and would invite them to take dinner with her at Kensington Palace without their wives.

When HRH was due to present the prizes for Best-in-Show at Crufts, Dom decided it was pay-back time. He persuaded Herself to give him a little help with his patented retractable dog collar, a spring-loaded device to which he had acquired sole rights and which was about to make his fortune.

Royal endorsement would ensure he'd sell a million.

The spring-loader had a choice of settings which could be clicked into place to accommodate the largest and heaviest of guard dogs, to little yappers small enough to tuck into a Chinese empress's sleeve.

The royal personage, invited to demonstrate the dog collar to a ring of interested photographers, managed to press the wrong button. Best-in-Show, a chihuahua no bigger then an anorexic guineapig, found itself dangling from the royal wrist with its tongue protruding from its well-scrubbed teeth and its eyes bulging like lollipops.

The only collaboration between Dominick and Nicholas that could be counted a success was literary, a slim guide to confidence trickery, *Refer to Drawer*, a phrase familiar to both men since it's what's written on a cheque when the bank refuses to pay.

The enterprise was cooked up during a long lunch with publisher George Weidenfeld, at the end of which the pair had extracted the promise of an advance of fifteen hundred pounds payable up front.

The sum was generous for the time and included the fee for the illustrator, the brilliant if somewhat unpredictable John Glashan. Glashan was a Glaswegian with an appetite for whisky. The authors divided the advance between the pair of them and spent it at the tables in the Clermont. True to the spirit of the enterprise, Glashan never got paid. But since Glashan was cunning enough to insist that all drawings were delivered in the pub and his collaborators had no option but to cover his bar bill, it was felt the cartoonist had got the better end of the deal.

Not long before the pair departed for Cannes, I picked up a copy of the *Evening Standard* to read on the top of the bus on my way back to the flat in Hyde Park Square after a shopping trip in Soho.

My firstborn was still portable enough to take with me and I had an uncontrollable yearning for fresh garlic and proper olive oil which didn't come in tiny bottles labelled for medicinal purposes only.

The headline, as it had been for the past few days, was a story about British and Russian agents in the Middle East – cloak-and-dagger stuff, appealingly John Buchan.

Someone, it seemed, had shoved a sheet of paper into a jacket pocket and his wife had taken the garment to be dry-cleaned. The manageress had checked the pocket and noticed that the paper was headed TOP SECRET, Ministry of Defence. So she rang the Ministry, who fetched the paper and handed it over to the police.

The letter was written in code but included a roughly scribbled map labelled something along the lines of 'Russian troop dispositions in the Arabian peninsula: Waddi to the left of big rock at 0600 hours on the road to Tashkent: 6 camels, 3 tents, 4 machine guns, 2 camel-drivers, 1 boy to make the tea.' On the other side of the paper was a list of telephone numbers with female names appended: Fifi, Mimi and so forth.

I settled myself on top of the bus, making sure the baby was sound asleep, before glancing at the headline.

'Letter begins "Dear Dominick"'.

I had had an uneasy feeling about the story from the beginning. Dominick had just returned from a visit to his godfather, Fitzroy Maclean, somewhere in the Middle East. Fitz was the kind of man who would know all about camels in deserts. Dominick was a man whose address book was loaded with Fifis and Mimis.

As I approached our front door, a figure darted out from behind a pillar. 'Thank God you're here. Quick – inside! I'm being followed.'

Since Dominick lived just round the corner, Nicholas's flat hardly seemed a suitable hideout. Once inside, Dominick rushed over to the window and closed the curtains. After a moment, he lifted one of the curtains and peered through the gap.

'There, what did I tell you?'

I settled the baby on the bed and walked over to the window.

Sure enough, on the other side of the street was a man in a belted raincoat with a hat pulled right down over his nose.

I let the curtain drop. 'So what's the story, Dom?'

Dominick slumped down on the sofa and pulled out a packet of cigarettes. His hands were shaking so much he could scarcely hold the match.

'It's such a stupid story; you won't believe how stupid. I was staying with Fitz and I needed to make a telephone call and I grabbed a sheet of paper to make some notes. Then I put the paper in my pocket and forgot all about it. And then Tessa took the jacket to the cleaners, and the manageress – well, you know the rest. And now the Special Branch want a word and I asked Nicholas to be my witness.'

Nicholas arrived. A few moments later the doorbell rang. Two burly men in raincoats were waiting for admittance.

The senior of them inspected the two men with interest, then spoke. 'No need to introduce us to your friend, Mr Elwes. We know all about Mr Luard.'

Dominick was let off with a warning not to waste Special Branch time and advised, should a similiar situation ever arise again, to choose a witness who wasn't already on file as a threat to national security.

*****

Meanwhile, there was the problem of the trip to Cannes.

I couldn't get any more information out of Nicholas, so I consulted Tessa, who could be counted on to know a great deal more about our husbands' goings-on than I did.

The plan, she said, was to make a movie about Jack Profumo starring his mistress Christine Keeler. Miss Keeler, subjected to a double barrage of charm, had agreed to play herself.

The story that had been unfolding in the papers every day sounded like something *Private Eye* might have dreamed up after a late lunch at the Coach and Horses. The Minister of State for War denied to the House of Commons that he'd had or was having an affair with a young woman he'd met at a weekend party at Cliveden, home of the Astors. Miss Keeler, it transpired, was sharing her favours with the Military Attaché at the Soviet Embassy, a post usually occupied by Russia's chief spook.

The go-between was society doctor and amateur portrait painter Stephen Ward. Dominick and Nicholas knew Dr Ward for his willingness to supply uppers and downers – amphetamines and barbiturates – to everyone who was anyone, including themselves.

Dominick, spotting a business opportunity, suggested to Dr Ward that his old friend Nicholas, a man with a finger in the business already, should arrange for Miss Keeler's photograph to be taken for publicity purposes by a professional.

Nicholas, spotting an opportunity for prodding the soft political underbelly, obliged by booking a session with photographer Lewis Morley in the studio above The Establishment.

When the session was over, someone fetched a chair from the bar. Miss Keeler, dressed only in bra and knickers after a tiring session in a hot studio, straddled the seat and rested her arms on the back. The picture was irresistible. Not only did the sitter appear to be naked, but the shape of the chair-back exactly mirrored her beautiful heart-shaped face.

Meanwhile Dr Ward, after a hard day in the witness box, went home and finished himself off with a lethal dose of the barbiturates he was accustomed to supply to his friends, making it impossible to pin the tail on any more donkeys, so to speak. The great and the good could sleep more easily in their beds.

The story had everything, Dom and Nicholas agreed. A government minister, a Russian spy, a drug-dealing gangster, a dead society doctor – and, best of all, a beautiful maiden in distress.

Which was why, explained Tessa, our husbands were off to Cannes with Miss Keeler to raise the money to make the movie.

Things didn't exactly go swimmingly in Cannes. Even with the gorgeous Miss Keeler in tow, the pitch lacked conviction. Hollywood producers had no interest in British political scandals. And with the festival already in full swing, accommodation was scarce, funds were short and bankrollers even shorter.

Which, no doubt, was what convinced Nicholas of the need to share a bedroom with his would-be star, an arrangement revealed, though not volunteered, when the bill for double occupancy, single room, fell out of his pocket.

'Reasons of economy,' said Nicholas, waving his hand airily, as if sharing a bedroom with a gorgeous call girl was not even worth discussing.

This struck me as a little short of what might be expected of a married man with a brand-new baby. However, I reasoned that a man with wife and newborn had enough on his plate without, as it were, helping himself elsewhere.

Which goes to show that woman with baby at breast has brain like jelly.

Soft-boiled Eggs with Toast Soldiers

A fool-proof method of soft-boiling eggs is important when you're making breakfast for babies. The usual rules about eggs apply. Myself, I pay no attention, since sensible cultures wouldn't dream of depriving their infants and new mothers (not to mention toothless old grannies) of a such a nourishing, perfectly balanced and easily digested meal. It even comes in its own bio-degradable wrapping.

SERVES MOTHER AND BABY

2 free-range eggs

To serve
Unsalted butter
2 slices freshly made toast

Start the eggs at room temperature – take them out of the fridge, if that's where you keep them – place them in small pan, add enough cold water to cover the shells generously, bring the water gently to the boil, leave it to bubble for 2 minutes, turn off the heat and wait for another 2 minutes – whether the eggs are large or small, the method is the same. Serve with buttered toast soldiers for dipping.

CHAPTER SEVEN

Olé Torero

'Oh, life is a glorious cycle of song, / A medley of extemporanea; / And love is a thing that can never go wrong, / And I am Marie of Roumania.'

Comment, DOROTHY PARKER (1960 – or thereabouts)

THE BATTERSEA HOUSE WAS READY AT LAST, AND I SETTLED DOWN TO the life of a young mother with a modest private income, a husband I loved but who wasn't around very much, a baby in the pram and another on the way.

If I thought about my life at all, it was to consider that I had not quite anticipated the loneliness and lack of adult companionship that was the price of motherhood, or the loss of independence that was the result of marriage. Amazingly for a young woman accustomed to making her own way around the world, I found that I could no longer open a bank account, change the name on my passport or apply for a mortgage without my husband's written consent.

All the same I felt no desire to return to the single life, felt no great yearning for my old haunts in Spain or Mexico or anywhere else, and considered myself fortunate to be where I was, pram-pushing round Battersea Park or shopping or cooking or doing all the domestic things for which a stint at the Eastbourne School of Domestic Economy and my upbringing had prepared me.

Never mind that evenings were spent either on my own with the baby, or entertaining those few of Nicholas's friends who could be persuaded to cross the river.

There was a distinct north–south divide, and Battersea was undoubtedly on the wrong side.

Sometimes, if Nicholas warned me in time, I could arrange a babysitter and join him for dinner elsewhere.

'Nicholas usually comes home at seven and says, "We've been asked to go out to dinner with the so-and-so's," ' I told journalist Dru Beyfuss when she interviewed me in 1968. 'And having no help, I'd say "I can't". In the early days of our marriage this happened time and time again. Nicholas would be out most evenings until two or three in the morning, and I would be stuck at home with the baby. I could get a babysitter, but what babysitter can you get who wants to stay up till three in the morning?'

Had it been up to me, I would have just picked up the baby and headed for the bright lights, as was always the way among the Latins. The Anglo-Saxons were different. Children were not welcome in mixed company, even in daylight, let alone after dark. In London and everywhere else in the land of my birth, there was little or no provision for mothers with babies in shops or other public places. Hotels, pubs and restaurants, I noticed with disbelief, thought it perfectly acceptable to display signs announcing 'No children or dogs'.

*****

As my second pregnancy wore on, I began to long for the freedom and sunshine of the Mediterranean.

So when Tim Willoughby rang from a little fishing-village south of Malaga to tell Nicholas he'd bought an interest in a local bar called Pedro's and needed help getting the place in order, I was happy for Nicholas to go down and investigate the possibilities of renting a house for us for the summer.

I had never been to Andalusia. What I knew of Spain was Madrid and the Basque country, a very different kettle of fish from the south. In the 1950s, my mother's friends, fashionable *Madrileñas*, spent the early part of the summer in Marbella and might visit Seville for the celebrations of Easter or the wine harvest in Jerez, but they rarely ventured anywhere more adventurous.

Of the big cities of the south, Huelva was an American military base, Granada and Cordoba were left to the culture-hungry tourists, and Malaga was a busy industrial centre with a growing trade in cheap-flight foreigners hell bent on roasting their flesh in the sun.

Houses were cheap in Torremolinos and everywhere else along the sun-drenched coastline, servants were paid little more than bed and board, and the early arrivals on the Costa all knew one another, or if they didn't, they knew other people who did. Pedro's was their gathering-ground, and Tim was the main attraction.

Nicholas, footloose and fancy-free as I was not, consulted Ken Tynan on what might be expected of life in Andalusia. Ken, brewing up *Oh! Calcutta!* and a regular barfly at Wips, had just returned from following the bulls with Bill Davis, owner of La Consula, a large and comfortable villa on the outskirts of Malaga just along the coast from Torremolinos.

'Bill's your man,' said Ken. 'He's a shit. But a hospitable shit. He adores writers. His wife has the money and Bill knows how to spend it.' The Davises, said Ken, had bought La Consula about ten years earlier on the advice of Cyril Connolly who had been visiting Gerald Brenan in Alhaurîn-el-Grande, a pretty little whitewashed village buried among the orange groves a few miles inland.

Connolly's ex-wife, explained Ken, was Annie's sister. 'So *sensible.* One should *always* keep on good terms with one's exes. They're like a pair of well-worn shoes; one simply never knows when one will need them.'

La Consula, he continued, was where Papa Hemingway had met the bullfighter Antonio Ordoñez and had written *The Dangerous Summer.* 'And then as you know, dear heart, the silly fellow blew his brains out with a shotgun. A lesson to us all.'

Nicholas was hooked. He had never been to Andalusia, never been to a bullfight, admired Hemingway more than any other writer, and there were rumours that Antonio Ordoñez, the greatest bullfighter who ever lived and Hemingway's mentor in the world of the bulls, was making a comeback.

A biography of a famous bullfighter with a Hemingway connection would be just the thing for Nicholas's new venture with Dominick, a book-production company.

Nicholas was sure he could sell the idea to George Weidenfeld. All that was needed was an author.

Ken rang Bill Davis and Nicholas booked himself on the next flight to Malaga.

'Preliminary investigations,' he explained. 'I won't be long.'

Three weeks later Nicholas telephoned me from Torremolinos. 'I've rented a house for the summer – what do you think?'

Brilliant, was what I thought. Just the thing for a mother with a baby and another on the way. My second pregnancy had come as something of a surprise to me since Nanny had told me you couldn't get pregnant as long as you were breastfeeding. Not true. So a month or two in Spain while I recovered my strength for the new arrival sounded like heaven.

Nicholas met us at the airport and took us directly to La Consula to catch our breath. Travelling with a small baby is never easy and I had had more than enough of the isolation my new life seemed to require of me. In Spain, I knew, babies were taken everywhere, and I was looking forward to an appreciative audience for the little fellow.

La Consula, it transpired, was not baby-friendly. Bill was exactly as Ken had described him, a big, shambling balding New Yorker who didn't look as if he much liked women, let alone women with babies. His wife Annie, who came out to greet us, was slant-eyed, flat-faced, brown-skinned and mercifully child-friendly. She was, it transpired, half-Mexican.

'I've put you in the annex,' said Annie. 'It'll be quieter for you both.'

Us both? Was my husband billeted elsewhere? Indeed he was. Nicholas, it transpired, was already installed in the main house. His reputation, Annie explained, had preceded him. Ken had sent down the reviews for Nicholas's first novel, *The Warm and Golden War*, a thriller loosely based on his experiences in Hungary. The book had received favourable attention in the literary heavyweights. So Bill, my husband explained, had insisted Nicholas occupy Hemingway's old room in the main house.

'Bill adores writers,' she explained. He'd never been good with babies, not even his own. What could one do?

There was no need for a man to share quarters with his pregnant wife and teething baby if he didn't have to – women were responsible for the children and good women knew their place.

Nicholas passed on these opinions with some amusement, but he didn't suggest we alter the sleeping arrangements.

'I have to be up early in the morning, sweetheart. Annie suggested I shouldn't disturb you, I hope you don't mind?'

I did. But I kept my thoughts to myself.

The main house, a nineteenth-century folly built by a Neapolitan trader, was large and gloomy enough to make me happy that I was where I was. There seemed to be a great many visitors in the house, many of them quarrelling with each other.

Gerald Brenan had just left after a row about Spanish Catholicism with Lady Violet Powell. Her ladyship had retreated to a swing chair on the veranda and was stabbing a needle into a piece of tapestry. No one, however, seemed in the least concerned about the row.

Among the other guests – the only one who bothered to greet me, cradling my baby and shy in such company – was a very tall, stoop-shouldered Englishman, Hugh Millais, whom Nicholas had met when both were running refugees out of Hungary.

As far as I was concerned, Hugh was the pick of the bunch. An opinion reinforced when, later in the evening, he produced a guitar and delivered a rather racy repertoire of Caribbean calypsoes. This, as far as I was concerned, was more what I had in mind. The baby slept soundly enough to allow me to join the group for dinner.

Meals were taken on the balcony at long tables set out for everyone to help themselves. The arrangement was something of a relief to me, what with a baby to listen out for and a feeling, not unfamiliar in such company, that I shouldn't really be there at all. The wine was plentiful and the evening, it seemed to me, was likely to end argumentatively and late. And I couldn't afford to stay up late with a baby sure to wake up at dawn.

And anyway I had grown accustomed to living life at a different pace from everyone else.

Next morning I woke early and found my way around to the servants' quarters for breakfast in the kitchen. As I had expected, the pair of us were greeted with delight. Andalusians – all Spaniards and everyone in the lands of the Latins – adore babies, and for the first time since I had become a mother, I began to feel welcome.

Next day, I packed us up into a rented vehicle, and we set off along the narrow coast road through orange and lemon groves with a steep drop to the beach on one side and dry, rosemary-scented hillsides on the other.

The house Nicholas had found was perfect, a pretty whitewashed villa in the hills behind Torremolinos. The owner was an elderly member of the local landed gentry, the Countess of Larios, who moved into the villa in the winter but was resident through the summer in a crumbling mansion fronting the main square in Torremolinos opposite Pedro's.

'Such a beautiful baby,' said the condesa as she showed me around the villa. 'You must bring him to me for luncheon. I shall enjoy practising my English with you and the baby can sleep in the shade.'

The condesa's house was quiet and cool. The rooms were shuttered and the curtains drawn against the heat. The garden was very formal, with box hedges enclosing rosebeds, marble pools edged with clumps of white lilies and gravel pathways littered with purple blossoms fallen from the judas trees. The place reminded me of the Casa Azul and Fanny Vernon, and I was happy in the old lady's company.

'It must be so lonely for you, my dear, without your family and your husband always in that wretched drinking-den across the road.' She waved her hand dismissively. 'So noisy, so many strange people – so *unsuitable.* They smoke marijuana, I'm told, though no one will arrest them because they're foreigners. They never eat at the right time and they take the siesta lying naked in the sun.'

The condesa ate at Andalusian times – lunch no earlier than three in the afternoon, dinner at midnight – and the dishes prepared by her elderly maid were always delicious.

'In Madrid,' said the old lady, 'the saying is that Andalusians eat badly but drink well. The reverse is true. Our wine is terrible but our food is excellent. My family laugh at me because I like to eat as the servants eat. But since what the servants eat is very good, why not?'

The condesa had an arrangement with a local fisherman to bring her the best of the catch. One day there'd be spiky sea-snails, *cañaillas*, which tasted like lobster and had to be coaxed out of their shells with a quick twist of a toothpick. Next time there'd be *chunquetes*, fish-fry, flipped through flour and fried with such precision that each tiny thread was separate from the other. Another time there were sea-anemones given the lightest possible coating in batter, and weird purple-juiced shellfish which tasted of iodine and which, said the condesa, inspecting my swelling belly, encouraged the conception of boys.

A little late for that, I said. And anyway, I hoped for a girl.

There were, too, exquisite pastries whose secrets, explained by the condesa, had been learned from the Moors. The ladies of the seraglio enjoyed *tortas de aceite*, oil cakes, flaky pastries crusted with sugar and sprinkled with aniseed, sticky squares of custard made with egg yolk and sugar syrup and darkened with caramel.

'Eat everything you wish, my dear,' the condesa would say. 'You English girls are much too thin.'

Suntans, she maintained, were just as undesirable as slenderness. 'I fail to understand,' she said as she watched me from the shade, 'why modern women think it right to brown their skin.'

Brown skin, she pointed out, was a sign you were a landless peasant, a fieldworker who couldn't escape the harmful rays of the sun.

The condesa approved of Franco. Life, she said, had been much improved under the dictator. Spain had acquired what it had never had before, a bourgeoisie. The bourgeoisie took their lead from the old aristocracy, many of whom were Franco supporters, and they wished to live as the aristocracy lived.

'And who can blame them? Life is so much more agreeable when there's no need to work.'

Andalusia's *latifundios* – hereditary landowners who paid the new regime for the privilege of continuing to enjoy their titles and revenues – still controlled vast tracts of the countryside. Most of them lived in Madrid, visiting their haciendas for the hunting and spending their money elsewhere. This, said the condesa, did not help the people of the countryside, but it brought prosperity and peace to the towns.

Prosperity and peace also brought foreign tourists, northerners in search of the sunshine they lacked at home. The condesa's lands had increased in value tenfold since the tourists came.

The blue waters of the Mediterranean and an easy way of life was also a draw for more permanent escapees from the rat race, rich and spoiled and looking for somewhere to settle where there was sunshine and freedom from the constraints of life under the eye of their parents. Most of them were a little older than I, some of them I knew from my year as a debutante.

None, however, seemed to be encumbered by children – or if they were, their infants were billeted elsewhere.

The house in the hills was cool and airy. I had little desire to spend my days at the beach, still less in the bar at Pedro's. In any event, Pedro's was empty throughout the day and came to life only in the evenings, when it was crammed to overflowing and the air was thick with suspiciously scented smoke.

Sometimes I would bring the baby down to the village for the evening *paseo*, a saunter round the square in the company of local families, with a pause for a glass of wine diluted with fizzy lemonade at one of the café tables.

On the other hand, Pedro's suited Nicholas well. Peter Kent, Tim's partner in the enterprise, ran the bar, while Peter's wife Sheilagh, a lank-haired blonde with a leathery skin and a permanently down-turned mouth, oversaw the kitchen. Sheilagh surely had reason for her discontent, since Peter – resplendent each evening in skin-tight white jeans thrust into cowboy boots tucked into the regulation blue-denim shirt open to the waist to show off his bronzed chest and gold medallions – rarely went home before dawn.

Tim came and went, no one ever quite knew where, returning with yet another beautiful girl on his arm and stories of Arab souks and piratical goings-on in Casablanca and Tangier.

Nevertheless, Pedro's was profitable enough for all those involved – including Nicholas – to eat and drink for free. Which was of little interest to me, occupied as I was with my small baby and a constant stream of visitors from London.

The food, as far as I was concerned, was not much of a draw – the condesa had taught me all I needed to know about shopping and cooking in Andalusia – and the drink was usually spiked.

Meanwhile, there was another amusement to keep Nicholas out and about elsewhere – which was something of a relief, as it happened, since the company in Pedro's, much like that at the Colony, was likely to lead to trouble.

Amusement elsewhere was provided by La Consula. Bill Davis had produced an author for the bullfighting book. His choice, Shay Oag, an American writer who had taken up with an English painter, lived in the hills behind La Consula and had a passion for bullfighters. Miss Oag's shortcomings, apart from the unpronounceability of her name, included a taste for shapeless dresses and an aversion to wearing make-up, preferences which had not endeared her to the bullfighting fraternity, which likes its women either dressed to the nines or wearing nothing at all. And as for letting her anywhere near the matador's dressing-room while preparing for a fight, no chance at all.

Which meant that Nicholas found himself obliged to spend a great deal of time in bullfighters' dressing-rooms, picking up the slack for his writer – or so he said. Truth was, he loved the bullfights and the excitement surrounding the matadors, the drinking-culture of the bullfighters' bars and the flamenco joints where the *cuadrilla*, the fighters' entourage, hung out with the dancers till dawn.

The culture of Andalusia has a dangerous edge. The fight to the death – man against bull – survives nowhere else in the form it takes in Spain. Few bullfighters die of old age in their beds, not least because their followers – men (and sometimes women) who live for the fight – have an appetite for blood on the sand. Nicholas wrote passionately about the bullfight and became as knowledgeable as any Andaluz about the breeding of the bulls and the bravery of the fighters.

I sometimes reflected, as I listened to late-night discussions of the latest boy-wonder of the ring, that he'd found in the bullfight a reflection of his own brief but bloody career as a boxer, or the thrill of a night at The Establishment when Lenny was on stage and the bar was full of Soho villains fresh from a punch-up.

*****

In the early 1960s – while just down the coast Marbella was a rich man's playground with a yacht basin and a golf course and a proliferation of villas with swimming-pools and expensive restaurants – Torremolinos was still a sleepy little fishing-village with a small population of dropouts, a few glamorous hippies and a revolving population of tourists, the source of such prosperity as there was.

The main attraction at Pedro's was the aforementioned Peter Kent, the young American with tousled blond hair and blue eyes who wore his shirts unbuttoned to the waist and tucked into very tight white jeans pulled down over high-heeled cowboy boots.

Tim had a house in the village and a half-share in Pedro's and a resident girlfriend, Clare Raab (funny how some names stick and others vanish from the mind) who wrote poetry and baked hash brownies to a recipe from Alice B. Toklas, best-beloved of Gertrude Stein who, it was supposed, had written the cookbook which bore her name.

Clare had a novel way of taking revenge when Tim had been misbehaving with some other lady. She waited till the evening's dalliance was over, then dragged a mattress outside his door and did what comes naturally with whatever or whoever had happened to catch her eye. The racket could be heard all round the village and drew an enthusiastic audience of onlookers, cheering her on.

Such behaviour was not unusual. Pedro's was always full of pretty girls in an advanced state of irresponsibility who were more than prepared to take a chance there and then with whatever good-looking young man took their fancy, whether or not there were onlookers.

This did very little for marital relations in the village, since the local youth were more than willing to oblige the pretty foreigners under the influence of substances which lowered their inhibitions.

Regular supplies of marijuana – mostly in the form of crumbly brown blocks of cannabis resin smoked in little clay pipes – were delivered by the smugglers who crossed the narrow straits that separate Europe and Africa in small boats less profitably employed in the inshore fisheries. Cannabis pollen, a yellowish powder which clings to the leather chaps of the harvesters and could be scraped off and sold cheap as a perk of the trade, was baked into brownies. It could also be sprinkled on spaghetti bolognese, one of the few dishes the kitchen was capable of producing, as a trap for the unwary.

Meanwhile, the house on the hill rapidly filled up with escapees from London, among them Dominick Elwes.

The condesa's winter residence, inevitably, had no telephone, which meant that all communication was relayed at second-hand through Pedro's. Depending on who took the message and whether brownies were on the menu, news travelled slowly, if at all. And when the call came through that Dominick was on his way, I had barely an hour to negotiate the pot-holed coast road and reach the airport.

When Dom limped off the plane, last in the line, he was a dismal sight. A broken nose under a thick wedge of white plaster, two black eyes and a split lip made him look as if he'd just been in a bare-knuckle fight well outside the rules laid down by Lord Queensberry.

If this was indeed the case, I said, he had my sympathy.

Not at all. The injuries, Dom explained with some indignation, were the result of a minor disagreement with his wife. Surely not? Tessa was half Dominick's weight and not, as far as I knew, inclined to physical violence. Though there were certainly circumstances under which even the most tolerant of women might resort to fisticuffs.

Indeed not. And although there were times when this might have been true, his injuries were caused by nothing more than a desire not to disturb his wife's night's rest by ringing the doorbell.

Because of this entirely laudable ambition, he had fallen from his own balcony on to the line of railings. Fortunately the railings were blunt rather than pointed. The result was not only the obvious injuries that had prompted my question, but he had been lucky to escape permanent damage to that part of his anatomy which makes a man what he is.

As a result of this, Dom explained, he was obliged to wear a protective box of the kind worn by cricketers when taking their turn at the crease, a situation which had not only closed down his social life but made him a laughing-stock at the Clermont. Hence the urgency to leave the city and lie low till the crisis had passed.

I see the point, I said. And giggled. I notice as we get in the car that Dominick is indeed sporting a very large bulge in his trousers.

The house being full of babies – only one, as I explained with some irritation – Dominick and Nicholas, who had returned in triumph that same evening from a bullfight in Seville, went in search of a social life and a bite of dinner at Pedro's.

Pedro's was awash with social life. When Tim was around, there was a party every night. The condesa was right: very little food was consumed and wine ran like water. And if Tim's girlfriend had baked a trayful of Alice B.'s hashish fudge, mostly chocolate and nuts and sugar with a lethal amount of marijuana pollen, the atmosphere was inclined to get rowdy.

Dominick pronounced himself famished, announced that cannabis had no effect on him whatsoever, ate three brownies in quick succession, and passed out like a felled ox.

Nicholas decided to leave him where he was and came home without him. Dominick was never a man not to find himself a lift home. Judging by the racket at two in the morning, one of the young ladies at the bar had offered to oblige and the pair of them were howling and thumping at intervals through the night.

The howling woke the baby. In the morning, I was feeling less than amiable – it had been the kind of night that puts a mother in a bad temper at breakfast.

So when Dominick came to find me in the kitchen, I was less than sympathetic. Still less so when he explained that his female companion had mistaken his shouts of agony for cries of ecstasy and the whole experience had been a nightmare.

Adding insult to injury, would I mind driving her home? Please?

Drive her yourself, I replied.

Shortly after that, Timothy decided he had things to do and people to see in Tangier. The things to be done involved a very fast, very flashy motor boat in which he was accustomed to run around the Mediterranean on errands. The boat, inconveniently, was moored at Cap d'Antibes.

Just before he left, Tim promised to bring me a beautiful Moroccan boy as a present, though I had no idea what I'd do with a Moroccan boy, however beautiful. It seemed to me I had enough trouble on my hands already.

Somewhere between the Côte d'Azur and Tangier a storm blew up. The boat disappeared off the coast of Corsica and the bodies were never found. There were rumours that Tim had been unwise in his choice of playmates and that he'd become rather too friendly with the wife or mistress of someone who was more than capable of planting explosives on boats.

As soon as the news came through, Nicholas set off for the island – a complicated journey from Malaga – hired a car and strong-armed the British Consul into accompanying him round the coastline in search of wreckage.

Cushions from the boat were found – inflatable and yellow, they were spotted from the air – but nothing else. Rumours flew.

For years afterwards, there would sometimes be a message which the caller, a voice with a heavy Middle Eastern accent, said came from Lord Willoughby. His lordship was alive and well and would telephone us shortly. Tim himself never rang. Eventually, after we moved house, the calls ceased.

*****

Timothy's disappearance left a tangle of loose ends for Nicholas to unravel. Wips, the joint enterprise, was sold to an entrepreneur who renamed it the Ad Lib and turned it into what it had never become under earlier ownership, the most successful nightclub in London.

Pedro's had never made a profit – at least, whatever profit might have been made disappeared into the front man's pocket – but there were plenty of unpaid bills. Tim's share of the business had to be sold rather smartly to cover its debts, though somewhat mysteriously, the place ended up back in the possession of Pedro himself.

Once Pedro's had been disposed of, there was nothing in the way of business interests to keep Nicholas in Spain.

Had it not been for the fast-talking Hugh Millais, the tall, lanky, guitar-strumming playboy who had strummed the guitar that first night at La Consula, we might have returned to London and never built the house in the valley that was to become our family home for more than a decade.

Hugh was married to a beautiful French wife, an excellent cook, and lived about a hundred miles along the coast on the far side of Algeciras in La Serafina, a rambling hacienda which belonged to his father, painter Raoul Millais. The hacienda, on the far tip of Andalusia, overlooked the hills of Africa.

Hugh's plan was to build a development of rich men's houses in a remote valley a few miles further round the coast in the hills behind Tarifa, a wind-buffeted harbour town overlooking the Straits of Gibraltar, just across from the mountains of Morocco.

Tarifa, the legend went, was built by the Phoenicians to guard the approach to the Atlantic and exact tribute from passing ships obliged to take on water and food. Thirty years after the end of the Civil War, the military were still the most powerful force in the land, and the area from Gibraltar to Cadiz was *zona militar*, an area where no one but the army could move freely, still less own property.

The assumption was that Franco was fearful of invasion from dissidents who had taken refuge across the straits after the Civil War – though the real fear was the return of the Moors across the narrow band of water that separated Europe from Africa. No foreigner, whatever the reason, was allowed to own land in the military zone, let alone build a dwelling.

Hugh was a persuasive salesman. He appeared early one morning with an ebony-haired scarlet-lipsticked companion who, since her name was Henrietta Partridge, was clearly not his wife.

The pair scooped up Nicholas and Dominick and took them off for lunch at La Consula with the Davises. Over a long and wine-fuelled afternoon, the deal was done – such as it was, since

Nicholas's side of the arrangement seemed to involve little more than a commitment to build the first house.

Which, considering there were no roads, no electricity and no telephone and the military owned the land, was something of a leap of faith.

No matter, said Hugh, he had the military in his pocket. He himself would oversee the building and Jon Banneberg, a decorator friend of Dominick's who had just designed the interior of the QE2 – not, in my view, much of a recommendation for architecting a cosy family house in Andalusia's charming vernacular style – would draw up the plans.

I had little or no say in the matter, though I was happy enough to go along with whatever Nicholas decided he wanted to do. Next day, Hugh reappeared with the beautiful French wife, walked into the kitchen and handed me a lipstick.

'Yours I think, darling. You left it in the car.'

'Not mine,' I said, unscrewing the lid and inspecting the contents. Miss Partridge favoured scarlet-woman crimson and I was into Juliette Greco pink, if I was into anything at all. 'Wrong colour red.'

Hugh rolled his eyes in the direction of his wife. 'As I told Susie – '

'Oh,' I said. 'I see what you mean.'

I don't think Susie was fooled, but I pocketed the lipstick anyway and carried on rolling meatballs for lunch, cheap and easy and expandable when there were more people at table than had been expected. And anyway, the baby loved them.

*****

The house in the Andaluz valley took less than a year to complete. Hugh was anxious for a show-house and Nicholas was delighted at the prospect of builders and architects and deciding where things went.

My beloved Battersea house had to be sold to cover the spiralling cost of the architect's plans.

Even so, with the two elder children at a London primary school and Nicholas involved with his publishing company, we had no intention of doing more than spending holidays at the house.

Nicholas, meanwhile, had managed to secure the lease on a rent-controlled flat just off Sloane Square vacated by a supporter of the anti-apartheid movement in South Africa.

The supporter had reason to be grateful to Nicholas. He had managed to arrange for a few of the more prominent dissidents to acquire British passports which were, if not totally what they purported to be, good enough copies to get them through frontiers. And no, I have no idea how this came about, except that my husband's indirect involvement in the dissident movement in South Africa was entirely in character, and he had friends who were more than capable of making copies of passports.

Money was tight and getting tighter. There had been other unforeseen expenses before the house could be declared officially ours. Permission to register ownership had to be bought from the mayor of Tarifa, the town council and the military authorities who controlled the stretch of coastline which ran from La Linea, the frontier with Gibraltar, round as far as Cadiz.

'It'll all be fine in the end,' said Hugh, with an airy wave of the hand.

Actually, it wasn't. We never managed to elevate ourselves from clandestine squatters to official residents. Every year, along with everyone else in the valley including the farming households who had lived there for generations, we had to pay an annual fine to the Guardia Civil to overlook our presence. Finally, two years after completion, the house in a cork-oak forest in a remote Andalusian valley became our family home, a story I have written about elsewhere, in *Family Life: Birth, Death and the Whole Damn Thing.*

The children were enrolled in Spanish schools and Nicholas, still based in the London flat, came to visit us whenever his business affairs permitted – not often, it seemed. Nevertheless, the house was large and airy and had a magnificent view across the straits to the hills of Africa – never mind that the walls leaked and there was no heating and I was too overawed by the architect's vision to disobey his instructions and curtain the floor-to-ceiling windows.

There were friends who came and went. The poet Christopher Logue took up residence for a time, publishing his poems in booklet form at the printer in Algeciras. Playwright Michael Hastings arrived for a fortnight and was still there six months later, courting, as I remember, a young Spanish grandee who remained strictly unavailable in anything but the intellectual department, but was happy to permit him to keep her company from midnight to dawn in a local nightclub.

Meanwhile, I returned to London with the children for the summer – the Spanish school year runs from October to June, leaving three months for the long summer break. And as the children needed me less, I was beginning to return to painting as a way to supplement the family income.

Alice B. Toklas's Hashish Fudge

Take this with hot mint tea as they do in Morocco, where it's valued as a cold cure. Hashish fudge can also usefully be served to a meeting of the Daughters of the American Revolution and is suitable for a Parisian tea-party. Consume no more than two pieces at a time.

MAKES ABOUT A POUND

1 teaspoon black peppercorns
1 whole nutmeg, roughly crushed
4 average sticks cinnamon
1 teaspoon coriander seeds

Pulverise the spices in a mortar. Add a handful each of stoned dates, dried figs, shelled almonds and peanuts: chop and mix together. A bunch of cannabis sativa should be pulverised with the spices. Knead the mixture with about a cup of sugar dissolved in a big pat of butter. Roll it all into a cake and cut into pieces about the size of a walnut.

Top left. Bertha Baron, my maternal grandmother, painted in the 1930's by Simon Elwes. *Top right.* My maternal grandfather, Eddie Baron, studio portrait from the 1950's. *Bottom left.* My mother Millicent with my father Richard Maitland Longmore on their wedding day. *Bottom right.* My father and grandfather, Air Chief Marshal Sir Arthur Longmore, on their way to Buckingham Palace.

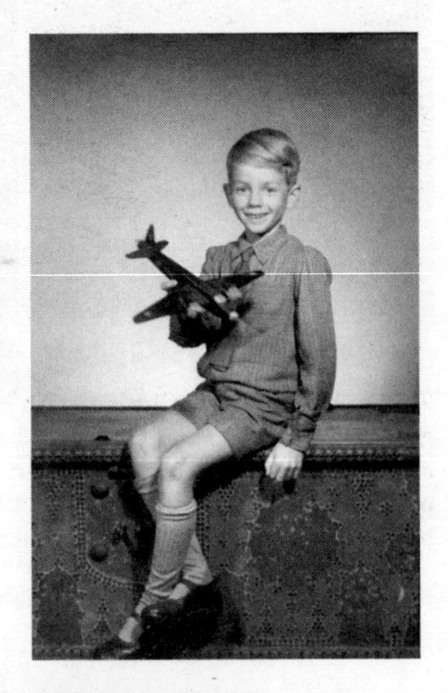

Top left. Nicholas' father Jock McVean Luard in Saudi Arabia circa 1940. *Right.* Nicholas aged 8, dreaming of higher things. *Below.* Nicholas' father and mother, Susan Lamert, on their wedding day.

Top. In Venice at the Cipriani with Nicky Mountain, first beau (Baron grandparents on the other side of the table). *Below right*. Receiving line at the Savoy: my mother and myself in Hartnell finery (mine's lipstick pink, my mother's is midnight blue). *Below left*. Deb dance at the Savoy: both parties evidently looking for action elsewhere.

Above. Opening night at The Establishment: Nicholas and Peter Cook in the middle; Peter's wife Wendy 2nd from right on floor, Dudley Moore at bottom left on stool, set-designer Sean Kenny cross-legged in front; Eleanor Bron under the ladder; John Bird back row 4th from left. *Right.* The Eye under new proprietorship (photo by Jane Bowen for *The Sunday Times*). Clockwise from left: Christopher Booker, Richard Ingrams, Willie Rushton, Nicholas on the floor.

Top. Shotgun wedding, Mexican style: on the river Uxumacintla by the Guatemalan border. *Below right.* Checking the racing results with tipster Jeff Bernard and playwright Frank Norman. *Below left.* Contemplating matrimony in Nicholas' flat in Hyde Park Square, Lucien Freud's 'Charlie' looking on.

Top. No going back: wedding day at St. Margaret's, Westminster. *Bottom.* wedding guests, left to right, designer Matt Carter, broadcaster Colin Bell, *Eye* editor Richard Ingrams, Mary Ingrams behind on right. *Left.* Bride and best man Nicholas Garland.

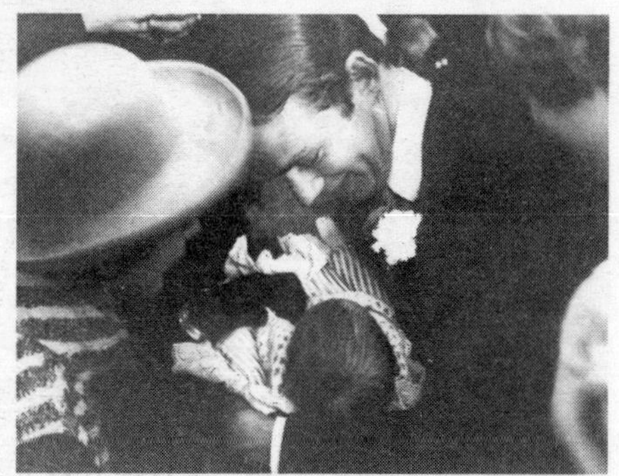

Clockwise from top. Listening to best man Nick Garland's speech: Kim Waterfield brandishing the bridal bouquet; Nicholas admiring Anneke Wills' baby; Willie Rushton up to no good.

Clockwise from top left. Nicholas plotting the next step in the flat in Hyde Park Square; me listening to the next step; cartoonist Nick Garland with wife Harriet; gang of four with Peter Bellwood and Harriet.

CHAPTER EIGHT

Sunshine and Donkey Droppings

'Perhaps all artists were, in a sense, housewives: tenders of the earth household.'

ERICA JONG, *The First Ms. Reader* (1972)

THE HUERTO WAS THE FIRST OF WHAT WAS INTENDED TO BE A development of secluded houses set in their own grounds where the rich and beautiful might spend their summers in comfort and privacy. With an accent on the privacy.

'Brilliant,' said Dominick happily. 'Twice as much fun as Mustique and you don't have to put up with Princess Madge and dear old Colin Tennant.'

The Huerto, it must be admitted, was not much of an advertisement for the lifestyle of the rich in search of comfort. Not only was it, by the end of 1968, packed to the rafters with four noisy children – their number regularly swollen by their Spanish schoolfriends – there was little evidence of the Mustique lifestyle. There was not even a swimming-pool, let alone a tennis court or any of the other luxuries Dominick and Hugh needed to persuade the punters to part with their money.

Terms of the lease on the house – ownership was out of the question – forbade public displays of suburban activities such as kitchen gardens and washing-lines.

I paid no attention to such nonsense. There was washing not only flapping on the line but spread out over all the bushes, the Andaluz method of bleaching linen in the sun. There was also a very obvious patch of kitchen garden in which tomatoes, aubergines, peppers and chickpeas were in full production.

The house was open and airy and built of porous building-blocks lime-washed to keep out the weather. The floors were tiled and the windows were floor-to-ceiling smoked glass with huge wooden shutters. Easy to keep clean, though not exactly cosy.

I employed help in the house, an au pair who had worked for us in London to help look after the children, and I soon found a brisk, efficient young local girl, Ana, to live in and do the housework – I loved to cook, but I was never any good with a mop and a bucket.

All that we lacked was a household pig. A house without a porker, Ana assured me, was a household without a soul. Manolo the dustman supplied a piglet and installed him with much ceremony in the tumbledown sty at the end of the garden.

We also needed a donkey. A household without an ass, said Manolo, is a house which lacks reliable transport. Bernardo the donkey arrived, retired from active service as a beast of heavy burden, and took up residence under the cork trees.

Hugh put up little resistance. He was not a man for a fight. And anyway, the Huerto and its inhabitants, four-footed as well as two, were invisible from the road, since we were tucked out of sight at the end of a bumpy road hidden among the tallest trees in the valley.

With the essentials in place, I set about acquiring the information that would allow us, a young family in the wilds of Andalusia, to live in way which was not at odds with our surroundings.

What I learned from my neighbours in those years of my children's childhood taught me to respect an ancient way of life already vanishing as fast as snow in summer. Money was a crop like any other. Its absence brought hardship but not despair: subsistence farmers are careful not to depend on a single crop. Nevertheless the life was hard and material rewards were few: physical labour ages like nothing else. None of my contemporaries expected to live to a comfortable old age. Couples, if both survived the middle years, would often separate as soon as they became grandparents, spreading the burden of responsibility for their welfare in old age. And when the last of those who knew how to live the life of the valley moved to the town, the mortarless walls of their stone-built dwellings crumbled back into the mountainside, unmarked and unlamented.

Our own house in the valley, the Huerto Perdido – the Lost Orchard – occupied the site of one such long-vanished homestead. The wellspring essential to human habitation remained, though the cork oaks had long since replaced any productive orchard trees. With one exception. A fig tree shadowed the Huerto's wellspring, evidence we were not the first to build a shelter in this beautiful place. Our predecessors had drunk the water from the well and waited, as did we, to taste the sweetness of the ripened fruit.

The climate was wet in winter, bone-dry in summer. The land was stony and hard to crop. My neighbours kept chickens for eggs and meat, and goats for milk and cheese. Wandering herds of pigs, semi-wild *ibéricos* of the old Mediterranean breed, foraged the forest for free. Ancient terraces hacked into the steep hillsides produced cabbages, onions and potatoes through the winter. In summer, there were tomatoes, peppers, aubergines and garlic for stews. Bread was baked once a week and most households kept bees.

Chickpeas and beans were sown as a catch crop, protected from the wind by neat rows of maize, food for the chickens. Although height and wind and damp made it impossible to grow grapes or olives, the cash crops of the region, the hardier fruit trees thrived: pomegranate, medlar, persimmon, mulberry for the silkworms. And the fig trees fruited twice a year – green in spring, purple in autumn – and the fruits that were too high to crop provided winter food for fig-peckers and the beautiful scarlet-winged goldcrests which migrated across the straits to their winter feeding-grounds in Africa.

The Gaudalmesi, the little river which watered the valley and never ran dry, had carved itself a steep channel through the mountainside, providing irrigation all through the year. In the absence of olive trees, sunflowers were grown for oil, though wine, essential to the wellbeing of any Mediterranean household, had to be bought. The community, such as remained, were otherwise self-sufficient. Money to pay for things that needed to be bought came from the sale of eggs and cheese traded through the *corredera*, an errand-runner who took the goods to market and exchanged them for cooking-implements and needles and buttons and thread and all things a household cannot make for itself.

There was also a little money to be made by taking employment in the small fishing-settlement which had established itself as a trading-post where the river flowed into the sea. The fishermen supplied fresh fish in exchange for crops grown further up the valley, but were always glad of a hand on the boats. The grain was threshed by donkey power and winnowed by hand on a beaten-earth threshing-floor, and the grain was turned into flour in a water-powered mill built during the Moorish occupation.

No one had access to electricity or a telephone line, though there was a little *venta* at the foot of the valley which ran a television on a petrol-powered generator. Every household baked bread at least once a week in an outside oven heated by bundles of sweet-scented sage brush and wild olive twigs.

The cork-oak forest that surrounded us was of particular interest to the bristle-backed pigs, all of which were known to their owners though no one would admit this when they rooted up my struggling crops. The pigs – known as *pata-negra*, black-foot, for the colour of their dainty little hooves – were the last remnants of the herds which had once cropped the woodlands of the Mediterranean littoral. Our own sty pig, provided by our neighbours so that the household's leavings would go to a good home, was also a black-foot, an adventurous brute with a ferocious appetite and a habit of escaping his sty to demand his dinner at the kitchen door.

Cork-oak acorns are good forage for pigs, and the herds provided their owners with an alternative source of income from the sale of the haunches for ham. The meat and fat was used for *chorizo* and salt-cured bacon, which flavoured the robust soup stews everyone ate in the winter.

At times of year when the sea was calm and there was neither planting nor harvesting, the little wooden boats tied up at the jetty by the river mouth put out to sea, trawling for sardines and anchovies to sell in the market at Tarifa, or to barrel up in salt as winter stores. Salt was gathered from the salt flats thirty miles or so round the coast at Cadiz.

Domestic animals and barnyard fowl were treated without sentimentality. Hens were popped unceremoniously in the boiling-pot when their days were done; poultry was women's business and I was soon taught how to kill and pluck a chicken. Donkeys went to the slaughterhouse to be turned into *chorizo* – a job for the butcher rather than the householder. The household pig, however, an altogether more manageable animal emotionally – only the English fall in love with their pigs – met his end every autumn in the yard. Pig-slaughter, I'm happy to say, was the business of the men, though I could always count on help from their wives when the meat arrived in the kitchen.

In the old days before the invention of nylon killed the trade, the silkworms provided strong thread for the fishermen's lines as well as barter goods for the *corredera*. Households who lived at the upper end of the valley had been accustomed to exchange the silkworm cocoons for fresh fish. In the old days, they said, shimmering towers of pink and yellow and cream cocoons tottered down the track on donkey-back and the trade made the upward trip worthwhile.

'You couldn't fry fish when the silkworms were spinning,' said Ana. 'The silkworms took fright and snipped the thread.'

Some of the fishermen made a living from the tuna which ran through the straits in spring and autumn, and there were others who traded in shellfish and the spider crabs which took refuge from storms in wrecks. But the real profit, reliable in a way that the fishing was not, came from the smuggling-trade. The fishermen of the Guadalmesi were always at loggerheads with the inhabitants of the neighbouring valley who made their money by informing the Guardia when a shipment was due.

*****

The development above the road was of no interest to those who lived below. The upper hillsides had never been inhabited, apart from the Huerto Perdido, the Lost Orchard – though no one remembered when it had been anything but lost.

Negotiations with the military and, I could only imagine, fistfuls of money in the right direction, finally paid off. Hugh managed to secure agreement from the military to allow the development to go ahead. Dominick managed to raise the finance for a luxury development to be known as El Cuartòn.

Work began first on a little village with apartments which could be sold or rented to finance the rest of the development. There was, too, a swimming-pool, a shop and a restaurant, facilities sure to attract guests from the villas just as soon as these were built.

Building proceeded at a snail's pace. A broad concrete ribbon of road snaked up the mountainside behind us, only to snake right back down again as soon as the rainy season began.

Progress on the villas, happily, was even slower. I had no desire to find myself marooned in a suburb of Mayfair and Manhattan in the middle of nowhere. For which, no doubt, I would have had only myself to blame.

The peasantry below the road held their lands through payment of an annual fine which decreased every year until, after ten years, title could be registered and the land passed on to the incumbent's direct descendants, though it couldn't be sold to anyone else.

The ten-year rule had been introduced by General Franco in the aftermath of the Civil War as an encouragement to the surviving peasantry to return to the land. The moratorium did not, of course, apply to foreigners in the military zone, who could only hold title in the name of a Spanish national, making it almost impossible to resell a property without lengthy negotiations and bribes.

By the time the house was complete, the cost of the building and the need to pay our household bills had absorbed the rest of my dowry. The Huerto was mortgaged to the bank which provided the publishing company with its working capital, which also happened to be the money behind the development, and there was nothing for it but to hope that Nicholas's publishing enterprises would succeed, or that, with one well-received thriller under his belt, he'd decide he was really a writer and write another.

I was never certain that Nicholas had ever really wanted to be a writer. Writing was a means to an end rather than something he could not exist without. Which is not to say that he wasn't a fine writer, lyrical and elegant, a wordsmith to his fingertips. But he had inherited the entrepreneurial spirit of his mother's family, loved politics, enjoyed the rough and tumble of the marketplace, made friends as easily as enemies. Success had never been a problem. He was the golden boy, and whenever an enterprise came unstuck, there was always something else to take its place. Perhaps, at least in those early years, a wife and four children never really figured in Nicholas's view of how he wanted to live his life. While I was always Mum or Ma or Mother – or whatever variation came to mind – the children never called their father by anything but his given name.

Whatever the reason for Nicholas's long absences from the family circle, we muddled through in our house in the valley.

For me, observing the comings and goings both above and below the road, the self-sufficient farming community which had always lived in the valley taught me all I needed to know about how to keep house and care for my growing family. For the rest, there was entertainment and company to be found in the houses and among the summer visitors who rented apartments in the tourist village, the latest development Hugh and Dominick fervently hoped would be a money-spinner.

The second house to be built high on the hillside above us had an uninterrupted view across the Straits of Gibraltar to the mountains of Morocco with the Sahara beyond.

On a clear day, said Hugh persuasively, you could see all the way to the Cape. The price of the view was the wind. The reason the view was uninterrupted was that there were no trees. There were no trees, said those who lived below the road and had never built on the mountainside for a very good reason: if you planted trees in the summer, in the winter the rain carried them all the way down to the sea.

The house, nevertheless, had a swimming-pool, underfloor heating, sunken baths and all the luxuries the Huerto lacked. The first owner was a young English beauty, widow of a French industralist thrice her age, who had left her well provided for on condition she remained a widow. Since she couldn't marry her lover for fear of losing her income, she needed a bolt-hole.

The house was built to the orders of the beauty, entirely composed of hexagons. The bedrooms were hexagonal, the roof was hexagonal, the swimming-pool was hexagonal, there was a hexagonal living-room and a hexagonal dining-room. Even the bathrooms were hexagons.

The glasses, plates and floor tiles were hexagonal, as was the hexagonal dining-table surrounded by a hexagonal bench. Both bench and table could be raised or lowered to fit flush with the floor. The raising and lowering mechanism was triggered by setting the hands of the grandfather clock to midnight. Very ingenious.

As soon as the beauty and her lover moved into the house, an inaugural dinner was arranged and invitations hand-delivered. Delivery by hand was all that was available up or down the valley since there was no official postman and all mail had to be collected from Tarifa, twenty miles away.

Unofficial deliveries were the business of Manolo the dustman. Manolo knew everything about everyone and, possibly as a result of this, had accumulated large amounts of cash which he was prepared to lend at rates of interest slightly above those available at the bank, but which did not require borrowers to go through the usual formalities.

Memories of the Civil War had left the valley's inhabitants unwilling to sign their names to anything, incriminating or otherwise, and anyway, few had had the benefit of schooling and not everyone could write.

Invitations to the inaugural dinner at Hexagonal Hall were eagerly accepted. Quite apart from all the hexagons – said to be good karma or at least to prevent bad karma – everyone wanted to see the famous table in action.

When the guests arrived, the table and bench were snugly tucked into the floor. As soon as dinner was announced, the table and bench were raised to sitting and eating height by the secret device hidden in the grandfather clock.

Dinner, a Moroccan feast prepared by a chef imported from Marrakesh, was couscous with chicken cooked with salt-pickled lemons, a dish which, if properly made, requires lengthy preparation since the grains must swell to at least four times their original size. The scent was heavenly – reminiscent, everyone agreed, of a particular lemon grove in the garden of the king's palace in Riyadh.

There were, too, elegant little pastries stuffed with cinnamon-spiced pigeon breast, dishes of rosewater for rinsing the fingers, dishes of mint and parsley folded with yoghurt, all of which also required care and time, delaying the arrival of dinner till just before midnight.

No sooner had the guests taken their seats when the clock struck twelve. The hexagonal table and its delicious burden began to descend slowly towards the hexagonal bench which, in its turn, began to rise to meet the table, threatening to amputate the diners just below the hip. With a piercing shriek, our hostess leapt for the clock and wrenched at the hands. The table and bench paused in mid-slide, allowing the guests to scramble to safety, then continued its descent, clicking and whirring as its clockwork innards digested the feast.

A day or two later, hoping that the memory of the disaster might have faded and I might acquire the recipe for chicken with salt-pickled lemons, I made my way up the hill.

The house was shuttered and Dominick and Hugh were sitting disconsolately on the doorstep. The chef had fled back to his homeland, the flame-haired beauty had retired to the comforts of the Hotel Alfonso XIII in Seville, and Dom and Hugh had been left with responsibility for clearing up the mess.

The remains of the Moroccan feast were still trapped under the hexagonal table. They were, said Hugh gloomily, beginning to smell less like a lemon grove in the king's palace in Riyadh and more like the Tangier rubbish dump.

The day was hot and the situation could only get worse.

Furthermore, said Dominick, the flame-haired beauty's lover's mother was the legendary Diana Vreeland, editor of American *Vogue*. She was due to arrive that very afternoon with a view to using Hexagonal Hall for a fashion shoot which, if all went well, would put the development on the map and make everyone a fortune.

Couldn't someone put her off?

Absolutely not, said Dominick. You didn't put off the editor of *Vogue*. The editor of *Vogue* didn't get put off by anything.

Nevertheless, they were working on alternatives.

They were, I suggested, welcome to move the location to the Huerto. If I tethered the donkey elsewhere and shut the pig in the sty and removed the washing from the line, the editor of *Vogue* might not even notice the difference. Apart from the hexagonals, of course, but we might be able to fudge that.

What we lacked in the way of swimming-pools, I pointed out, we made up for in rustic charm. New York sophisticates adored rustic charm. And I'd be happy to cook a rustic dinner and provide charming accommodation for the night, if that would help.

Hugh brightened. Only to have his hopes dashed.

'What about the owl?' said Dominick.

Ah. The owl might indeed be a problem. I had to admit that not everyone wanted to share accommodation with a full-grown eagle owl, a stripe-feathered glamour girl with a six-foot wingspan, ferocious talons, enormous orange eyes and a beak which made a noise like a trapdoor in a force-nine gale.

The eagle owl, I confirmed, was indeed still in residence in the guest-room cupboard, confined to barracks till a broken wing had mended. Dominick had met the owl the last time he found himself in need of overnight accommodation at the Huerto.

Dom had an apartment of his own in the village but his girlfriends tended to be on the feisty side, just like Tessa, and locked him out when he misbehaved. On the most recent of such evenings, I had showed Dom to his quarters but omitted to mention the presence of a very large avian predator in the guest-room cupboard, a floor-to-ceiling affair with plenty of room for movement.

Dominick, having drunk rather a lot of aniseed brandy before retiring to his billet, had woken in the middle of the night to find a hungry raptor perched on his bedpost, rocking from side to side and clattering her beak as if getting the measure of breakfast.

'Thanks for the offer,' said Dominick.

'Perhaps not,' said Hugh.

I wasn't convinced that they were right.

I explained that my good friend Edie Coulson, an elegant New Yorker and herself a friend of the editor of *Vogue*, had told me that cheetahs, even more ferocious beasts than eagle owls, were all the rage on the catwalk and were quite the thing in chic gentlemen's clubs.

As far as I was concerned, Edie had her finger on the pulse. She was the author of a seminal work on feminism and, conversely in the days when bra-burning was a statement of sisterhood, a woman who never appeared in public without her make-up, even at breakfast. She also had the good taste to rent my house in the summer and had struck up a friendship with the owl.

What did Edie mean by chic gentlemen's clubs?

Bordellos, said Edie cheerfully. Members only, very exclusive. She herself was in the habit of joining her husband, a Bostonian banker of impeccable credentials, for tea and cake in the foyer. The cake was home-made, the tea was lapsang, the *Wall Street Journal* was provided and wives were welcome in all the public areas. What went on upstairs was no concern of those enjoying refreshments downstairs. All very civilized, said Edie.

Tea in a bordello with your husband, however chic the surroundings or classy the newspapers, struck me as a little on the tolerant side, but Edie didn't seem to think so.

'Nonsense,' she said. 'All the husbands go there. It saves everyone a lot of trouble.'

I see.

What would happen, I asked, if the vice squad came to call?

Edie waved her hand. 'Nada. Zilch. It happens all the time. The management gets ten minutes' warning and they always arrive at the tradesman's entrance. It happened when I was there. The rest of us didn't turn a hair. The hookers came sliding down the fire escape followed by the cheetahs followed by the husbands in their underpants. It was very amusing. Then we all left through the front door as if nothing had happened.'

So you see, I ended triumphantly, sharing accommodation with big spotted predators was right on the button. *Vogue* would be thrilled.

'Not the owl. It's not house-trained,' said Dominick. 'Don't be absurd.'

The third house, La Muñeca, the Doll's House, was a miniature palace with two turrets and an arched patio built by Hugh and Dominick for sale to whoever would buy.

Dominick managed to persuade a Swiss count with a well-stuffed bank account to rent it for the summer with a view to purchase. The count immediately shipped his elegant French wife back to Geneva for the weekend and imported a posse of young ladies from Paris courtesy of Madame Claude and her little black book.

To add a touch of respectability to the enterprise, Dominick was despatched to distribute invitations around the place – the local ducal family and their cousins, a few of the more amusing members of the English colony – to a gala dinner on the Friday evening to be catered by French chefs. There was, naturally enough, a great deal of excitement over the event, even though, unusually for gatherings in Andalusia where everyone arrived late for everything, we were warned we would be expected to arrive on time and leave before midnight.

This, said Dominick somewhat coyly, was because public entertainment would be over by then. By which was meant that the private entertainment would be just starting somewhere else.

Everyone arrived more or less on time, done up to the nines in beads, sandals and kaftans. Already resident at the palace were a dozen exquisitely groomed Chanel-clad beauties with matching shoes and handbags who moved smoothly among the guests, making polite and well-bred conversation in French, Spanish or English, depending on whom they were addressing.

Madame Claude's, it was abundantly clear, was more than a match for the rest of us.

A stupendous dinner – quail poached in Sauternes with truffles, followed by profiteroles and *glace vanille au chocolat* – was served under the arches in the candlelit patio. Gardenias scented the air. The attendants were magnificent in gold pantaloons, embroidered waistcoats and turbans. Then a bell rang and everyone except Dominick vanished.

'That's it,' announced Dominick firmly.

Obediently, the rest of us gathered ourselves together and a gloomy procession of kaftan-clad non-participants made their way to their parked vehicles and wended their way back down the hill, leaving the bright lights and laughter behind.

The children were always up early, so I was not particularly sorry to leave. And Nicholas, as usual, was in London, and although by now I was well accustomed to accepting dinner invitations on my own, tonight was one of the nights when I had felt a little lonely.

I walked back down the hill to the Huerto in the moonlight and had just settled myself at the kitchen table for a reflective nightcap when I heard the rattle of a heavy vehicle on the gravel outside.

I walked to the window.

Hugh emerged from the company Land Rover, with Dominick close behind.

'Darling,' he called, 'we're on a mission. Can you let us have a stash?'

I considered the question. A stash meant marijuana. The truthful answer was no. I didn't do marijuana. Never had done. Nicholas preferred liquor and pills and distrusted anything that wasn't sold over the counter or came from the chemist. Well, not since I was seventeen and never again.

But, considering the hopeful look on the two faces and my position as the resident hippy, it might be quite fun to say yes.

'Wait in the car,' I said. 'I'll see what I can do.'

It was late in the year and I had been drying a supply of herbs to see us through the winter. I took a jar of marjoram from the shelf, mixed it with a handful of black tobacco from a packet of Spanish cigarettes, added a good pinch of donkey droppings that the daughters had been saving for their dollies' tea party, and handed it over.

'Take care,' I warned. 'It's very strong.'

Two days later, Hugh reappeared with spinning eyeballs. 'Wonderful stuff,' he said. 'We're all still flying. Did you grow it yourself?'

'Donkey droppings and marjoram,' I said shortly, somewhat irritated by the pink eyes and evidence of too much partying with the ladies from Madame Claude. 'And serves you right.'

By the look on his face, I don't think he believed me. And if he did, he certainly wasn't going to share the information with anyone else.

The development's tourist village, designed as a luxury version of an Andalusian *pueblo*, turned out to be nothing of the sort. There was a problem with leaking roofs and drainage. Nevertheless, the apartments sold like hot cakes to friends of Dominick and Hugh, many of whom seemed to be in need of rest and recreation without their wives, several of whom, I noticed when I took the children to swim in the pool, were vaguely familiar from the Clermont.

The apartment owners took up residence in the summer. In the winter, the *pueblo* was virtually deserted and Dominick would drift up from his apartment to the Huerto, where he would make himself at home. If there was no else around to amuse him, I would often find him asleep in one of the guest-rooms in the morning. Dominick's love affairs rarely ran smoothly.

There were two guest-rooms at the Huerto, one of which was more often than not occupied by my best friend Venetia. Venetia had been one of the residents in Nicholas's bachelor flat in the days before we were married, and we had remained friends thereafter.

Venetia's love life was almost as complicated as Dominick's, and a great deal more entertaining, as far as I was concerned, since she attracted hopeful young men like bees to honey.

She was, however, being enthusiastically courted by another of the Clermont regulars, Richard Parkes. Richard sported a luxuriant moustache which made him look not unlike the Earl of Lucan. And when Lucan went on the run after the murder of the nanny in his estranged wife's house in Ebury Street, rumours began to fly.

Dominick was in London at the time of the murder and had been despatched by the Clermont regulars to charm Veronica Lucan into not dishing the dirt on her husband. None of the Clermont's regulars was prepared to discuss what might or might not have happened on the night of the murder.

Police inquiries centred on Lucan's friends – particularly those who had seen him that night. Aspinall, it was thought, might have persuaded the gambler to do the decent thing and fall on his sword, and have thereafter fed the evidence to the tigers at his private zoo. On the other hand Jimmy Goldsmith, went the rumour, was more than capable of aiding Lucky's escape by providing a private plane to fly him out of the country to somewhere where he could hole up till the business blew over – Switzerland, South Africa, Australia, or, for that matter, the wilds of Andalusia.

When the London trail went cold, Scotland Yard contacted their opposite numbers across the Channel and elsewhere and asked them to look out for the mustachioed peer in places where a man might have friends prepared to protect him from justice.

The news trickled down to the police post nearest to our valley, the Pelayo branch of the Guardia Civil, an outpost of Galicians sent to Andalusia by General Franco after the Civil War to ensure that the law was administered by out-of-towners considered less likely to take bribes or settle scores.

Since the Galicians had been there for thirty years, they had acquired family and friends in the neighbourhood and were considered to have gone native. Up to a point. You never quite knew where you were with the Guardia Civil.

The villagers of Pelayo, a half-horse *pueblo* halfway between the valley and our local market town of Algeciras, had a weakness for draughts played for money, a source of income from the tourists since they were very good at the game.

There were excellent snails available in season at the *venta* where the gambling took place, and I would sometimes take guests at the Huerto for a bite to eat and a quick turn at the boards. This was a costly affair for the visitors, though much welcomed by the home team, since the Pelayo players were more than capable of breaking the bank in Vegas should the opportunity arise.

When we first moved to the valley, the two eldest of our children had attended the little state-funded one-class schoolroom in Pelayo which shared premises with the Guardia's barracks. To the amusement of the Guardia, we usually arrived on donkey-back, money being short at the time.

When our finances had recovered somewhat, the children were moved to more exalted educational establishments in the town. Meanwhile, a regular order for bread and eggs from the wood-fired bakery opposite the Guardia's flag-draped barracks kept me in touch with news from the village.

'*Señora*, I think I should warn you,' said the baker's wife one morning as she wrapped a crisp-crusted two-kilo loaf in a square of brown paper, 'the Guardia has been asking questions about your visitors, particularly the one with the moustache.'

Questions from the Guardia were something to be avoided. Perhaps, I thought, information and denunciations about the marjoram had reached the authorities – the moustache was a bit of a worry since Richard, I knew, had a penchant for exotic tobacco – and the Guardia had decided to verify what was growing in my garden.

I had no reason to expect denunciations since relations with my farming neighbours had always been friendly. However, I had lately been involved in a dispute over the right of a herd of foraging pigs to join the resident sty pig in digging up my newly planted lemon trees. And when one of the four-legged foragers had crashed through my bedroom window – floor-to-ceiling plate glass which cost a fortune to replace – I had publicly announced my intention to discover who might be held responsible.

Not, I explained to the baker's wife, who could be counted to pass the word along the line, that I wished for the damage to be paid for by the swineherd, since everyone knew that Iberian pigs had an inalienable right to roam the forest and crop whatever they pleased. I rather hoped, however, that my willingness to pay the bill for the glass myself might mean that the pigs might be persuaded to forage elsewhere.

Two days later, the Guardia Civil came to call.

'We have information, *señora*, that the English milord wanted in your country for murder is hiding in your cellar. We are under instructions to inspect the premises.'

The cellar, an excavation beneath the house intended as a store-room, had never been usable since it filled up with water during the rainy season.

'I think it unlikely there's anyone in there,' I said cheerfully as the inspectors contemplated the subterranean swimming-pool. 'Don't you?'

The premises having been duly inspected, the Guardia withdrew, leaving me with a grainy photograph of the renegade earl – who did indeed look remarkably like Richard – and a promise to inform them immediately if any such person should appear at any time in the future.

For the next week or two, the Land Rover and its uniformed occupants were to be seen lurching up the mountainside to take up a commanding position on the ridge above the house, binoculars trained on the valley below. Every time a vehicle left the Huerto, the Land Rover would bump its way back down the track and set off in noisy pursuit.

The Guardia's activities, while yielding nothing in the way of mustachioed runaways, since Richard had long since returned to London, disturbed the foraging pigs at the moment of optimum fattening on the acorn crop. The presence of the law also upset the valley's population of smugglers, who were accustomed to the Guardia turning a blind eye to their activities for reasons which might have had something to do with uninterrupted supplies of Swiss chocolate and American condoms.

Surveillance ceased abruptly and peace returned to the valley when the smugglers went on strike and refused to pay their dues, and the owner of the foraging pigs, a powerful businessman said to have the ear of General Franco, denounced the Guardia for harassment of his herds. The Pelayo gamblers and Enrico, owner of the *venta*, were also pleased when life returned to normal, since the Guardia's sudden burst of activity had discouraged passing trade and depressed their profits.

'The Lord moves in mysterious ways, *señora*,' said the baker's wife the next time I picked up the bread. 'The *sub-comandante* sends his regards and says rest assured you will no longer be troubled further by the pigs.' She glanced at me and smiled mischievously. 'And Enrico says to tell you that your guests are always welcome at the *venta*, with or without their moustaches.'

Snails with Tomato and Chilli

A dish of snails as served at the *venta* in Pelayo to sustain the backgammon players. You can leave them in their shells for this dish – the Spanish don't mind the little black intestine but love sucking the juices off the shell. If live snails elude you, tinned are fine.

SERVES 4 TO 6

1kg large live snails (petit-gris or Bourgogne)

The sauce
4 tablespoons olive oil
2 tablespoons diced serrano ham or lean bacon
3–4 garlic cloves, crushed
1 medium onion, diced
1 large green pepper, diced
1kg ripe tomatoes, fresh or tinned, chopped
2–3 dried chillies, crushed
2 bayleaves
1 glass red wine
Salt and pepper
1 heaped tablespoon chopped parsley

To prepare live snails, starve them in a bucket for a week, rinsing off the gunge every day. Then salt them and rinse off the *baba* – the white gloop they exude when subject to such unkindnesses. Continue with the salting and rinsing till there's no more gloop. Bring the snails gently to the boil in plenty of unsalted water with bayleaves and peppercorns. Simmer for 20 minutes, then drain. They are now ready for the recipe.

Make the sauce. Heat the oil gently in a shallow pan and add the chopped ham or bacon, onion and garlic. Fry for a moment. Add the green pepper and fry until the vegetables soften. Add the chillies, bayleaves and wine and bubble up to evaporate the alcohol. Stir in the tomatoes and cook uncovered for 10 minutes until you have a rich thick sauce. Stir in the snails and simmer all for another 10 minutes to blend the flavours.

This dish will keep hot without spoiling. Serve with twice-fried chips cooked in olive oil and a salad of crisp lettuce. A glass of Spain's robust red wine to accompany.

CHAPTER NINE

Trouble Comes in Threes

> *'The reasonable man adapts himself to the world. The unreasonable man adapts the world to himself. Therefore all progress depends upon the unreasonable man.'*
>
> OSCAR WILDE, *The Soul of Man under Socialism*

BY 1968 I HAD FOUR CHILDREN, ALL BORN IN QUICK SUCCESSION AND not easily either. For every baby that survived, one died. The fault was mine. Wrong rare blood group, incompatible with the father, treatment still experimental. And every time I lost a baby – two little boys at full term, another still-born too early – I started another.

Four small children are a full-time occupation. When we returned to London in the summers, I could see that my city-based contemporaries were in much the same situation as I was. Husbands, though perhaps not as geographically absent as mine when we were in Spain, spent little time with their children. And as a family, we were fortunate. In Spain I could afford help with the children and the housekeeping.

Social life in London meant inviting people to dinner when the children were safely tucked up in bed, while in Spain, where children were welcome everywhere, I could take them with me wherever I went, and did. And anyway, I loved the company of my children, their fearlessness, the way they saw the world exactly as it is, their ability to create anarchy.

The state of marriage, in any event, was considered pretty old hat in what *Time* magazine had dubbed Swinging London. Everyone who wasn't in therapy was on LSD or one of the new chemical compounds imported from California. Liberation was everywhere, though this, as in the days when I was footloose and fancy-free, still seemed to benefit the men more than it did the women.

Those of us who had made the alliances our parents had mapped out for us did not seem to be doing any better than those of us who had chosen our partners for ourselves.

My closest schoolfriend, a beauty as well as an heiress and the first of my year up the aisle, skipped out of her marriage on Derby Day with a plausible rogue in an Aston Martin she'd bought for him herself. Her husband, she explained, was far too fond of other men's wives, her life was dull as ditchwater and her children were far better cared for by their devoted nanny. The note she left for her husband, she said, explained it all: 'Your dinner is in the oven. Ask the second footman where the oven is.'

The husband was rich, the lover poor, but my friend had money to burn. Whenever the lover needed to pay a bill, he would sell the vehicle to the dealer in Berkeley Square, and his inamorata would buy it back. The arrangement worked perfectly. For a time. Thereafter she repeated the exercise with other lovers whenever the fancy took her, and has lived a merry life in sunny places where millionaires dock their yachts. Still does.

Whatever was happening elsewhere, free love was not for me. Heterosexuality was out of fashion and I was certainly out of step. Bisexuality was normal, and if you didn't fancy your girlfriends, too bad for you. My own view was, well, thanks but no thanks. I even felt obliged, to Nicholas's disappointment, to turn down an offer at a literary party from a lady dressed head-to-toe in Ossie Clarke to make a threesome – even though she had flowing red hair and carmine lipstick and was a poetess to boot. And anyway, I was pregnant at the time. A normal state of affairs, no doubt, but one that meant, I would have thought, that my tastes might lie elsewhere.

Nicholas had no such scruples. To this day, I don't know the half of what he got up to. And how. Unless I intended to do something about it, what was the point? I was never much of a schemer.

So what does that mean for a wife?

Heartbreak, of course, what else? But I find it easy to be cheerful. If it's a matter of finding the silver lining, I'm your woman. If it's a question of what the errant husband gets up to, I was living proof that the wife's the last to know.

Even so, there comes a moment when even the wife has no option but to draw her own conclusions – a road-to-Damascus moment when everything falls into place.

It took me seven years to work out what everyone else already knew and no one had bothered to tell me. Perhaps they had.

I hadn't read the signs. I had assumed that since Nicholas's business affairs kept him in London for weeks at a stretch, sometimes months, the marriage was most at risk when he was living the high life in the big city.

Which is why, one bright morning in the house in the cork-oak forest, the penny didn't even drop when I found the au pair sobbing in the kitchen.

'What's the matter?' I enquired with real concern.

Reliable au pairs are hard to come by, and an au pair in a state of unhappiness can lead to the need to find a replacement. And this particular au pair was a qualified nursery nurse and she fitted easily into the rhythm of the household.

Rather too easily, as it happened.

She was very pretty, very curvy and very blonde – attributes much admired by visitors when she was sunning herself in a small bikini on the terrace.

She was sobbing for the usual reasons which afflict a young woman whose thoughts have turned to choosing a suitable mate. The mate she had chosen, however, was not up to scratch.

'I'm in love with a married man, and he with me,' she sobbed.

'Really?' I said. 'Anyone I know?'

I hoped I wasn't responsible for a situation that might lead to the break-up of some otherwise happy family.

'Yes,' she sniffled. 'But I can't say who.'

I put my arm round the shaking shoulders.

'He says he'll leave her,' she added, blowing her pretty little nose into my nice clean hankie.

'Does he have children?' I enquired, thinking that if he didn't, I might identify the bounder and maybe have a word.

'Four,' was the answer.

'That's a bit of a problem,' I said, distracted by the obligation to peel potatoes for my four children's supper. 'I'll find Nicholas. He's good at things like that. He'll tell you how to handle it.'

Nicholas happened to be in residence at the time, and I'd noticed he was working rather hard on a new book in his studio well into the night.

'All right,' said the self-confessed strumpet, and dried her tears.

A short time after this, we both – myself and the strumpet – found ourselves separately obliged to pay a visit to the doctor in Algeciras to obtain a prescription for a gynaecological condition requiring treatment with antibiotics, a misfortune I assumed to have been acquired – not being entirely a woman of the world in spite of my experience of childbirth – from a lavatory seat.

We passed each other in the corridor, the strumpet and I, both clutching identical prescriptions, both making our way to the chemist.

And even then I didn't guess.

Trouble always comes in threes.

By the turn of the decade, as the 1960s became the 1970s, my marriage was probably already in trouble, though with the children to occupy my time, I admit I wasn't really looking.

Life in the remote valley in Andalusia suited me well. I had no fears that the children's education would suffer if they were educated in Spanish. I had had the same experience myself, and while I knew that sooner or later we would all have to return to the land of their birth, for the moment, it was the most sensible option.

And anyway, there were practical considerations. We no longer owned a family house in London. The remainder of my trust that hadn't gone into the house had vanished into the book-production company, which seemed to need constant injections of cash. With the Battersea house sold, although we had found the rent-controlled flat, life in London was pretty crowded now that we were six.

The reality was that there was no more money in the kitty.

Nicholas, true to his Huguenot ancestry, was undeterred by the slings and arrows – or so it seemed. Truth was, I knew little of his life. Once the babies were born, I was busy caring for my growing family. The au pair had returned to London, but with a little money coming in from the publishing business, I could just about afford help in the house.

And if we lived frugally throughout the rest of the year, renting the Spanish house in summer paid for the upkeep.

It didn't quite work out like that. While Nicholas continued to visit us intermittently, he always seemed in a hurry to get back to London. His career as a thriller writer, after a stupendous start, had been put on hold in favour of his business interests.

When the book-production company moved into larger premises and turned its attentions to packaging handsomely illustrated books for other publishers, cashflow became even more of a problem. The company seemed constantly in need of what's euphemistically known as refinancing – borrowings at the bank. The house in Spain was the only collateral available – though I think perhaps the bank, one of those that springs up in the boom times and disappears in a slump, might have thought that I was richer than I was.

Meanwhile, seven years on, my friends' marriages were beginning to break up.

Feminism had caught the *Zeitgeist*. To young wives – and most of us were no more than twenty when we married – at a time when everyone else was claiming freedom, female empowerment meant behaving like men. Fidelity and attitudes to faithfulness had begun to change.

We had no easy answers. We still knew we needed to make it work, but hadn't yet worked out how to do it. Some of us threw in the towel. Some of us turned a blind eye. Some of us knew and didn't make a fuss. Some of us, including me, sailed blithely into the sunset and didn't notice a thing.

Maybe, as I've said before, I didn't want to know. Whether from innocence or ignorance, it didn't occur to me that marriage meant anything less than it said it did. This, if I wasn't much mistaken, meant forsaking all others till death did us part. And until a higher authority told me otherwise, the arrangement stayed in place.

I found out about the business with the au pair when Nicholas was in London and I was boxing up old manuscripts in his study. The house was porous and soaked up water throughout the winter like a sponge, releasing damp into the interior as soon as the weather warmed up. This didn't matter in the larger rooms, since the windows ran from floor to ceiling and could be opened and aired. But Nicholas's writing-room was rarely used, and I had decided to move the manuscripts to a drier place.

Nicholas had beautifully elegant handwriting – clear and well formed, a result no doubt of his left-handedness – as I had had reason to appreciate in the days when, before he had learned to type, I had had to transcribe his manuscripts for his publisher. The letter was dated several months earlier, just before he had returned to London after Christmas. It had not been posted, I could only assume, because the sender had decided to return to the arms of the recipient in person.

Certainly Nicholas had seemed unusually short-tempered and had found it necessary to spend an unreasonable amount of time on the telephone to London in the bar in the village. We lacked a phone line and I knew he was preoccupied with what was happening in London since he had changed his flight several times, arriving just before the Eve and booked to leave again before New Year.

He had also been even less affectionate than usual – coming to bed long after I had fallen asleep and not appearing in the morning till I was busy with the midday meal. I had not been unduly worried by his lack of demonstrative affection, since this was not really a change. Over the seven years of my troublesome pregnancies and small babies constantly needing attention, expressions of affection had rather gone by the board.

I stared down at the letter. The message, written in the elegant hand I knew so well, left me in no doubt that my husband's affections lay elsewhere.

I had the blueprint for what to expect of my marriage. I should have paid more attention to the message. When asked by journalist Drusilla Beyfuss, how people were all coping with the state of wedlock, the answers were instructive.

Not good. In such times, what can we do but run wild? And if we're running wild, are we having fun?

Some of us are, some of us aren't.

With hindsight, I should have read these interviews more carefully – there was much to be learned from the answers we gave at the time, 1968, around the time my marriage was already in trouble, though I didn't yet know it.

Nicholas on his expectations: 'When Elisabeth married me she came across into another world and brought no one with her.'

And what do you admire about your wife? 'She's stubborn.' And then, maybe to soften what might not be taken as a compliment: 'She has a stubborn sense of right and wrong.'

He's right.

The best way for a wife to get over a philandering husband is to take a lover. A lover taken on the rebound should be nothing too serious – out of the frying-pan, don't jump into the fire. A kindly fellow, long hair and beard, and considerate. Passionate, naturally. No point in a lover if there isn't passion. That said, passion is all very well in its place, but it's not the whole story. And it's also – how shall I put it? – time-consuming.

Not that I felt guilty. The very reverse. Not yet thirty, I needed the reassurance I wasn't yet on the rubbish heap. With my husband's enthusiasms directed elsewhere, taking a lover wasn't so much a serious commitment as a decision taken in much the same way that a man might embark on a mistress. Which, under the circumstances, seemed to me perfectly sensible. It seemed my husband didn't want me as a lover or for anything else, not even for company. The children – his and mine (the deal from the very beginning was that nothing was ever 'ours') – were rarely involved with their father. And when they were, it was usually in the form of 'do not disturb'.

Nothing for it but to cut my losses, pack up the children and run. In London I might, just might, manage to salvage something from the business. There was, I knew, a backlist of books in the warehouse and the Official Receiver called in to wind up the business would have no interest in anything but a fire sale.

There was another problem. Marriage and life in Spain had left me without friends or family to turn to. Nicholas had been very clear when we married that this was the way it would be.

He was right when he said that I had brought no one with me into our marriage. I could talk to Nicholas's friends, but there was no one else I could turn to for advice. Of the two men I consulted, both writers, one made a half-hearted pass and the other advised me not to commit my affections elsewhere.

The third – well, let's call her a friend of a friend – suggested a new career as an escort for foreign businessmen, some of them awash with oil money, who would pay a thousand pounds for my company over a weekend in New York.

Really?

I'm a mother of four, of limited experience in such an enterprise – surely not. Respectability is much sought after, the friend of a friend explained. A respectable married lady brings class without commitment.

No commitment? A thousand pounds, no strings?

Well, any extras would be up to me.

Extras? I think not. Not even for a thousand pounds, which, at the time, was as much as a respectable shorthand typist could earn in a year.

No money, nowhere to live, no father for my children – all this was, to put it mildly, a bit of a problem.

I had already emptied what remained in my own London bank account into a Spanish bank so that Nicholas had enough to keep him going while he stayed at the house and finished a novel. The novel, he hoped (and so did I), would attract a decent enough advance to allow him to settle our debts. Hope is the lifeblood of every author – and of every author's wife, present or absent.

*****

In London, absent as I was and taking no responsibility for anything but the welfare of my children, the flat had been rented out and the tenant, a young man heading for a career in the law, not only refused to pay the rent but was in no hurry to vacate his comfortable billet.

The children and I needed somewhere to live while I reasoned with the tenant's father. The father happened to be head of the Law Society, and I had hopes he might be able to reason with his son.

So when Nicholas's sister Lip offered us temporary accommodation in a disused basement by the Thames in a house she had bought as an investment but which was due for demolition by the council, I accepted with gratitude. The basement lacked heating – though it did have running water – and it hadn't been lived in for months. My sister-in-law couldn't be sure when the bulldozers would arrive, but the council was inefficient and we'd probably be safe for a few weeks. Actually, she said cheerfully, she'd be glad to have us there since our presence would discourage squatters. And by the way, we should set traps for rats.

Any port in a storm. The basement was below the waterline and the demolition – for a road-widening scheme – was proceeding apace, but we were housed.

The next problem was money. Perhaps, I said to myself, Nicholas's family might help. My mother was in Chile, and anyway I felt my own family had already provided more than their fair share. And I reasoned that my mother-in-law would be sympathetic once she knew of Nicholas's involvement with the strumpet.

My mother-in-law listened to my tale of woe in silence, then passed the buck.

'I suggest you contact Jock. He borrowed money from his son when Nicholas first came into his trust. As his trustee, I had to sign the transfer. Actually, I was a little shocked. It's unusual for a father to borrow money from his son, but I suppose Jock took a different view.'

This was useful information. I telephone Nicholas, check that the money lent hasn't been repaid, and ask him to make arrangements with his father.

My father-in-law agrees he owes the money but refuses to hand it over to me because he's heard all about my deplorable behaviour from my mother-in-law and knows me to be a bad lot.

My mother-in-law agrees she passed on the information to my father-in-law. And anyway, what did I expect? I knew all about Nicholas when we married.

No I didn't. I knew that he was wonderful and brilliant and we'd live happily ever after.

The mistake, no doubt, was to come clean about the barefoot lover.

Surely, continued my mother-in-law, my own behaviour cancelled out whatever Nicholas had got up to – didn't it?

Not really. But thank you for saying so. At least a bit of arm-candy made me feel better about myself. Actually, I'd taken to kicking the poor fellow out first thing in the morning to earn the grocery cash driving a mini-cab – very unsuitable for a gentle long-haired hippy who didn't wear shoes.

Meanwhile my mother-in-law decides the marriage is over and decants the hamperful of beautiful clothes I had left stored in her attic into the village jumble sale. And serves me right. All my finery – Dior, Saint Laurent, Balenciaga, Hartnell and everything else left over from days of wine and roses – had gone for ever. Poignantly, the hamper bore my father's name, Richard Maitland Longmore, and had been used to store my mother's wedding trousseau.

The message was absolutely clear. I could expect no help from anywhere. So I delivered the children to spend the day with their cousins, returned to the rodent-infested basement and cried my eyes out until it was time to fetch my children home.

The following morning, I dried my tears, congratulated the barefoot lover on the purchase of a pair of shoes required by a man who drove a mini-cab, and set about restoring order to our lives.

A brief conversation with Social Security revealed that I had no chance of claiming any additions to the statutory child allowance. As soon as there was mention of taking my children into care, I removed myself smartly from the office without leaving an address.

That was that. At least I knew where we were.

There was life to be salvaged from the debris.

We were still a family and the mini-cab driver was providing us with groceries. Better still, the day after my visit to Social Security, news came through that the tenant, under threat of not being able to complete his bar exams, had agreed to leave our flat.

Emboldened by these successes, I made an appointment to meet the Official Receiver in charge of winding up the publishing business. If assets were to be stripped, I knew exactly what they were and how much they might be worth.

Everyone knows that crying over spilt milk gets you nowhere.

It occurred to me that I was crying in the wrong place. So I took myself and my hankie to the bank where, fortunately, I had kept my own account running throughout my marriage.

I needed £500, I explained to the manager through my sobs, to rescue the stock of Moviebooks, the only bankable asset left in my husband's bankrupt company. I was confident, I assured him, that the loan would be short-term, since I already had orders for £750 worth of the books, invoice to be settled on delivery.

'You'll need a guarantor,' said the kindly fellow. 'I suggest you contact your mother. Better still, I shall contact her myself. You may take it the money is yours.'

And if that seems like a fairytale, I should explain that the bank was small and privately owned, two branches only, and that I had banked there since I was six years old and I bank there still, bless them. To this day, through thick and thin, they've never bounced a cheque.

By now Nicholas, bored with life in Spain, had returned to London and taken up residence elsewhere. Quite possibly with the strumpet, though I didn't feel the need to enquire.

Perhaps, he suggested, it might be better to declare ourselves bankrupt. He would, he said, consult his friend, property tycoon David Hart, an expert on matters such as this. David had been bankrupt himself when a deal had gone sour and the family trust had refused to pay up.

We – if we could any longer call ourselves a partnership – had no family money and no trust. And since the house in Spain was in hock to the bank, we had no assets.

'Whatever you do, don't do it,' said David. 'Bankruptcy is hell.'

Things – finances, though not the marriage – were beginning to improve.

The stock I had purchased from the Official Receiver with the bank loan had paid for itself and was beginning to produce a modest income, enough to cover the groceries as long as we stuck to shepherd's pie and bought everything at the street market in Pimlico, where the butcher threw in a couple of pig's trotters for free.

Better still, a London gallery – the Tryon in Cork Street, specialists in natural history and sporting pictures for the hunting and shooting set – offered me a one-man show based on work done during my years in Spain and France. Mostly these were eagles, vultures, flamingoes and owls. Eagles were saleable, the gallery pointed out, but they couldn't do vultures. Flamingoes are borderline, and herons only for specialists. What was needed was owls. Plenty of owls. Owls were easy. With their big brown eyes and solemn expression, they looked quite human.

And pigs, of course. We don't suppose you could do pigs? We can sell as many pigs as we can get. Next time, perhaps.

This, of course, was the moment when Nicholas decided he wanted to be married after all and took to leaving bottles of champagne on my doorstep with charming little notes and flowers.

He had also, he said, secured a contract for the new novel. From now, all would be sweetness and light.

I considered the proposition.

The house would have to go, and so would the lover – mine that is. And there were our four children to consider, a shared responsibility. I knew only too well what it meant to lack a father. The simple truth – if there's ever a simple truth for matters of the heart – was that I loved the man I married. Nicholas was not a man you could love a little – he was far too troublesome for that.

Just the same, I held out for a time, ignoring the declarations delivered daily to my doorstep, uncertain that things would ever change.

And did they change? Up to a point. Nicholas had to learn to live with a wife who had taught him a lesson no husband wants to learn. And I had learned to live with what I couldn't change.

Pig's Trotters with Garlic and Parsley

Choose an old-fashioned butcher who cuts up his carcasses himself and has bones and offal and other goodies going cheap. Once he knows you, you might even get your pig's trotters for free. Ears, tail and head can all be prepared in the same way. Start the cooking in the morning and leave the pot to simmer in the lowest possible oven all day. At the same time, dry out any leftover bread crusts in the bottom of the oven and use the space to bake potatoes and beetroots – so much better when oven-roasted.

SERVES 4 TO 6

4–6 pig's trotters, split in two

For the cooking broth
Onion, carrot, celery, bayleaf
Salt and peppercorns
1 glass dry white wine

To finish
4–6 tablespoons fresh breadcrumbs
1 garlic clove, finely chopped
2 tablespoons chopped parsley
125g unsalted butter, melted
Salt and pepper

Wash the trotters and singe off any little whiskers. Tie them together in pairs, cut sides facing each other, and pack them in a casserole along with the cooking-broth, vegetables and herbs. Add the wine and enough water to submerge everything generously. Bring to the boil, cover loosely and leave to bubble steadily for 30 minutes. Top up with boiling water, turn down the heat, and cover tightly, sealing the edge with a flour-and-water paste if the fit's not perfect, and leave to simmer very gently in a low oven (275°F/140°C/Gas1) for at least 8 hours, until the trotters are really soft.

Leave the trotters to cool in their cooking broth. Saving the broth for a soup, drain the trotters, untie each pair and remove the hard central bones. Arrange the de-boned trotters in a gratin dish, cut side up, and top with breadcrumbs, parsley and garlic, season with salt and pepper, trickle with melted butter and slip the dish under a very hot grill to gild and crisp the topping.

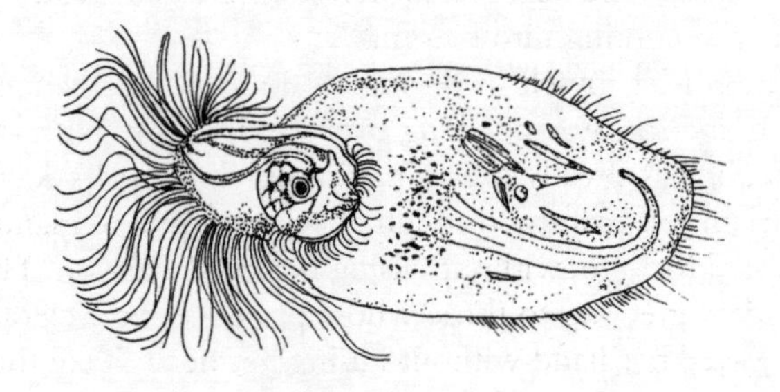

CHAPTER TEN

Of Flukes and Fleas

> *'Violet Elizabeth dried her tears. She saw they were useless and she did not believe in wasting her effects.'*
>
> RICHMAL CROMPTON, *Just William* (1922)

'FLEAS,' SAID MIRIAM ROTHSCHILD WITH DREAMY SATISFACTION, 'are the most fascinating creatures on the planet. Much more interesting than humans.'

I had arrived early that day at Ashton Wold to work on a drawing Miriam needed for a new project. From the moment I turned off the main road to drive down the long pock-marked driveway – left untended, said Miriam, so that people would drive slowly enough to avoid crushing insects – my spirits lifted.

Miriam had lived at Ashton for more than half a century. The house and its gardens served her as both laboratory and workplace. It was the place where her children had grown to adulthood – five in all, three her own, two adopted.

Miriam worked either in her ground-floor bedroom, where bats hibernated through the winter behind the curtains, or in the beautiful book-lined drawing-room where light streamed through windows framed by rambling roses heavy with bees. There were fresh flowers everywhere – daisies and meadowsweet and lilac just coming into bloom.

Today, as I let myself in through a door left permanently on the latch, the sun was not long over the horizon. Nevertheless, the sunlight was already streaming through looped-back curtains and Miriam was halfway through checking a pile of manuscript.

'Ah,' said Miriam, without raising her head. 'It's you.' This was her standard greeting to those whose presence she welcomed.

She waved her hand without raising her head. 'Take the mice to Pammy. Don't forget the goggles.'

I walked over to the door which led into the garden. Next to the step was a cardboard box without a lid. Inside was a pile of laboratory mice. They looked very dead.

Pammy was a tawny owl, by no means tame, who lived in one of the glasshouses in the walled garden where Miriam spent most of her working hours. A fierce little night hunter, Pamela had had a broken wing and had been brought to Miriam to convalesce. After the wing had mended and Pammy was free to go, she had chosen to stay, roosting among the vines, invisible among the leaves. Every year she laid a batch of imaginary eggs, sat on an imaginary nest, reared imaginary fledglings and, presumably, fed them imaginary mice.

'So convenient,' said Miriam. 'All the pleasure and none of the pain.'

Pamela was named for one of Miriam's closest friends – not, she added, for any particular reason unless that one was as beautiful and unpredictable as the other and she enjoyed talking to both.

Pammy, I knew from experience, had a nasty habit of swooping from her perch, talons to the fore, at anyone she considered a threat. You never knew which direction she was coming from. And if you forgot to wear goggles you might well lose an eye.

Ashton Wold was an hour's drive from the farmhouse we had borrowed on the Easton Neston estate. Lacking central heating or any of the modern conveniences which would make it saleable to commuters from London, the farmhouse was no longer needed to house the farmworkers.

It was, for a time, a haven at weekends from our crowded London flat. We were grace-and-favour tenants, an arrangement that suited our benefactor, Alexander Hesketh, Easton Neston's owner. We kept the house warm and lived-in while he decided if the farmhouse should be sold. Many of the tenanted houses on the estate were being modernized and rented out as weekend cottages, and we knew we might have to move out at a moment's notice.

We had spent the previous year in France in a little stone-built cottage high on the windy plateau of the Languedoc while the children attended local schools, adding French to their fluent Spanish. The house in Spain was on the market, and things were beginning to settle into something approaching a normal family life. Nicholas had no choice but to spend more time with his family, and at last he was getting down to the serious business of earning his living by his pen.

In Northampton at the weekends, there was fun and amusement to be had for Nicholas at Easton among Alexander's guests – motor-racing folk and wheelers and dealers from London. Alexander's mother Kisty, one of Nicholas's oldest and closest friends, lived in the dower house and entertained politicians at weekends.

As for me, while the show at the Tryon had been a sell-out, the work had taken five years to complete and we needed a more regular source of income than the gallery could provide. I couldn't afford another five years without reward. In Spain, I had found a ready market for my botanical paintings in the playboy enclaves of the Costa. There were people prepared to pay good money for water-colours to match the wallpaper.

Nicholas's income was sporadic. Few authors, even those who publish one book a year, earn enough to pay their own bills, let alone support a family. Nicholas published a novel every two years at best.

As for my own contributions to the family income, a show in a central London gallery hadn't convinced me I was an artist. But I was enough of a craftsman to be able to deliver what Miriam wanted of an illustrator. And I valued what she could teach me – not least that there were other ways in which I might be able to use the talents I had.

There were things I wanted to do. I didn't yet know what they were, but the children were growing older and needed me less all the time.

Nicholas found his amusement in London and at Easton. He stood for Parliament three times throughout his life, always as an independent on a platform of his own choosing.

And I had the freedom to come and go from Ashton as I pleased. Among other projects – Miriam always had half a dozen on the go – she was working on a study of cabbage white butterflies and the methods they used to choose leaves for egg-laying.

As a butterfly you need to look ahead. No sense in entrusting the future of the species to a leaf that has already received its full complement of caterpillars. Cabbage whites are the chief predator on oil-seed rape, prime candidate for the production of fossil fuels. Oil-seed rape, said Miriam, was a plant with a future.

'Go where the money is,' said Miriam. 'Scientists depend on grants.'

She sighed. 'That's how it is. The things we really want to do never pay.' She looked at me over her glasses. 'You, for instance. You'll never make enough money as an artist, just as I've never made any money as a writer. But what matters is to do something nobody else has ever done – and we're all capable of that.'

Such as?

'Whatever you do best. You have a good brain. Draw your own conclusions. Work out what you want to do and do it.'

Miriam had already drawn her own conclusions about the butterfly's selection process. The insect, she knew by observation, identified a plant already laden with eggs by drumming a leaf with its feet, much as a baker might tap the underside of a loaf to discover if it was done.

'Which is exactly what I mean. I drew my own conclusions and proceeded to prove what I already knew. That's the way to do it. They didn't believe me till they did the chemistry. And then they knew I was right.'

Miriam, as a Rothschild – not that the money had come from her father; she had inherited her fortune from an aunt – could afford the time to work in the way she did. She didn't have to earn a living.

'Of course. Time and money is an advantage like any other. I'm perfectly happy to use what I have. Scientists are like the rest of us. They enjoy good company and good food and the recognition they deserve. Ashton provides that. And in return, I have all the collaboration I need whenever I need it.'

And if what Miriam wanted was an unknown with little in the way of a track record to illustrate her work, that was exactly what she got.

Under her instruction, I forgot that I had had no formal scientific training and began to trust my instincts. Miriam was as close to self-taught as I was. Lack of formal education was an advantage like any other. Miriam used it to break the rules.

'Draw what you see, my dear, not what you think you're supposed to see. I'll correct you if you're wrong.'

And indeed she did. Working on *The Butterfly Gardener*, the first of the wildflower manuals which encouraged planting for the benefit of butterflies, I'd sit for hours in the meadow at Ashton watching butterflies take off and land.

Miriam tolerated no fancy artistic footwork.

'Antennae *down*, my dear. An orange-tip *hangs* from the petal when it's resting. You've made it *perch*. Use your eyes.'

I began to change the way I worked.

Any skill I could deliver as a draughtsman became secondary to trying to understand what I was watching. What I was learning was to trust myself to tell the truth. To deliver what I really saw.

For the first time I began to understand that I had a skill that might be of use in other spheres.

I wasn't a writer. Nicholas was the writer. I did, on the other hand, contribute a cookery column to *The Field*. Simon Courtauld had offered me the job when he moved over from the deputy editorship of the *Spectator.* I had been an occasional contributor to the magazine, and Simon, a visitor to the house in Spain, already knew that I could cook. Since I was providing illustrations as well as text, the money was useful and Simon seemed to like my writing.

It was, however modest, a start. And I wasn't writing fiction, a job for a real writer. Nevertheless, the idea that I might be a real writer was no longer impossible.

Miriam took the view that everyone could do everything, and the sooner the better. Life was short, no time to waste. By the time she finally boxed up her microscope and left the planet, she was a Dame and a Fellow of the Royal Society and held every honour the scientific world could bestow. Although the Rothschild name and fortune were undeniable, Miriam was a woman with a fierce need to make her own mark on the world at a time, the 1920s, when women were struggling to achieve the vote. A woman might pursue a career if no other course was open to her.

Miriam's brother Victor, as highly educated as Miriam was self-taught, had been an academic all his life. Watching and listening to the two of them together when I accompanied Miriam on occasional visits to her brother at his house on the outskirts of Cambridge, it seemed to me that Miriam's intelligence was of a different order to her brother's. His was an orderly mind. Hers, while not disorderly, ranged free. The connections she made were instinctive as well as informed – and Miriam was formidably well read. The conclusions she drew from her own observations of the natural world – and as a Rothschild she had the leisure as well as the patience – were those a more regimented mind would never attempt.

'One should always keep one's wits about one. One never knows when one might need them.'

Indeed so. Miriam was more than a match for anyone's wits. She disliked gossip, was intolerant of boredom, admired skills of a kind she didn't share, had never eaten meat or worn leather. She adored children, particularly her own grandchildren, but preferred dogs.

She particularly didn't approve of useless members of the aristocracy. It should not be forgotten that wealth, she observed, brought responsibility as well as privilege.

Walking through the woods one day when the bluebells were in bloom, she demonstrated the point when she paused at a clump of white blossoms, creamy little tassels, incongruous in the sea of blue, and poked them with her stick.

'Albino forms in nature tell us the species is in decline. Bad breeding will out.' Whiteness is weakness, she concluded, an indication of lack of choice.

'Consider the British aristocracy, a species in decline. Foolishly they marry heiresses. In a system which favours the male, the emergence of an heiress indicates lack of choice. Heiresses are used to getting their own way. They pick inferior mates who can't threaten their power. Which leads to the birth of more girls. And so on till the line has gone for good. Which is why,' she concluded, 'they'd do better to let the roof fall in and marry a barmaid.'

My own grandmother, I pointed out, had been an heiress, and both her children were girls.

Miriam shook her head. 'Your mother had the good sense to marry your father. A hero, a man who would certainly, had he lived, have challenged her power.'

She paused and smiled. 'I chose a hero myself for precisely the reason your mother married your father – because he was both remarkably handsome and unusually courageous. I couldn't live with mine, of course. But his children are splendid.'

'As for your grandmother,' she said. 'Bertha was spoilt. But she was a beauty. And one always has time for beauty.'

Miriam was right. My grandmother was certainly spoiled, and she certainly married someone she bullied. If something displeased her, everyone within earshot knew it, including my grandfather.

What I knew of her early life was that she was brought up by her Aunt Sadie, a woman who tolerated no argument. I also knew that she had been educated at a Catholic convent, an unusual experience for members of Baltimore's enclosed Jewish community. She had married early, controlled her own fortune, and after her marriage, did more or less what she pleased.

This I had always thought, until I worked for Miriam, was unusual for her time. Women of her generation, I had imagined, were like my mother, subservient to their men. 'Here is my husband. Admire his brilliance. Envy his success. Laugh at his jokes. Was ever a woman as fortunate as I?'

My grandmother, however, did not grant her husband unconditional approval. Which made her, Miriam pointed out, the perfect heiress.

'My mother,' I say by way of defence, 'says her mother made her father unhappy and that was why he gambled.'

'Your mother,' said Miriam, 'didn't get what she wanted. So she blamed her mother. Children always do.'

Miriam rarely talked about her own family. Particularly recently, when there had been questions over her brother's role in the spy scandal which uncovered Anthony Blunt.

She was, however, willing to talk about the Rothschilds in the context of the Barons. She pointed out the entry in the *Encyclopedia Judaica* which told me where my family came from, and for me she was the only reliable source of information on my mother's life before she married my father.

The two were the same age, both were rich, both were born of prominent Jewish families at a time when anti-semitism was perfectly normal. Distrust of the Jews, however, fortunately for anyone as identifiable as a couple of heiresses, didn't take the same form in Britain as it did elsewhere.

Miriam was prepared to expand a little.

'We were outsiders, of course. But we were tolerated if we were rich. But we had to fit. I always say that countries get the

Rothschilds they deserve. The Austrian Rothschilds are the aristocrats, the French are the parvenus, the English – well – we're the bourgeoisie.'

What of my own family? Did they fit?

She considered the question. 'You can be proud of old Bernard, your great-grandfather. He was an admirable man, the best kind of Jew. He was a guest at Tring when Uncle Walter was alive.'

To have been a guest at Tring was a considerable accolade. Walter Rothschild was Miriam's childhood hero and the subject of her only biographical writing. 'Bernard was helpful to Uncle Walter when he was building London Zoo. I imagine they ran out of money and he stepped in.'

What about my mother?

'Silly woman. No business marrying that second husband of hers. I had more time for the elder brother. Homosexual, of course. Such an English habit. The brother came to Ashton to ask my advice about a garden. Didn't do what I told him – no one ever does – but one can forgive much of those who garden. No doubt one of the family had to marry an heiress because of the house. A mistake. It makes everyone unhappy and solves nothing.'

Exactly so.

Miriam had a remarkable way of hitting the nail on the head in her professional as well as her private life. Her early writings, product of the years in which her reputation was made, was a pioneering study of the lifecycle of the rabbit flea.

The rabbit flea, she observed, had adjusted its lifecycle to suit its host. The flea waits to lay its eggs when the rabbit itself is breeding. When the babies are born, the newly hatched fleas transfer themselves to their new hosts. The rabbit flea cannot breed on any other creature but the rabbit.

All parasites, she concluded, are species-specific. This is a useful tool for taxonomists, those who separate one species from another, and leads to the conclusion that everything living is dependent on every other living thing. Which was why – a revolutionary suggestion when first proposed in the 1930s – we must learn to see the planet as a single living organism.

'The risk for the flea,' said Miriam, observing me over the top of her reading-spectacles, 'is that the rabbit will not breed. And if the rabbit fails to breed, so will the flea. The flea does what it has to do because it's a flea. You do what you have to do because of who you are. As a species, we are less successful than rats and not as well adapted as the cockroach. We can, however, change our minds.'

Later, driving home through the dusk, I considered what Miriam had said. As a family, as soon as my own money had been spent, we had always depended on what Nicholas could earn.

This had always meant that I favoured his work over my own, researched his material, tidied up his plots, worked out his storylines, wrote bits of chapters when he was bored with his characters – whatever it took to meet a delivery date and pay the bills.

What if I too could write? I didn't need to write the kind of books that Nicholas wrote, my own experience and skills were very different. And *European Peasant Cookery*, the book with which I made my name as a food writer, began to take shape in my head.

*****

Nicholas greeted me enthusiastically on my return that evening to the house at Easton Neston. He had a project to discuss: an expedition in the steps of David Livingstone across the Kalahari Desert to the Okavango Delta. The book already had a title, *The Last Wilderness.*

It had been twenty years since anyone had made the crossing by land. These days, the journey took three hours or so in one of the little planes that supplied the diamond mines in the north and the tourist destination at Maun, a much more practical alternative.

The Last Wilderness was a story Nicholas had always wanted to write.

Although he'd made his name as a thriller writer and his books sold respectably enough for the genre, his most successful book to date was *Andalucia*. A departure into travel writing suited him as much for the ready-made audience it attracted as for the fun of spinning a tale that required neither complicated plotting nor the need to invent characters in which he was more than likely to lose interest halfway through.

What *Andalucia*'s publisher had expected was a straightforward guide to the geography, history and architecture of southern Spain. What Nicholas delivered was a pilgrimage, a voyage of discovery which took him from life in the cork-oak forest to the glories of bullfighting, the delights of propping up bars with sherry salesmen in remote villages with Moorish names, the rewards of watching eagles and storks migrate across the Pillars of Hercules.

The Last Wilderness was also to be a pilgrimage, a search for what Nicholas remembered of a magical time in his childhood, a place where lions prowled and leopards hunted and elephants came down to the waterhole at dusk to drink.

The advance for the book, though generous by publishing standards, was not enough to cover the cost of an expedition that had to cross a thousand miles of desert for which the minimum requirement was two Land Rovers, a back-up truck, one white hunter, a mechanic and two local guides, members of the Tswana tribe, who knew the territory.

The journey was likely to be expensive. Volunteers were needed to share the cost. Anyone who came with us had to know how to handle a gun, not mind a little discomfort – a relaxed attitude to personal hygiene was essential since baths would not be available for the duration – and be willing to contribute to the storyline.

Alexander Hesketh's brother Bobby, idle and bookish with a taste for adventure, was the first to volunteer. Next came David Towill, escapee from the London rat race to our house in Spain, first brought to the Huerto by Dominick.

Towill had remained a friend of us both after we left Spain. Particularly of mine, since he was an enthusiastic trencherman and appreciated my cooking – unusual in a man who drank as much as he did. Since David's mother had been a friend of my Longmore grandmother, his company was doubly welcome since it provided me with a link to my own past. David was also very funny, particularly when not in his cups. Drink and careless living had given him what Nicholas described as the bulk and temperament of a silverback gorilla – a description David protested about but rather enjoyed.

'Elephants, my dear,' he said, when provided with a list of the fauna of the Delta, 'will suit me very well.'

Third man in for the trip was David Grenfell, Towill's friend from their days at Eton. Grenfell – known as Grumpy, though his nature was a great deal sunnier than Towill's – was equally hard-drinking, though in considerably better shape. He was also possessed of a laconic wit and lean, hard-edged good looks, which made him irresistible to women – particularly impressionable young women who hung around the watering-holes of Chelsea.

'Not many women in the Kalahari,' I said. 'Are you sure you won't get bored?'

'Rest assured,' said Grumpy. And left it at that.

Grumpy's qualifications for inclusion were that he could handle a gun and was already what was known in the region as an old Africa hand through family connections in Ian Smith's Rhodesia. In fact, he and the other David intended to take a swing across the border to check on the family's holdings.

Inspecting the list, it was clear to me that not only would I be the only woman on the trip, but that these were men who had more than their fair share of ladies waiting for them at home and would probably be glad enough to get away from them for a spell. Towill was married, Grenfell and Bobby were not. I had grown accustomed to being the only woman in the gang – matron to a bunch of schoolboys. It also occurred to me that I would be the only member of the party who was sober. Which meant that I should take a good stock of books to amuse myself in the evening round the campfire, while the rest of them got down to the serious business of drinking. A minor consideration to anyone else on the trip, but important to me.

On my next visit to Miriam, I explained I wouldn't be around for a month or two. I had never been to Africa and the chance was too good to miss.

'The Kalahari?' says Miriam thoughtfully. 'Weaver birds, I think. The nests are reused and in continuous occupation – an excellent habitat for parasites. We might discover a new species. I'll give you the bags for transport. A dozen will do. Make sure they're fresh.'

It never occurred to me to argue with Miriam. Whatever she wanted, she got.

It did occur to me, however, that flea-infested weaver birds' nests are not easily explained to customs officers when passing through airports.

While I am usually untroubled at border posts – many years of passing through the diplomatic channel have left me with an unshakeable belief in my own innocence – I wouldn't like to have to explain myself to a sniffer-dog crazed by fleas.

Miriam laughed. 'Don't worry. You're perfectly safe.'

Safe?

'They're species-specific. They certainly bite, but they won't survive for long.'

We had less than a month to prepare for the trip. Three weeks after the first planning meeting, with all arrangements completed in advance, the expedition assembled in Gabarone, Botswana's dusty little capital.

It was mid-October, the end of the rainy season, and the land was as green as it would ever be. At the time – the city has expanded since – the only tall building in Gabarone was the Holiday Inn, a holiday destination for the bruderbond, redneck South Africans from the Transvaal in search of a little rest and recreation of a kind prohibited under apartheid.

Comedian-of-the-month at the Holiday Inn was Tommy Trinder. Dinner was fish and chips, which had arrived in ready-prepared form in Mr Trinder's specially converted refrigerated lorry. Once reheated, the arrangement came wrapped in yellowing copies of *The Sun*, complete with a little sachet of Sarson's malt vinegar.

Tommy cracked Blackpool-friendly jokes about Chelsea Football Club and seaside landladies. Never mind what the inhabitants of Gabarone made of this, since alternative rest and recreation was provided by a line-up of ample-bottomed local ladies in tight white satin perched on barstools in the foyer.

'Just what's needed,' said David Towill, patting one of the ladies on the buttock with one hand and expertly upending a tinny with the other.

A 'tinny', there's probably no need to explain, is beer in a flip-top can.

There were thirty crates of tinnies in our truck, along with twenty cardboard boxes, each containing a dozen bottles of what Grumpy described as perfectly acceptable South African claret. There were, in addition, two dozen catering packs of baked beans, ten sacks of mealies for our guides, fifty pounds of flour for bread-making, coffee, condensed milk and six sacks of onions. I had insisted on the onions. Bread and onion, it seemed to me, was a perfectly acceptable well-balanced diet. Beans and beer, on the other hand, were a recipe for gastric disaster, particularly when bouncing around all day across unmarked territory in a truck.

The provisions list met with the approval of white hunter Sid Youthed – now gone to the great elephant graveyard in the sky – official organizer of the expedition and the man responsible for our welfare in Botswana. With the addition of a large water tank in the back-up truck, this was all that was required to keep seven men and one woman fed and happy for the full forty days in the wilderness, provided we shot our own meat.

Sid referred to himself as a white hunter, an accurate description: he was indeed both white and a hunter. There were no black hunters in Botswana, explained Sid, since any Tswana clever enough to hold down Sid's job wouldn't want to do it anyway because he'd be in Gabarone, running the country.

Sid was the only one of us with a licence to hunt game for the pot. No matter. We had guns, we had marksmen, we had ammunition and once we were in the desert, there was no one to see us. Which, as Grumpy observed, might prove a problem if we ran into trouble.

What kind of trouble?

'Ran out of gas. Sprang a leak. Broke an axel. Lion. Hyena. Curtains.'

With these thoughts in mind and all participants assembled, the expedition was on its way.

A brief delay in departure – allowing David Towill to become rather better acquainted with one of the ladies on the barstools – was caused by Grumpy and Bobby nipping a hundred miles north on the only road worthy of the name for a raid across the border into what had just become Zimbabwe to check on the Grenfell family farms.

Not good, they reported. The natives were restless. There had been trouble at Beight Bridge, the crossing-point, where someone had blown up the middle bit and the makeshift bridge was a little wobbly.

Family retainers, on the other hand, seemed to be still in place.

The news about the trouble at Beight Bridge was a little worrying. On the other hand, the border crossing was due north and we were headed west, which, said Sid, was a good thing because all the attention would be on the border and there was no danger of anyone interfering with what we were up to.

What were we up to?

Nothing really. Except that in our safari gear – boots, camouflage jackets and the like – we did look rather like a gang of mercenaries about to foment discord in the colonies.

My own contribution to the expedition's wellbeing in the untracked African wilderness was a boxful of papers from the Smithsonian. The revered institution had just conducted a survey of the San people – usually known as Bushmen, though the San never applied the word to themselves – and the information was fascinating. There was also, roped down against the dust, a suitcaseful of books written by nineteenth-century explorers – missionaries and hunters – who'd made the journey in ox-drawn wagons and killed everything that moved and might be considered edible or trophy-worthy, including the San.

'Any tips?' asked Towill, contemplating my stock of heavy-duty literature without much enthusiasm.

'Try this,' I said, passing over a copy of *Shifts and Expedients of Camp Life* by Thomas Baines and W. B. Lord. 'Eight hundred pages. That should keep you busy. Tells you how to build an earth oven in a termite mound and what to do when you're savaged by a lion.'

'Just what I need,' said Towill, and buried his nose in the book.

Thereafter he popped up at intervals with information on how to convert an ox-drawn wagon into a flat-bottomed boat for river crossings, how to prepare elephant biltong and how to make candlewax with hippopotamus fat.

Thomas Baines travelled with David Livingstone, chief converter of the natives. Not, as it happened, that the natives felt much enthusiasm for conversion. In all his thirty years in the region, Dr Livingstone managed only one, Sechele, paramount chief of the Tswana, a gentleman not in the first flush of youth who could see the advantages of trading in a bunch of argumentative old wives for one young wife who could encourage him in ways the others couldn't.

Researching Nicholas's books was a self-imposed task – and one I much enjoyed, since it gave me reason to search through books in libraries I would never otherwise frequent. Permission to enter places of scholarship was not easily obtained without bits of paper proclaiming me already a scholar. Nicholas had all these bits of paper, but didn't much enjoy the research. Still less when someone else could do it for him.

Most of the books I wanted to consult were available only in the library attached to the Natural History Museum. The dragon at the admissions desk refused me admittance, even when I offered my passport as surety. Absolutely not. I couldn't use the library unless I had a university degree. I pointed out, somewhat unnecessarily, that people who didn't have university degrees were exactly the people who were most in need of a library. And I wanted – needed – to use the library, since there were books there which were not available anywhere else.

This was not true, said the dragon, since all books ever published were available in the British Library.

I pointed out that I couldn't gain admittance to that exclusive establishment unless I had a recommendation from a university. And a university wouldn't be able to recommend me unless I had a degree. And I didn't have a degree since I didn't have the educational qualifications which would allow me to gain admittance to a university. All of which seemed a little insurmountable, considering the urgency with which I needed access to the books.

Too bad, said the dragon. Rules were rules. And the rule, as applied to my request, was no. Absolutely not.

Really? Absolutely not? We'll see about that. I removed myself from the fray and returned at the time when all librarians take their midday break.

The staircase was unguarded – you simply walked up the steps and there you were, in the holy of holies, the stacks that contained the books. Entrance, I had observed during the course of our discussion, was refused only to those who actually asked for it. One young woman had sailed past the dragon with no more than a wave of the hand.

Confidence, that was the trick. The dragon was absent and her place had been taken by a bespectacled young man with his nose buried in a book. All librarians should be short-sighted and have their noses buried in a book – the public demands it.

'I'm just popping up to the Africa section,' I announced briskly, and headed up the stairs.

One whole wonderful week later, the dragon tracked me down and threw me out.

But by then I had everything I wanted. I had made a transcript of botanist William Burchell's travels in the veldt in the 1790s with an eye-witness account of slaughtering bushmen for sport. The bodies, the naturalist recorded, were to be skinned and stuffed and displayed in lifelike positions – hunters throwing spears and setting traps, women performing bare-breasted tribal dances or feeding their babies – in a panoramic display in the Cape Town museum. There was also the biter bit: David Livingstone on what it felt like to be eaten by a lion. Not at all painful and rather dreamy, he said, till the animal let go and it hurt like hell. And Frederick Courteney Selous on the excellence of elephant's trunk cooked in the jacket – tender and glutinous, he said, rather like well-stewed pig's trotter.

The Kalahari draws the romantic and rootless, and our companions were both. Nicholas was romantic to his fingertips, and rootless too, when it suited. Wilderness is good for the soul, and Nicholas was always content under African skies.

The men were happy in each other's company, and I was busy with my reading and my sketchbooks. When we pitched camp for the evening – an uncomplicated affair since no one considered it necessary to sleep under canvas – I joined the guides for a cup of tea and a slice of bread to eat with sugar. George and Elvis were the trackers and fire-builders, while Mtimbe was in charge of the catering. The menu was always the same – bread and onion for me and baked potatoes with beans for everyone else. Unless we had time to hunt for meat, and then the cooking was of a different order – thick stews with gelatinous winy broth flavoured with desert herbs and rich with animal fat.

Breakfast bread was freshly baked and eaten with Camp coffee stirred with condensed milk. Every evening as soon as we pitched camp and lit a fire – desert nights were icy and the flames gave light as well as warmth – Elvis dug an earth oven and Mtimbe prepared a batch of dough. The loaves were shaped into tins, left to rise, then placed in the oven and left overnight to bake slowly in the embers shovelled in from the fire. By morning the crust was dark and crisp and the crumb was soft and white and wonderfully chewy, ready just in time for breakfast. With it came a mug of freshly made coffee, unstrained so you had to suck it through your teeth, sweetened with a thick swirl of condensed milk. Those who were hungover from the previous evening's drinking added a dash of hair-of-the-dog.

There were nine of us out in the desert. As I lay on my narrow canvas bedstead, listening to the desert noises under the stars, it struck me that the only sober members of the party were those of us who didn't have guns.

By day we were guided by compass and the position of the sun, following the faint tracks of earlier travellers through the labyrinth of thorn thicket and red earth punctuated at oddly regular intervals by termite mounds, russet-tipped mopane thicket, slender ridges of grey rock crowned by the weird upside-down trunks of baobab trees.

The Kalahari is not a desert in the usual sense but a vast ocean of dry vegetation, grey and spike-leaved, which draws its moisture from the dew and the earth beneath.

There's water beneath the desert for those who know how to find it. In daylight, traces of life were everywhere – footprints and hoof marks, the patterns made by scuttling lizards, debris of beetles and ants – though the creatures that made the marks were rarely seen.

At night, when the air was still and the bustling of the camp had ceased, I slept fitfully, aware of the presence of predators like ourselves, night hunters who might resent our presence in their territory.

By day the land was ours. We had guns and men who could hit a moving target, bird or beast, at a hundred paces. As we moved further in the wilderness and our senses became more attuned to what was there, we began to understand the small movements that told us where to look. The creatures of the desert, perfectly camouflaged in the golden landscape, have ways of showing themselves to one another, and to us.

The predators – lion, hyena, jackals, wild dog – have ear tufts tipped with black whose tiny movements betray their presence. Elephant, a moving grey stream in the distance among mopane thicket, are visible only when the eye is trained to find the shapes. A clearing in the woodland, seemingly empty of life, suddenly reveals the patterned necks of tall giraffe, dark-eyed females with their long-legged young, weaving among the branches, cropping thornbush. The dust of the desert softens the outline of zebra, kudu, wildebeest. Impala, russet and gold, stand motionless, heads turned towards danger, then run, a flock of guineafowl rising in their wake. Most memorable of all for me, a leopard sleeping on a branch above half-eaten prey, one paw delicately extended towards its prize.

I painted what I saw, taping the water jar to the dashboard and holding my paintbox flat on my knuckles, sketchbook in hand.

At night, we slept under the stars, firelight and the heat of the flame our only protection. Predators ourselves by day, at night we were prey. When I woke in the silvery moonlight, propping myself up on an elbow to watch the sleeping forms beside me and listen to the noises of the night, I was aware of shadowy shapes in the darkness. By morning there were tracks all around.

There were, too, signs that others were interested in who we were and where we were going. The San, the little golden-skinned hunters who live and die in the desert, leave few signs of their presence – and when they do, said Sid, it's by choice, because they want whomever they're watching to know they're there.

Anthropologists, authors of the papers from the Smithsonian I carry with me, have studied the customs of the San and written down their stories. By the light of the fire, when I cannot sleep, I learn what I can.

The San, say those who study them, are one of the oldest tribal groups on earth. Their gods are the spirits of water and air and earth. They respect the creatures they hunt and ask their forgiveness for the sacrifice they have made. They have no fear of death, no understanding of possession, no thought of the future. Their myths are of miraculous beginnings without endings. They walk lightly on the earth, take what they need and leave no print.

If the San appear only when they want to be seen, the first time they showed themselves was when they knew that we had killed for meat.

We had pitched camp early that day, and the Tswana guides were stripping off the feathers from half a dozen guineafowl. Bobby, the best shot among us, had managed to line the birds up in his sights and get three with each shot. There was, too, the carcass of a klipspringer, a dainty little antelope, being made ready for skinning.

The meat was more than enough for our meal that evening. Fresh meat must be eaten within an hour or two of slaughter, or it toughens up and must be kept for a week till it softens.

The San were willing to exchange meat for trade goods. They spread out the wares on the sand: necklaces made of ostrich-shell beads threaded with porcupine quills, salt-tanned skins of desert cats, bone-tipped arrows, bows strung with sinew.

When the trade was over, as a way of prolonging the visit and to establish a form of communication, I took out my little paintbox and showed the traders what I did and how.

A painter has the advantage over a photographer in such situations – everyone can see what you're doing and no one feels threatened. As I worked, a few of my completed sketchbooks were passed from hand to hand. The images were rough but accurate, since I was learning to paint exactly what I saw: leopard and lion, zebra and impala, hyena and jackal, eagles and vultures, the stork-like secretary bird which feeds on carrion.

The books were returned reluctantly with smiles and laughter. The headman spoke a little Tswana. Beckoning one of our guides to help translate, negotiations began anew, this time over the contents of the sketchbooks. If I would give them this one and this one and that one of the little paintings, what will I accept in return?

New trade goods appeared. A wedge of honeycomb dark with unborn bees, an empty ostrich shell filled with little white ant eggs, another with termite pupae, still another filled with the blue-green caterpillars that live on mopane leaves.

I shook my head. None of these things. What I needed, I explained, was weaver birds' nests, freshly vacated and complete with their fauna.

No problem.

But what did I need them for?

For the fleas, I explained, making jumping movements with my fingers.

Did I eat fleas?

No, but I had a friend who wanted them for other reasons.

Of course. There was no accounting for tastes.

But the gathering would take a little time. They would return in due course with what I wanted, strange though this might seem.

They would meet us at the end of the journey, on our return from the reedbeds of the Delta. The Okavango Delta, our destination on the northern limit of the desert, is the watery wilderness where the Okavango river empties its waters into the Kalahari sands.

It would take time to gather what was required. And neither I nor they would want to disappoint my friend, who would clearly put live fleas to good use.

Indeed she would.

'Did they bite?' asked Miriam with interest, emptying my hard-won prizes on the dining-room table at Ashton.

No idea, I answered truthfully. For the past month or so I have been eaten by every insect under the sun. I wouldn't have noticed the difference.

'Pity,' said Miriam. 'I was rather hoping they might.'

A couple of days later, Miriam rang with news of the nests. 'Plenty of fleas. Mostly dead. Nothing new. But the museum says there's a rather interesting scorpion they've never seen before. Very toxic. Check your luggage. They're hoping for a pair.'

Kalahari Peppercpot

An all-in stew designed to be reboiled every day with new additions, depending on what's fallen to the hunter's gun. Seasonings can be wild-gathered: feel free to include any flavouring herbs you please. Heads and sawn-up bones should also be included for strength in the broth – though you'll need a really big pot.

SERVES 8 TO 10

3–4 guineafowl, roughly chunked
1 spring hare or wild rabbit, roughly chunked
2kg deer meat, off the bone
2 onions, thickly sliced
3–4 chillies or 1 teaspoon grains of paradise, crushed
1 short length cinnamon stick
2–3 sprigs thyme or other aromatics
1 glass vinegar or sour red wine
1 tablespoon Worcester sauce
2 tablespoons molasses
Salt

Put all the ingredients in a large stewpot with enough water to submerge everything, bring to the boil, turn down the heat, cover and simmer for at least 4 hours – longer if you like – until the meat is perfectly tender. Add more water if necessary. If you prefer to use the oven, allow the same length of time at 300° F/150° C/Gas 2.

Taste and adjust the seasoning – a little more sugar, a touch more vinegar? That's all. Good today, better tomorrow.

CHAPTER ELEVEN

Alarms and Interventions

'Anybody can be good in the country.'

OSCAR WILDE, *The Picture of Dorian Grey*

MIDNIGHT IN THE CITY. NICHOLAS IS ON THE LINE.

He's travelling north with Chris Brasher. The two of them are spending the night in the Lake District, a convenient stopping-point on the way to Edinburgh.

Tomorrow is the first meeting of the John Muir Trust, a maverick attempt to save the wildernesses of Scotland from the depradations of private landlords and the National Trust. The others involved are Denis Mollison, Professor of Mathematics at Edinburgh University, and Nigel Hawkins, a Dundee Scot. All are veteran hill-walkers and admirers of John Muir, the Scots-born naturalist who set up America's network of National Parks. Nobody in Scotland knows this, but the founders are undeterred.

Nicholas tells me he means to run the New York Marathon. It's happening next month. Brilliant, don't I agree?

Absolutely not. You're not in training.

'It's all arranged.' He sounds aggrieved.

You must be crazy.

'Maybe.'

But why?

'Because it's there.'

This, in my opinion, is not enough reason to put an untrained body through twenty-six miles of tarmac hell.

If Brasher can do it, says Nicholas, so can he.

I consider this on its merits.

Brasher, I point out, is an athlete.

And so, says Nicholas, is he.

Chris Brasher, Olympic gold medallist, winner over the jumps at the Melbourne Games, is just about the most famous athlete in Britain. He's also hard-drinking, hard-thinking and fit as a fiddle. And he has no need to raid the family coffers. He's a successful businessman. He's made a fortune promoting his own line of hill-walker footwear. And anyway, even now, pushing sixty to my husband's fifty, Brasher could climb the Eiger blindfold. No doubt he already has.

For now, I'm pretty sure they're drunk.

You've raided the cellar, I say. Go to sleep.

Chris is – or was, since he left the planet half a dozen years back – a man who prides himself on his cellar.

'Château Talbot 1966,' says Nicholas with dreamy satisfaction, as if the name of a *premier cru* claret might adequately explain a decision which could very well land him with a heart attack on the Veresano Bridge.

I tell him we'll speak in the morning.

It seems to me that Chris, a man as susceptible as my husband to the charms of claret, is capable of running a marathon whether he trains or not. Nicholas, naturally wiry and tough, has never seen the need to train for anything in his life.

Which leads to an argument I'm never likely to win.

Nicholas is determined to run a marathon and I'm just as determined he shan't. Naturally I give in. Of course I do. In all our years together, I had never knowingly changed my husband's mind. So I decide what would make me feel better when I'm a widow, and insure his life for the duration of the New York Marathon for a million dollars.

Nicholas breasts the New York tape in a little under four hours – not bad for an amateur. Ah well. Bang goes a million.

The following year, Nicholas and Chris embark on a year-long battle to set up a marathon in London.

Stuff and nonsense, say the powers-that-be. Why should anyone be interested in a bunch of skinny athletes pounding twenty-six miles of London pavement?

The public disagrees. As soon as news of the plans leak out, applications to run the race come flooding in. Many of these, for lack of an organization ready to respond, are stacked in my corridor for weeks, awaiting sorting.

Plans begin to take shape, as does the organization. Limited, to be sure, but enough to take decisions.

Greenwich is to be the starting-point with the finishing-line planned at the end of a straight run down the Mall to Buckingham Palace.

Since the Mall bisects a royal park, permissions are required from the royal owner. With only a week to go, royal advisers refuse access to the royal parks.

Insufficient public interest is the reason given. The organizers have no choice but to move the finishing-tape to Hyde Park Corner.

County Hall, rather more in tune with Londoners than the Palace, gives in to pressure from Chris and agrees to close a bridge and some of the access roads.

There's no money to pay professional race marshals, so these are co-opted members of the organizers' families, including the two eldest of our children.

On race day, Brasher takes to the streets while Nicholas takes care of the starters at Greenwich.

All it takes, said Brasher, is willpower and string.

As the runners assemble, the heavens open and unleash a downpour. Over the lull which precedes the starting-gun,

Nicholas's voice booms out over the loudspeaker: 'Courage, ladies and gentlemen. It may be raining at the start, but there's sunshine over the finish.'

And in the way that miracles sometimes happen, as the first runners reach the tape, the clouds part and the sun shines through.

*****

Election day (12 June 1987) and Mrs Thatcher's expected to be a shoo-in.

Max Reid, son and heir of impresario Carol Reid, throws an all-night party for what everyone knows will be a walkover.

Max's cousins, the beautiful Fox girls, are there. So's their impeccably tailored Uncle Edward, the Duke of Windsor's lookalike. In the main, however, the company is drawn from regulars at the Sporting Page, last bastion of the Chelsea set, lean and hungry and just a little on the seedy side, prowling the room and eyeing up the talent.

Talent abounds. The brotherhood of the Sporting Page are oddly attractive to successive batches of young women fresh from the country and possessed of more money than sense. Wives, in the main, are elsewhere. Present talent includes a curvy young woman in a lycra bodysuit who says she's Kermit the Frog. The suit is a luminous green and she's waving a leaf. Since every room seems to have at least one Kermit the Frog, I assume there are several.

The layout of the house – actually two long thin houses knocked into one – is confusing. Many small rooms lead one into another, each more dimly lit than the other. Things are already happening in corners.

Nicholas makes straight for the bar. There are cocktails and champagne circulating on trays. I hope there's catering. I can't manage an entire political evening on Twiglets and crisps. The waiters are unusually handsome and their trousers are unusually tight.

In the middle of the waiter action is Peter Cook, his hair – white last time I saw him – dyed a fetching shade of Rita Hayworth red.

Peter is drinking either vodka or water. Hard to tell from a distance. Sometimes he's on the wagon, but by the way his hands are waving around, he's back on the sauce.

Nicholas heads purposefully through the throng. I follow cautiously, searching for familiar faces in the crowd.

I've always been wary of Cookie. There's an edge, an unpredictability, something just beneath the surface which makes him a hard man for a woman to like – or perhaps I was never his type. There's always that. And anyway, few Englishmen educated without women are comfortable in their company.

There were also, I'd noticed, times when Peter was just a little camp. He had a way of standing with one hip thrust out, flicking a couple of fingers in the air to punctuate a story. Nothing obvious, just enough to suggest he might – just might – be up for what my good friend David Towill called bum-boy stuff. Sorry for the indelicacy, but Dave, veteran of the Kalahari expedition, was always a man who said what he thought.

Tonight the warning lies in the flaming hair, the flushed cheeks, the attention Cookie is paying to a young man with yellow-blond hair in skin-tight jeans and lace-frilled shirt unbuttoned to the waist. Nothing unusual about that. In the company in which we are to celebrate a Tory victory, skin-tight jeans and frilly shirts abound.

Soon after the stroke of midnight, Mrs Thatcher claims her victory. No surprises there. Just the same, the room explodes.

I search for Nicholas to tell him I'm heading home.

I find him on a stairway clasped to someone's bosom, shoulders wracked with sobs. The bosom's ample. The bosom's face, now turned to me, is plump and pink and full of sympathy.

Nicholas finds sympathy like cats find mice.

'He's had a dreadful shock. Are you the wife?'

The wife is what I am.

I ask my husband what's the matter.

Ample Bosom shakes her head. 'Poor dear. He's had a dreadful shock.'

Poor dear hides his face, but not before I recognize the symptoms. The tears, it seems to me, might just as easily be joy.

'What's upset him?' I ask the comforter.

I know my husband. He's up to something.

Nicholas shakes his head and burrows deeper.

'He's upset,' says Ample Bosom.

Upset by what?

'A terrible betrayal. As he should be the one to tell you.'

Please continue.

'He found them in the broom cupboard – it's all too dreadful.'

I first inspect the comforter, and then my husband.

'Nicholas,' I say with mock severity, 'what were you doing in the broom cupboard?'

'I heard a noise.'

Finally, triumphantly, Ample Bosom pulls the rabbit from the hat.

'His friend, his oldest dearest most special friend, was in the cupboard with a man.'

I inspect my husband with interest.

'A friend?' I say. 'Would that be a very old friend? Not by any chance red-headed?'

Nicholas nods. His eyes are bright with joy.

I leave my husband to his mischief-making and call a cab.

While I usually paid little attention to what Nicholas was up to when he was working – not that there was much I could do about anything even if I wanted to – I was beginning to notice that there seemed to be an unusual number of empty bottles knocking about his workroom of a morning.

We were approaching our silver wedding, a landmark in any couple's relationship, and this, I hoped, might be a moment to tackle what was becoming more of a problem than even he knew.

Sometimes I thought I was the only one who knew, or who even noticed the amount he drank. In the early years, it had had little effect on the way Nicholas lived his life – and anyway, there were always drugs to soften the effects, the uppers and downers prescribed by respectable Harley Street doctors without turning a hair.

There had been plenty of casualties already. Dominick had swallowed a cocktail of prescription pills when he ended his time on the planet. David Towill used both drugs and drink to wash himself down the eternal plughole.

******

A silver wedding is worth a party. A quarter of a century of marriage – give or take the odd hiccup along the way – is something to celebrate.

I plan a gathering of family and friends. Good food, no speeches. Nicholas announces his intention to attend a meeting of Alcoholics Anonymous instead.

This is news to me.

But then again, there's much about my beloved I am the last to know. He had just returned from a walking-holiday in Switzerland in the company of a lady friend. We'll call her Madeleine.

Nicholas had always enjoyed the company of women like Madeleine: elegant, rich, impeccably groomed sophisticates with motherly instincts.

Nicholas appealed to women like Madeleine because they knew they alone could change him. And, I sometimes felt, it was possible they were right.

If Madeleine could change Nicholas, make him see the folly of his ways, I'd be delighted. I'd never been any good at making Nicholas change. As far as I knew nothing I had ever said or done had ever made the slightest difference to how he lived his life.

Madeleine was married to her second or third husband, a heavyweight industrialist. She led a busy social life among influential people, and sometimes needed someone – Nicholas – to escort her to a charity event. There would also be last-minute invitations for Nicholas to make up the numbers at one of her elegant dinner parties thrown for whoever was the latest social lion in town.

Madeleine, said Nicholas, knew I'd understand.

Did she really?

Of course. Madeleine knew I was busy. She considered me a friend and was sure I wouldn't mind.

Nobody can be friends with the rich, said Miriam, who considered herself not truly rich, just comfortable. The rich know how to use you, but they're never your friend.

Nicholas soon fell into the habit of taking Sunday lunch at Madeleine's home among her family in her highly decorated fully staffed villa in the luxurious neighbourhood of Holland Park.

Sunday lunch at home with his own children was inclined to be quarrelsome. And I did indeed have work to do, a book to finish, a column to write in a national newspaper, articles to deliver to magazines. Someone had to pay the bills, and Nicholas's income, though he could command much higher advances than I could ever attract, was dependent on what P. G. Wodehouse identified as the source of all success, the application of seat of trousers to chair.

And anyway, there were times when I welcomed a little outside assistance, a respite from responsibility for what was beginning to seem an increasingly impossible task: keeping my husband sane.

Sophisticated Frenchwomen advise their daughters to choose their husband's mistresses. Far better a married woman with everything to lose than an ambitious young strumpet who'll steal your man.

So when Madeleine proposed a walking-holiday in the Alps, I raised no objections. In any event, said Nicholas, Madeleine's family and husband would certainly be present throughout.

Madeleine owned a chalet in the mountains, comfortable but simple, where she and her extended family – there were children and stepchildren from other marriages – went in winter for the skiing. She herself preferred the place in summer for the tranquillity of the surroundings, the beauty of the flowers and the clarity of the air.

Madeleine had business affairs to settle in Geneva, and Nicholas would be free to wander where he pleased. The solitude, she told me, would soothe my husband's soul.

When I met my husband at the airport on his return, his soul had indeed been soothed. Madeleine, he explained, had been wonderful. They had walked and talked together for many hours while climbing the mountain peaks. Clarity had come to him in waves.

How about the husband and the children?

Nicholas waved his hand. They'd had to leave early.

How early?

Soon after he and Madeleine arrived.

Was he sure it wasn't before he and Madeleine arrived? A long time before?

Not at all. After the husband and family had gone, the house had been peaceful and all had been made clear.

How clear? There are degrees of clarity a wife might not welcome.

They had grown close.

How close?

Very close. Nicholas never admitted to anything unless he had to.

Very close seemed a little too close for comfort.

Nonsense, he said. What did closeness matter when a man's life is at stake?

He had seen the light.

He would never drink again.

Never?

Never. Nicholas was and is and will always remain an alcoholic and he doesn't care who knows it.

I recognize the mantra. AA requires that every alcoholic declares his addiction in public as a precaution against backsliding. Once an alcoholic, always an alcoholic.

I think about this. How about an announcement in *The Times?* Births, Deaths and Taking the Pledge?

'Don't be facetious.'

I'm not. I'm serious.

Actually, he said, I'd rather you didn't labour the point. People don't trust a man who drinks.

Really?

Furthermore, says Nicholas, although he will make an exception for the silver wedding, from now on he proposes to attend meetings of Alcoholics Anonymous every evening. The Chelsea chapter comes highly recommended.

Every evening?

Every evening.

He plans to attend the meetings in Chelsea because the meetings in Stockwell, just down the road from where we live, are for a different kind of alcoholic.

I inspect my husband. Does he mean the sort of alcoholic who lives under a bridge in a box?

Nicholas wouldn't put it quite like that, but close.

The Chelsea meetings are timed so people can get home in time for dinner at eight. The Stockwell meetings are timed for six o'clock tea, which doesn't suit people who take dinner at eight.

And Madeleine has agreed to accompany Nicholas to the first meetings. She'll show him the ropes. He'll make new friends – writers, artists, actors, journalists – people just like him. Madeleine said he'd be surprised at how many there were whose faces he'd recognize, and they his.

I'll bet.

Nicholas was never a man to do things by halves.

From now and this time forward and for all eternity, never again. Wife, family, work, all these things were of no importance.

Right. And how, I enquired, could I help?

I couldn't. Family and friends can't be involved.

What about Madeleine?

'That's different.'

Really? Doesn't that make her your co-dependant?

You see, I'm learning the jargon already.

'No.'

Right. So what can the rest of us do to help?

Go about our business and leave him to his.

Even though Madeleine has advised him to avoid social situations which involve the family, he's willing to make an exception and attend the dinner provided no one expects him to drink.

As if anyone would.

With family alerted, the menu needs planning. Unusually for me, I can't remember what we ate first time round. Exquisite little Claridges canapes no doubt, very labour-intensive. Vol-au-vents, foie-gras mousse in choux pastry buns. Caviar, if my grandmother had anything to do with it.

All these things are somewhat beyond me. I settle for pheasant with walnuts and stuff the choux with cream. As a centrepiece, I order up a copy of the wedding bouquet from the same Sloane Street florists who provided the flowers first time around.

The day of the party, Nicholas registers his feelings by taking the opportunity to apply fresh paint to the door frame between the kitchen and the dining-room, making it impossible for anyone to enter or leave without acquiring a sticky residue of magnolia gloss.

My sister-in-law Priscilla, arriving early to give me a hand in the kitchen, is helpless with laughter.

'I don't how you put up with it,' she says.

I don't either.

At times of anxiety triggered, as now, by lack of alcohol, Nicholas sees himself as mad King Lear. Which of the three daughters is allotted the role of Cordelia depends on his mood. Membership of Alcoholics Anonymous hasn't improved his temper.

Never mind. Sooner or later, all will be well. Meanwhile, the addict in recovery explains that he can't put pen to paper since he's been advised to avoid all situations in which he usually reached for the bottle. Since bottle-reaching includes all those times when he is either working or not working, windows will be hard to find.

Furthermore, the waifs and strays he brings home for dinner after meetings are not such as I would have chosen for company, not least for the evangelical tone the conversations take.

No one more reformist than a reformed alcoholic.

Part of the twelve-step programme was the obligation of co-dependants – as wife and family would henceforth be known – to believe, as did the dependant himself, that alcoholism is a disease.

If it was a disease, I say, it seems to me I'd have caught it.

Someone had to work to pay the bills.

My mother-in-law offers me her house in Lewes – a forty minute train journey from London – to use as a weekday workplace while she visits her youngest daughter in Australia.

She would be away for a month, just long enough for me to finish the book on which I was working, *The Barricaded Larder*, a follow-up to *European Peasant Cookery*. A collection of store cupboard recipes, all of which had to be tested, needed quiet concentration and no diversions.

I arranged for Priscilla to fill the fridge once a week, and left London, the newly pledged non-alcoholic and those of the children who were still in residence – two, as I remember – to fend for themselves. The eldest was just starting on a career in the City and newly back from training in Tokyo, and the youngest was awaiting enrolment for her first year at university.

For the time being – things might change – Nicholas was resolved to avoid everyone and everything which reminded him of the times when he was accustomed to reach for the bottle.

The truth was, whether writing or not, Nicholas drank quietly after breakfast. Discreetly through the morning. Amusingly at lunchtime. Steadily through the afternoon. Complainingly in the evening. And angrily at night.

A Jekyll and Hyde situation, some might say. But I'm not so sure. To an outsider – even close family – he would never appear to change, never seem more drunk at one time than any other. I never counted bottles. What was the point?

All was well, as far as I was aware. I returned at weekends to clean the house and set up the catering – for the rest, I left the family to its own devices. Until one bright morning, working away in Lewes, I had an early-morning call from London.

Madeleine was on the line. She had just delivered my husband to Accident and Emergency at St Thomas's down the road, where he was recovering from an alcoholic overdose.

No need to worry, she said. He'd sleep it off through the morning and soon be right as rain.

No need to worry, repeated the nurse when I arrived to collect my errant husband. The stomach pump would have dealt with the hangover. He might have a bit of a sore throat from the tubing – the doctor was young and inexperienced – but he'd be ready to leave as soon as he woke.

Care in the community, that's me. It's the first time I've heard the phrase, and it rankles. A negation, it seems to me, of the role of those of us who pick up the pieces.

And there are plenty of pieces. A drinker drinks because that's what he does. Drinking is not against the law. Anyone can walk into anywhere where drink is sold and acquire whatever it takes to kill himself. There's tough love and rehab and all the other things a man or woman can do to keep themselves out of trouble. But if the drinker is a writer, a solitary occupation which tolerates neither interference nor interruption, if he wants to drink, he will.

Meanwhile, I am rather hoping the memory of the stomach pump, option of last resort for the self-poisoner, is unpleasant enough to discourage repetition.

Nicholas, however, is unrepentant.

What stomach pump? I see no stomach pump.

And anyway, as far as he's concerned, it was the drink itself which poisoned him.

What drink?

The stuff in the bottle on the dresser. The stuff he drank when he'd finished the half-finished bottle of sweet Sauternes – a touch of the Bluebell Girl – I'd been saving for an evening treat.

The bottle on the dresser reveals itself to contain the dregs of a medicinal Chinese wine in which, clearly visible in the murky depths, is a full-grown Chinese lizard, small but perfect in all its parts. Never mind how it came to be there. I'm a food writer; these things happen.

Any man, it seems to me, who could gulp down the contents of such a bottle at a single swallow is not a man to heed a warning.

After the episode of the lizard wine, Nicholas returned to his usual habits. The wine flowed, the visits to Alcoholics Anonymous ceased, and he began once again to write. I had – still have – no way of knowing whether the writing and the drinking were so deeply entangled that the one was impossible without the other. Whatever the truth, as soon as Nicholas returned to the bottle, life returned to what was normal for a novelist, writing books.

With *The Last Wilderness* delivered and well received, Nicholas embarked on a contract with a new publisher for a blockbuster set in Africa, *Gondar*, with a second in the same genre to be set in India, *Himalaya*. The books were to be much longer and more ambitious than anything he had ever done before.

*****

Meanwhile, I had turned my attention to my own first novel, *Emerald*, a romantic fantasy of an unwanted daughter of Wallis Simpson and the Prince of Wales, and was happily settled into the stacks in the London Library, dividing my time between researching Ethiopia in the 1900s for Nicholas, and the home life of the Duke and Duchess of Windsor in the 1930s for myself.

Libraries always make me happy. And the London Library was set up for people like me – those of us who can't get past the dragons. As a writer, I took the decision to use my married name. In my previous wage-earning existence as artist and illustrator, professions which pay little attention to qualifications, I used my mother's maiden name just because I liked the sound of it. But as a writer – well – Luard is unusual enough to be memorable, and I figured if one of us wrote a bestseller, so much the better for the other.

Nevertheless, if I wrote on a subject unrelated to recipes – say, in the *Spectator* on the problems of Romania under Ceaucescu, or on scientific collaboration between Israel and the Saudis when the Middle East was at war – Nicholas was sure to receive congratulations. Presumably if Nicholas had ever written recipes – never likely – I would have been held responsible.

No matter, as long as one of us banked the cheque. We never argued over what was in the bank account. Whoever had the money settled the bills.

*****

'Take a look at this.'

Nicholas dropped an estate agent's brochure in front of me on the desk. It was 1990 and Nicholas had managed to bank a decent advance for an adventure-novel set in Africa, *Gondar*, his most successful book to date. Translation rights had plumped up earnings and things were looking good.

I glanced down at a photograph of a little stone-built cottage set in woodland on the island of Mull. The details described a two-room dwelling, a crofthouse with a lean-to on the back and a walled garden tacked on the front.

'I've bought it.'

Sight unseen?

Not exactly. Nicholas had visited the little house when he was a child on Mull, and he knew it would be perfect as a workplace.

Flush with an advance on the new novel and newly back on the bottle after his flirtation with Alcoholics Anonymous, Nicholas has decided he always wanted to be a gardener.

In the middle of the garden is a single overgrown cyprus, tall as a skyscraper, of the kind planted in Italian and Greek cemeteries.

While a century ago the rich earth had supplied a large Victorian household with fruit and vegetables all through the year, there's very little left. Evidence of former fertility can be seen in a line of crippled moss-draped apple trees, a thicket of raspberry canes and a tangle of currant and gooseberry bushes.

At the far end of the garden is a wall of Japanese knotweed, scourge of the island, planted as pheasant cover by the laird.

I consult a Japanese cookbook and learn that the shoots are edible and good. I think it unlikely I'll be able to convince the entire population of the island to switch to a diet of knotweed prepared in the Japanese way, with dipping-sauce of soy and ginger. Islanders don't like change.

I had visited the island first as a young wife soon after our wedding.

Nicholas's grandmother, Flora McVean, was island-born, and his father owned a crofthouse opposite the little island of Ulva, where David Livingstone spent his childhood.

The family mansion, Kinfinnichan, on the Ross, the southern end of the island, had long since been sold to a property developer from London, the fate of most of the island's larger houses. Mostly it was only the crofthouses that remained in the same families for generations.

Nicholas loved the Hebrides, and I too had come to love the tranquillity and beauty of his islands. Throughout the years of the children's childhood, we'd take them to visit their grandfather on the island at Eastertime, or rent a cottage for ourselves just down the road in summer.

Jock now treated me with wary courtesy, and I was careful not to intrude on his relationship with his grandchildren. Whatever he felt towards his daughter-in-law, he was a rewarding grandfather.

He kept a little rowing-boat moored to a buoy in a sheltered cove just below the crofthouse, and when the skies were clear and the water calm, he would start the little two-stroke motor and they'd all head out to sea to drop lines for mackerel, or check the creels for lobster. And if there was nothing there, the ferryman would leave a pound or two of crayfish in the postbox.

All in all, I felt, a good place for both of us to settle down and work, leaving behind the alarms and diversions of city life.

Nicholas has also acquired a clinker-built Fairey Huntsman, a motor boat with an insatiable appetite for fuel and a habit of springing leaks in its planks just below the waterline, where it matters. To celebrate the acquisition, he spent a week at a residential navigation school learning whatever you need to know to turn the engine on and plot a course.

The Huntsman was trucked up on a low loader and slipped into the calm waters of Tobermoray Bay. Nicholas, however, after a single triumphant victory ride round the bay and a bumpy encounter with open water in a force 9 gale, normal weather conditions in Hebridean waters, immediately turned over care and control of the boat to Archie Simpson, part-time fisherman and full-time joy rider.

Thereafter the boat could be observed on stormy days and calm, merrily churning up the waters between Mull and the adjoining island of Ulva, while Nicholas paid the bills. Nicholas's enthusiasms were short lived. He was ever a man for pursuit rather than fulfilment.

The cottage was built as a black-house, a house without a chimney. The outer walls were curved at the corners, evidence that the original stone-built dwelling had lacked openings of any kind apart from the door, so that soot from the hearth fire could be scraped off the walls and transferred to the land as fertilizer. In the old days, soot was an important resource and the land's fertility a matter of life or death.

Windows and chimney were added in Victorian times, when the garden wall was built. Modern conveniences more recently installed included electricity and telephone and running water piped down the hill from a spring. All, however, are subject to interruption from various sources. In the winter when the pipes froze and the water no longer flowed, I was obliged to fetch a bucket from the stream and cook one-pot stews and be very sparing with the washing-up.

With the London flat on the market – financial respite offered by *Gondar* didn't last long – finances once more dictate how we live. And we decide to exchange life in London for

Mull, at least until the garden is restored and work on the cottage completed.

Both us travel regularly, though rarely in the same direction.

Nicholas plans another trip to Africa, a return to Kenya, where he lived as a child. And I have a commitment to make a television series based on *European Peasant Cookery* for an Australian production company which will take me away for weeks at a time.

On Mull, there are people around whose company Nicholas enjoys, work to be overseen in the house, and the garden to be attended to. Just the same, island life breeds island fever. The only cure for island fever is to leave the island for the time it takes for the fever to pass, or head for the pub. Nicholas prefers the latter.

*****

There's another reason for welcoming what the island has to offer. We need a haven, somewhere where Francesca, the eldest daughter, can find privacy and peace when she needs it. As she surely will.

At first we had thought that the bursts of illness which sapped her strength and seemed hard to shake were nothing serious. As a busy journalist with a shopping-column in a national newspaper and a hectic social life, occasional bouts of exhaustion were normal. She never did drugs, her love affairs were never casual. There was nothing in the way she lived her life that might lead anyone to suspect that her inability to shake off a persistent lung infection had a more sinister source. No reason not to suppose that a week or two on the island – fresh air, home comforts, long walks – wouldn't restore her strength.

We know now that this is not the way it's going to be. Tests show that the weakness of the lungs is the first sign of a worsening condition. The cause, the big illness with a little name – the one that no one wants to know about and everyone thinks won't happen to them.

We didn't know how long this thing would take. Impossible to tell how long it's been there. Impossible to know how far it's progressed. Twenty years ago, little was known of how the virus which attacks the human immune system takes hold, still less how it might be held at bay. The only certainty is that the diagnosis is irreversible.

Francesca, always practical, tells the rest of us to go about our business and let her get on with hers. She decides on a change of career and books herself into art school. She means to be a painter. Life, she says, is too short for shopping.

We lost Francesca four years later, at the bleak end of the year which leads up to Christmas. We buried her in a little country churchyard in the shadow of the Sussex Downs. Not yet thirty, a beauty and a wit, when she walked into a room, heads turned. She was ready to find a good man, have babies, live happily for ever, just as they do in fairytales. No drugs, no excuses, no unforeseen risk which might somehow explain how it happened. She was young and unlucky – that's all. Aids is no respecter of youth or age, or good or bad, or man or woman.

In winter, in a place where roses bloom in summer, snow falls thick and white on the stone which marks her resting-place. Her life and death are still too close to remember without tears. And tears were never her way.

That year, Christmas came all too soon. We borrowed a house in a place where there were no memories to remind us of what we had lost, in the Garfagnana, high in the hills of Tuscany, bleak and cold and clean.

Nicholas and I arrived before the rest of the family, winding our way into the clouds through the chestnut trees of the beautiful valley, just in time for a raid on the little mobile shop for bread and ham. The old lady who had care of the house showed us round. We lit fires, made the beds, did what was needed to make the place welcoming and warm.

Fran's brother, eldest of the siblings, arrived from New York just in time for the Eve. His two sisters drove up the valley from

Milan the day before, arriving in darkness, following the white ribbons Nicholas had tied on to the lamp posts to lead them through the winding streets till they found the house.

The village, noisy with holidaymakers through the summer, was quiet in winter. Those who lived in the few inhabited houses had set lighted Christmas trees in the street, and the little farmhouses on the way up the valley had placed Christmas cribs outside their doors.

By the time we are all assembled, the fire is blazing, the candles lit, the stove glowing in the hallway, the larder crammed with the best that the nearby town could yield. Good food is comforting at times like these.

We speak of unimportant things, make lists for the market in the morning, talk of recipes, seek advice from neighbours, chatting in the street about what might or might not be proper for the festival.

There are no words to make it right. A family which loses one of the number under such circumstances has to find healing in any way it can. The eve of a festival is a solemn time. This suits us. I find, as always, comfort in warmth and food and company to share it.

In the market on the Eve are sacks of hazelnuts ready roasted in their shells, pyramids of pineapples, crates of oranges, nets of tangerines, boxes of Sicilian tomatoes, strings of garlic, purple onions, green celery, fat white heads of fennel stacked root outward, posies of purple artichokes and bundles of woolly-furred cardoons.

And for those who had had the forethought to bring their own bottles, first-pressing green olive oil sold from the barrel by a white-haired olive grower who mills his own olives.

There are unfamiliar greens for the fasting supper, bundles of leaves like giant dandelions, mustardy greens which could be bought ready cooked as little round balls for stirring into soups, or for heating with garlic and butter.

The butter is white and salty and sold carved from the block. Tuscan bread is baked without salt – salt attracts damp and unsalted bread dries without mould and can be damped down and reheated in the oven, or toasted on a naked flame, or served as a layering for the fasting supper of the Eve.

We are not in the mood for feasting. The quiet supper of the Eve suits us best. Afterwards we cross the square to the little church to join the congregation, take comfort in the lighted candles, the crib with its promise that the birth of a child will bring us joy.

Time passes for the living. Not so for the dead. And if her spirit lives, it lives elsewhere. On the island she loved, among the silver sisters of the Hebrides, where the water falls white as a white mare's tail over black rocks to the sea.

Lasagne with Winter Greens, Hazelnuts and Cheese

The fasting supper of Christmas Eve in the Garfagnana is a simple bread-based lasagne made without meat. The dish can be made in larger quantities for a party. Simple food, but good.

SERVES 6 TO 8

8 slices buttered bread (not too fresh)
1kg spinach and bitter salad leaves, washed and rinsed
2 cloves garlic, chopped
2 onions, finely sliced
4 tablespoons olive oil
1 tablespoon dried sage and thyme
4 tablespoons toasted hazelnuts, chopped
Salt and pepper

For the sauce
500ml full cream milk
3 eggs
Salt and pepper
A scrape of nutmeg
4 tablespoons grated cheese

Cut the bread into fingers. Shake the leaves dry, and shred. Fry the garlic and onion lightly in the oil in a saucepan till the vegetables soften – don't let them brown. Add the leaves and stir over the heat till they wilt. Season with the herbs, salt and pepper.

Beat the eggs up in the milk. Season and add the nutmeg.

Cover the base of a gratin dish with bread fingers, buttered side down. Pour in ⅓ of the milk-and-egg, sprinkle with a little cheese, then spread on half the vegetables and a spoonful of chopped nuts. Repeat the layer with the rest of the ingredients, reserving enough bread, milk-and-egg and grated cheese to make a final layer.

Bake in a moderate oven (350° F/180° C/Gas 4) for 30–35 minutes, until golden and bubbling.

CHAPTER TWELVE

Politics and Postscripts

'Never try to lick ice cream off a hot sidewalk.'

CHARLIE BROWN TO LINUS, CHARLES M. SCHULTZ

IT'S 1997 AND THE TORIES HAVE BEEN IN POWER FAR TOO LONG. Tony Blair has taken over the leadership of the Labour Party and I for one intend to vote him in. I'll admit to a personal interest in the outcome of the election. My younger sister's married to Charlie Falconer, Tony's best buddy, and I have spent many a merry evening in their kitchen in the heights of Islington, and the atmosphere is heady.

Meanwhile Nicholas, always the political spanner-chucker, has decided to stand for Jimmy Goldsmith's Referendum Party against Michael Portillo in what's considered a safe Tory seat, Enfield Southgate.

I suspect the purity of his motives.

Nicholas knows Portillo and, as far as I'm aware, thinks him sound.

Michael was a regular weekend guest at David Hart's in the days when David owned a huge Elizabethan mansion in Suffolk and was close to Mrs Thatcher. David was the man reputed to have broken the miners' strike for Mrs T., though I was never sure quite how.

Nicholas and David always enjoyed each other's company, perhaps because both were demolition men rather than empire builders. When David organized a political weekend, Nicholas was always invited and I went along for the fun. There were always people around who could make things happen. Some of them were famous and in the public eye, others not famous at all and members of the CIA. David had a taste for the cloak-and-dagger, and so did Nicholas.

Portillo was David's choice to replace the leader when she retired of her own volition. And when she was pushed, it was David who organized Portillo's abortive bid for the leadership.

'He's sitting on the fence,' says Nicholas cheerfully. 'I mean to push him off.'

Europe is a subject on which my beloved and I agree to differ. I am quite certain we should be in the Union and Nicholas is equally certain we shouldn't. And although I have never met Sir James – maybe once or twice in passing with Dominick Elwes in the Clermont or in the dark at Annabel's – I am perfectly certain Sir James is not to be trusted.

No matter, said Nicholas. We share the same ambitions. Jimmy puts up the deposit and provides the back-up.

What back-up?

Pens and things, says Nicholas vaguely. Every now and again, ten years later, I still find Referendum Party ballpoints around the place – white, with blue writing, made in China.

Nicholas, offered a choice of seats, has picked Portillo, he says, because he's a government minister with a seat in cabinet and is fair game for the Eurosceptics.

The second and, I suspect, the real reason behind picking Portillo, is because Nicholas can see an opportunity to rock the political boat. There is enough dissatisfaction with the clapped-out Tory government to allow Portillo another crack at the leadership when the party replaces John Major as soon as Labour gets in.

Portillo's seat is not even marginal, but the pollsters are predicting that even the safest seats are vulnerable. Nicholas may not get in, but there's a good chance the voters who wouldn't consider Labour will vote for a man with a convincing accent and a nippy line in rhetoric.

Nicholas dusts down his Brigade of Guards tie, polishes his shoes to a military shine, assembles a motley crew of supporters, borrows a shopfront, and retires to the pub.

His agent, an enthusiastic anti-European, has an impenetrable German accent and his name is Josef Goebbels.

'Perfect,' says Nicholas. 'You're hired.'

Dr Goebbels, as he immediately becomes, takes delivery of a box of Referendum Party balloons – white with blue writing and also made in China – and spends an afternoon filling them with helium.

I, meanwhile, have given up the struggle with my conscience and am canvassing the area with as much enthusiasm as I can muster.

I soon encounter an undercurrent of opinion among the gay community – mostly antique dealers in the smarter part of the borough who have nothing better to do than chat to a canvasser – that Michael Portillo is a regular at a nightclub which serves as a pick-up joint. I have no way of knowing if this is true. Since the idea is presented as a good reason to vote Conservative, I attempt to undermine the rival candidate by suggesting that a man who sits on the fence politically is not to be trusted personally, particularly if he's in the closet with the door shut.

Shortly after this, a representative from Peter Tatchell's Outrage comes in search of the closeted Conservative candidate for Enfield Southgate.

Portillo refuses to be outed.

Nicholas, on the other hand, declares himself more than willing to vacate the closet. But since he's running on a family-man ticket – photos of children and grandchild available on request – and his wife's out on the stump, no one believes him.

Dr Goebbels decides to help things along by handing out the helium-filled balloons to mothers and children returning home after school. Labour – Stephen Twigg, as I remember – has set up shop a hundred yards further up the street outside McDonalds, a popular after-school venue for schoolchildren and their parents.

The balloons go bobbing up the street in one direction and come bobbing down the other covered in Labour Party stickers.

Dr Goebbels attempts to recapture the balloons and remove the stickers on the way back, leaving a trail of howling children. No one understands what Dr Goebbels is saying owing to the accent, and anyway they don't like the buttoned-up raincoat and the shades.

A small riot ensues.

Nicholas has to be fetched from the pub and warned by the law for creating a situation likely to encourage public disorder.

As if he would.

Dr Goebbels is taken off street duties and confined to the office answering telephones. Though this is probably counter-productive, considering the difficulties over the accent.

Election day is hotter than Hades.

It's so hot that the chewing-gum melts on the pavement and people have to make their way to the polling-stations trailing sticky grey threads, like refugees from a primeval swamp.

Dr Goebbels, unaware that election rules prevent canvassing within twenty-four hours of polling-day, has to be prevented from standing outside the voting-booths handing out bottles of water with Referendum Party stickers plastered over the labels.

As soon as the booths close, we make our way to the school sports centre where the count is to take place. The building has been cleared for action. There's a bank of televisions in the foyer and credentials are checked on the door. We all wear badges. Candidates' wives are allowed to enter, as indeed are their agents.

Nicholas and Dr Goebbels wander up and down the aisles, checking the count. There are six other independents on the list, including the Monster Raving Loony Party.

No sign of Portillo.

Actually, Portillo sightings have been rare throughout the campaign. The candidate has a safe seat and he's a government minister and he hasn't much seen the need to hit the hustings.

This is a mistake.

Young Twigg, it appears from the neat little piles of votes, is neck and neck with the potential next leader of the Tory Party. Nicholas is also doing very nicely thank you, considering he's an independent and the British voter doesn't much like independents. In fact, it appears that the difference between Twigg and Portillo is Nicholas.

At midnight, Portillo and his henchmen pop up. We know they've arrived because of the screaming sirens and the uniformed outriders and the gleaming limos which sweep through the school playground. Portillo is Minister for Defence. Military escorts come with the territory.

Those of us not actually engaged in the count crowd the foyer. Police clear a path, shouldering us aside. This seems to me rather undemocratic, though I know you can't argue with policemen. The henchmen and the minister are all wearing look-alike dark suits and heavy black shades. They look like a squad of Mafia hitmen.

Somebody must have warned Michael the count was close.

Silence falls. The vote's too close to call. A recount begins.

When the result is declared, Portillo makes a graceful speech accepting defeat.

The clip shown on TV at the time is the one which always pops up whenever there's a discussion of whatever happened to the Tories. Nicholas, needless to say, is bobbing around in the background, smiling and waving, the very picture of a man who's done exactly what he wanted and will do it again if he wants.

What neither of us yet know is that the drink has taken its toll and time is running out.

*****

The election is over and Nicholas is considering his future, and he doesn't much like what he sees.

We have just inherited a house in a beautiful place in the wilds of west Wales. While I welcome this as a stroke of good fortune, Nicholas remains unconvinced.

The house has come to us by a roundabout route, though we have known for years that the offer was there. Monica Rawlins, an artist by profession, daughter of the Edwardian aristocracy, had left the property jointly to both of us. Monica had known Nicholas for forty years. The official storyline was that Nicholas was her godson. The story put about by my mother, who had influential friends in the neighbourhood, was that Nicholas had met her on a train and taken advantage of her thereafter. The truth was that Nicholas had first come to Brynmerheryn when he was still at Cambridge in the company of his then girlfriend, Elizabeth Beddingfield, who was indeed Monica's goddaughter.

Nicholas had got on famously with Monica, less so with the girlfriend, but the friendship endured. As the years rolled on, Nicholas talked to Monica regularly on the telephone – the old lady was as sharp as a tack and the two enjoyed talking about painting and Paris. In later years, when she could no longer come to London, Nicholas would visit her in Wales, sometimes with me, sometimes on his own.

The old lady died when Nicholas was away in Africa. So it was left to me to attend the funeral and take over the house. By the time Nicholas returned, I was hooked. The house was in a sorry state of repair, but the bones were good and the place was beautiful. And anyway, as I said to Nicholas, we could happily transfer from the Hebrides. It was all sheep and Celts – and we were more than happy with both.

Nicholas is restless. Gardening has lost its appeal. He has no wish to retire to the country, nor is he prepared to count his blessings. He hasn't finished. He needs new challenges, new people, new places.

Actually what he really wants is not to be involved in anything which has gone before. He will give up everything – wife, family, work, women. He will travel in Africa, paint in Paris, do whatever he needs to do to change his life.

I listen carefully. What I hope he's decided is that it's time to give up the drink. No such luck. Madeleine is still waiting in the wings. Maybe she can do what I cannot. And anyway, I have a trip abroad to organize, work to deliver.

Children and their friends are due in Wales for the weekend. I will, I say, leave everything prepared and Nicholas will have company for the few days I need to be away.

The editor of an American travel magazine wants a thousand words on where to go and what to eat in Eastern Europe. I have suggested Romania, the Saxon villages of Transylvania. The most famous of these, the village of Viscri, has little to offer as yet, but new roads are planned and hopes are high.

In the bad old days under the dictator, the Saxons lived much as they had for a thousand years. These days the villages are all but empty, the inhabitants returned to Germany, the houses crumbling. The few that are left are hoping to attract Western tourists to stay in the empty houses, bringing new life and a source of income to those who remain.

The magazine agrees and I book my flight to Bucharest. American magazines pay well enough to cover the cost of travel, and I can pick where I go and what I wish to write.

Throughout the Ceaucescu years, the Romanian capital was a pock-marked city ruled by fear, its shops empty of goods, its streets deserted. Now, with the dictator gone, the streets are thronged, the cafés packed, and everywhere are advertisements for all the things the previous regime despised.

I meet Romanian friends for dinner that evening and immerse myself in the complicated politics of Eastern Europe after the Russians have retreated – larger questions than what's going on at home in Wales, and welcome.

We, the friends and I, have not seen each other since the fall of the dictator, and everyone's anxious to discuss the changes. The country's literati communicate in French, the common language which unites the educated of the region.

Borders have always drifted in one direction or another. Not everyone speaks Romanian. Romania is not even sure she's really Romanian. There are Moldavians and Transylvanians and those who live in the Carpathians, Hungarians and German-speaking Saxons and Slavs and those who trace their ancestry back to the Ottoman Turks.

There are, in addition, Romanies and Jews, the fall-guys when things go wrong. The conclusion, it's as plain as the nose on your face, is that it wasn't the Romanians who were responsible for the Ceaucescu years and the ruin of the nation, but the Hungarians, Jews and Gypsies. With a little help from Moscow, of course. The Russians, it's generally felt, were worse than the Turks.

At least, it seems to me, the Ottomans could cook. Most of the dishes considered really Romanian were actually Turkish. *Sarmale*, little rolls of rice-stuffed leaves, the national dish, is really Turkish.

Next day, I drive to the little village of Viscri to meet Carolina, a member of one of the last remaining Saxon families, a young matron with a husband and a daughter, who holds the position of mayor.

The other houses, she explains, are still owned by the original families, though some have been sold to people from Bucharest and others squatted by Gypsies. The empty houses are the ones they plan to convert for tourists.

Carolina says she dreads the Gypsies' appearance on her doorstep because she can refuse them nothing.

Why not?

'They have the evil eye.'

She walks to the door and shoots the bolt.

'And you, do you live where you have always lived?'

No. I've lived all over the place. I make myself at home wherever I am.

'You're fortunate. Me? I have no desire to go to Germany. They make fun of us. They say we speak like the Luxembourgeois, and everyone laughs at the Luxembourgeois. It was Hitler who told us that we were German, who made us think about who we were.

'Before then we were the Saxons of the Seven Villages, we knew who we were. After the war, our families were no longer together. It was like that for me. My mother was in Russia and my father was in Germany and we, the children, stayed here with the grandparents. We were very poor – you cannot imagine how poor. We had four years in school, but only in the winter. There was no school in summer.

'We had animals to care for, sheep and cows, pigs and chickens. The sheep and cows go out to pasture in the morning and come back in the evening and always stop at the right doorway and turn in. These days we employ a shepherd who looks after the sheep and takes over the milking. He's black but he makes good cheese.'

Black, Carolina explains, applies to anyone darker than the blond, blue-eyed Saxons.

We climb the tower for a view of the village.

'This is my corner. From here I can watch the whole village. The Saxon houses are the ones closest to the church. Look down there, by the gate, where the earth is bare. That is the dancefloor where we used to dance the Saxon dances. On Sunday, after church, the musicians played, and we would dance.'

Freedom did what oppression never could – empty the village of Saxons. Once the barriers came down, those who had hopes of a future got out while the going was good.

All that's left is the old folks, the ones who don't wish to bury their bones in foreign soil.

I know what they mean, I say. I'm a grandmother now and am happy that my grandchildren associate me with such a beautiful place.

It's beautiful here too, says Carolina. But the Saxons are not likely to return. Those who remain must find another way to live. Whether the future of the villages is an improvement on the past matters little. The situation is as it is. And there are advantages. There are schools and new roads and the hope of prosperity brought by tourists. There may well have been much to value in what was there before. Not least the thrifty use of the earth's resources, a community which cared for the old and the young because society needed both, a value placed on good neighbourliness and the kindness of those who expect no material reward.

My thoughts return to Wales.

Nicholas may not yet be reconciled to leaving his beloved Hebrides – never for good, we can always return to visit the silver sisters whenever we wish. Meanwhile, well, there are Celts here too. And mountains and valleys and woods and the wilderness he loves.

We have reason to be grateful for what Nicholas is inclined to see as an inconvenient legacy. We have been made welcome in the place we now call home. The Welsh value their writers and poets. There is, too, a tolerance for eccentricity in those who earn their living by the pen. And Nicholas is popular among the locals not only for the interest he takes in things that matter to isolated communities such as this, but for his fondness for the pub and the entertainment afforded by the scrapes he gets himself into when the drink takes hold.

When I take the risk to travel, I expect the trip to be cut short and ring home daily. But since the Saxon villages are not equipped with telephone lines and mobiles don't work unless you're on top of a mountain, I had to trust that if there was a crisis at home, someone will know and call help.

When I finally ring in, Nicholas is fine. He's had an excellent weekend. The friends were all young and admiring. Particularly one, a female doctor, who has convinced him he has to change his life or he will surely die.

The young woman has promised to arrange for Nicholas to be admitted to the care of a specialist, a brilliant surgeon, the best in the land.

I cannot imagine how kind she is, how happy he is, how fortunate – how wonderful.

I've heard that word before, and in similar circumstances. Perhaps this time it'll work.

And by the way, he adds, there's other news.

My mother is in hospital. Admitted for a minor operation, there are fears she won't survive.

In her hospital bed in a private room, my mother is already deep in a morphine slumber.

My sister has taken up the offer of beds for us both. It won't be long, says the doctor. Better stay close.

I'm an imposter. I don't belong here, at this deathbed which has nothing to do with me. I shouldn't be here at all. My mother wouldn't want me here, but my sister does, and that's enough.

'Care for the living,' said my daughter Francesca, sending me home from the hospital where her final days were spent.

I take my work into the room where my mother sleeps. I write recipes. I am guilty of inattention, conscious that what I am doing would not please the woman in the bed. The woman whose daughter I am.

The hours pass.

There is a subtext, a business of hospital life. People come and go – a doctor, a nurse, the brothers, mine and my sister's. Morphine flows through a slender tube into my mother's veins. Her eyelids are transparent, blue-veined, veiling the flickering pupils. Morphine softens pain. No pain says the nurse. The modern way of dying is no pain.

It's dying none the less.

My mother said she would never want to be a burden to her children. In that at least she's had her way.

I have no memory at all of my mother's embrace. Even her scent, the print of a mother on a child, eludes me. I remember the touch of bone on bone, her habit of pulling her mouth aside to proffer a cheek.

We talked, my sister and I, of our mother and our lives and the things we shared.

My sister was born in Madrid. I was fourteen and a schoolgirl, no longer at home. My sister was three months old when we first met – a red-haired pink-cheeked baby in a big black pram dressed in exquisite little clothes trimmed with lace and ribbon.

My mother told me at the time – a rare moment of confession – that she hated her last pregnancy. Hated the demands it made on her and the way it made her look. The pregnancy had not been planned. It had been seven years since she had last carried a child, she was thirty-five and had never expected to go through it all again.

She set aside her beautiful clothes and hid herself in flower-printed smocks in ugly colours she would never have worn at any other time. Usually she dressed at Cristobal Balenciaga, keeping appointments for fittings in his little walk-up studio just off the Gran Via, Madrid's main shopping-street. The couturier was at the beginning of his career, stitching impeccable little black dresses for the elegant *Madrileñas* my mother met at the Puerto de Hierro, the country club where the wives of diplomats and Franco's government officials spent their afternoons.

Occasionally, when I was in Madrid, I would be allowed to accompany my mother on a shopping-trip. Opposite the entrance to Balenciaga's workshop was a busy café where my mother would order coffee for herself and vanilla ice cream for me.

In later years, when crossing the Spanish capital with my own children sleeping behind me in our camper van as we made our way south, I drove down the Gran Via in the dead of night to see if the coffee house was still there. The waiters were closing the shutters and the tables had been stacked inside, but there it was, a reminder of a very different life.

Once my sister was born, my mother handed the baby to Nanny and that was that. She was always beautifully powdered and painted, exquisitely dressed, perfectly coiffed, deliciously scented. She returned to the life of a diplomat's wife, ornamental, a wonderful hostess – everyone said so.

Once I was married, I rarely saw my mother except on formal occasions, or when I myself had suggested lunch or that we meet in the morning for coffee. Her evenings were never available. She was a Hildyard now – and as far as the rest of the world was concerned, she'd never been anything else.

And now, in this hospital bed with its tidy corners and its plumped-up pillows and the instruments which control her pain, my mother is dying. Her breathing softens, halts, returns, then halts once more. Dark shadows rim the sockets of her eyes, closed in sleep. Her face is tranquil, smooth-skinned, peaceful, almost childlike.

I try to remember her in the days when she was young and I was a child myself. Childhood memories call physical things to mind. Rope-soled sandals shimmering with leaf-shaped sequins and tiny pearls bought in Capri and worn in summer. Soft silk flowers with tiny veils worn in the hair for a party.

There are other things I can learn to forgive but cannot forget. That my father was good-looking but stupid and the marriage would never have lasted. That I had changed the spelling of my name because I had always thought myself something I was not. Some time later, I had reason to check my birth certificate. My mother was wrong. The spelling of my name – Elisabeth rather than the more usual Elizabeth – had never changed. Later still, I asked my father's sister if she knew the reason for the unusual spelling. 'Your Longmore grandmother insisted. She was born a Maitland and Elisabeth was a family name. To spell it with a "z" would have been unthinkable.'

My mother has not been happy these past few years. Toby died of cancer three years back and our mother, says my sister, had never recovered.

My mother has closed herself away from all but her younger children of recent years, and I have seen her rarely. There were always reasons for a visit to be inconvenient, and I had been too preoccupied with other things to insist.

Too late now to say the things which might have been said, the things a daughter needs to say: I was your child, we loved each other as best we could. We were as alike as we could be. Had things been other than they were, there might have been things to share. You might have learned to love your grandchildren, to know who they are. 'I'm too young to be a grandmother,' said my mother when my children were born. 'I'm sorry. That's just how it is.'

We are all of us someone's child so long as one of our parents lives. After that, the roof is open to the sky.

The order and content of the funeral service was settled by my younger siblings, Hildyards both. Instructions were left that this was how it should be. This was the way my mother had wanted it, a Hildyard funeral, a Hildyard wake. My mother was to be buried in hallowed Hildyard ground.

My younger brother delivered the funeral address. His mother, he told the assembled mourners, had been a devoted wife, a caring mother, selfless and dutiful. No mention was made of my own father, that there had been another life before the life he described, another existence.

As my brother spoke, I studied the paper in my hand, the phrase I had agreed to read, a quotation from a poem, bland and uncaring and suitable.

When it came to my turn to speak, I set the verse aside and spoke of what was in my head. Of who my mother was to me, of the days when she was young. Of her pleasure in the paintings on her walls, the excellence of her table, the warmth of her friendships.

To illustrate my memories of her later years, I told a story of a shopping-trip we had taken together when she returned to

London on leave from Chile. There were, she explained, certain inexplicable shortages in the capital under the communists.

What did she need?

She smiled. The full-length sable she was wearing, dark and soft, which would serve her well when she went to the opera in Santiago. Chilean women were very chic, they dressed in Paris.

What else?

Picture hooks to hang her paintings.

What I mean to say, I felt the need to explain, was that the coat was beautiful and the picture hooks were practical. And that my mother loved beauty as much as she loved order.

I did not speak of my father. Well, good-looking but stupid was the way my mother described him: not much of a reason to choose a husband. And yet there was a time when she thought otherwise. After my mother died, among the papers in her safe was a letter addressed to the children of her first marriage. My younger brother found the letter, read it and – careful to send a photocopy rather than the original – passed it on. My brother is a lawyer and lawyers are careful. My mother had moved house at least a dozen times during her lifetime, transferring the family records from place to place, and yet she had failed to pass the document over to her children, the two to whom it mattered.

The dateline on the letter is London, 1944, the year the war in Europe ended and, I could only presume, my father's death had been confirmed.

'My darling children,' my mother began. 'When you are both old enough to understand I will do my best to hand on to you as many memories of your father as I am able. They will all be happy and cheerful ones – no thoughts of him could ever be anything else. I cannot in any way replace him for you, but I can pass on to you an account of our brief four years together. You must know, I am sure, my thoughts and memories are nothing but happy.'

There followed some thirty hand-written pages describing how two young people met soon after Munich in 1939. How they fell in love and were married and the joy they took in the birth of their children. For proof of this, there were letters transcribed in her hand but signed by my father.

The story was never finished. Unfinished stories leave unanswered questions. Questions I wasn't yet ready to ask.

Afterwards, when my mother's effects were cleared from her apartment in Onslow Square – instructions had been left that this should be done only by the children of the second marriage. My Hildyard brother found the letter with a formal little note.

Inside the parcel was a tattered mink coat from the 1940s, box-shouldered and losing its pelt, the only such garment, the note assured me, my mother had ever owned.

I recognized the coat. It had been my grandmother's, saved against a rainy day. I didn't argue with my brother. Any more than I could argue with my mother's will.

In death, as in life, my mother kept things tidy.

She left what remained of her fortune – a million or three, though I never checked – to the children of her second marriage, declaring them, to all intents and purposes, her only legitimate heirs.

Romanian Sarmale

Rice wrapped in leaves, Turkish *domades*, is the national dish of Romania – or it would be if the Romanians would ever admit to such a thing. Recipes are very variable and the method and content vigorously disputed. Cabbage is the usual wrapper in late summer and autumn, vineleaves in spring and early summer, and salt cabbage in winter.

SERVES 6 TO 8

1 small green cabbage
2 carrots, scraped and finely chopped
2 sticks celery, finely chopped

The filling
250g round rice (risotto or 'pudding')
4 tablespoons oil
1 medium onion, finely chopped
2 garlic cloves, finely chopped
1 tablespoon finely chopped parsley
1 tablespoon finely chopped marjoram
1 teaspoon ground cumin
1 teaspoon ground cinnamon
(optional) 1 egg, lightly forked
Salt and pepper

Settle the cabbage in a roomy bowl and pour in a kettleful of boiling water – leave it just long enough to soften the bases of the leaves. Drain. Remove about 18 of the large outer leaves and lay them flat, ready for stuffing, pressing down with the flat of your hand. Cut out the hard stalk and discard, shred the remaining inner leaves and put them in a roomy casserole with the carrot and onion.

Heat 2 tablespoons of oil in a frying-pan and fry the chopped onion and garlic until soft and golden – don't let it brown. Add the rice and stir it over the heat until the grains turn translucent. Season and add enough water just to submerge the grains. Bring to the boil, turn down the heat and simmer for 10 minutes, when the grains will be chewy but most of the water will have been absorbed. Tip the contents of the pan into a bowl. Work in the herbs, spices and egg thoroughly with your hand, squeezing to make a firm mixture.

Drop a tablespoonful of filling on the stalk-end of each leaf, tuck the sides over to enclose, roll up neatly and transfer to the bed of cabbage in the casserole. Continue till all is used up. Sprinkle with the remaining oil, add enough water to just cover, bring to the boil, turn down the heat, lid and simmer gently for about an hour, until all the liquid has been absorbed.

PART TWO

25 MAY **2004** WRITERS DRINK, SAY THOSE WHO WRITE, BECAUSE they're writers. And because they drink, they die before their time.

Hemingway, Fitzgerald, Dylan Thomas, Kingsley Amis were drinkers all, all dead before their time.

The genes were good. Nicholas had every chance. Both his parents lived well into their nineties. Nature was on his side. His body was strong. Wiry and tough, well-formed, muscular, broad-chested, with a weightlifter's shoulders and a prizefighter's neck. As a young army conscript, not yet twenty, he boxed for his regiment. At university he pulled an oar for his Cambridge college. In his middle years, he ran marathons without the need for training.

The hell with it. The hell with all of it. The hell with what was once and will never be again.

That's right, says the counsellor allotted to soothe my grief, let the anger out. Anger is normal.

No it's not.

There's nothing normal about what's happening here. Nothing normal at all.

Left. Early days in Spain with daughter Francesca aged five. *Below right.* Nicholas and Hugh Millais mulling over plans for the house. *Below.* The house in the Andalusian cork-oak forest.

Above. A break on the annual Whitsun pilgrimage to the Virgin of Rocio, middle daughter Poppy at front left. *Below left.* A glass of wine and a tapa. *Below right.* Nicholas and youngest daughter Honey ride to Rocio.

Above. David Towill, David Grenfell and me on the Makgadikgadi salt pans, central Kalahari. *Above left.* Bobby Hesketh with reading-matter and cheroot, central Kalahari. *Above right.* Me in Stockwell kitchen celebrating the publication of European Peasant Cooking. *Right.* Pitching camp in the Okavango delta.

Above. Family Christmas in Provence circa 1986 - from left, daughter Honey, son Caspar, daughter Francesca, me. *Below.* Celebrating our silver wedding.

Above. The little cottage with the big garden on Mull. *Right*. Picnicking at Quinish Point. *Below left*. Nicholas gets down to the shearing. *Below right*. Nicholas in the garden-room at the cottage, dreaming of Africa.

Above left. Chairman of the John Muir Trust with Patron HRHR at Sandwood Bay, 1993. *Above right.* Nicholas does battle for the Referendum Party against Michael Portillo, 1997. *Below.* Lineup of trustees at Sandwood, 1993. *Below.* New York marathon 1980, Nicholas crossing the finishing line with beard and hat.

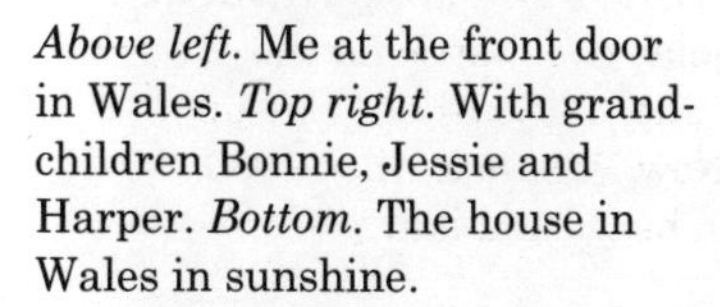

Above left. Me at the front door in Wales. *Top right*. With grand-children Bonnie, Jessie and Harper. *Bottom*. The house in Wales in sunshine.

Happy memories, summer 2003. Nicholas with eldest granddaughter Jessie, mowing the meadow in Wales.

CHAPTER THIRTEEN

Call in the Plumbers

'There aren't many left like him nowadays, what with education and whisky the price it is.'

EVELYN WAUGH, *Decline and Fall*

ON THE DAY WE WERE MARRIED, THAT BRIGHT DAY OF HOPE IN THE sunshine of our lives, neither of us could have foreseen such an ending.

The signs were there, had I but kept my wits about me.

There was a restlessness even then, a need to convince himself that things were other than they were. Whatever Nicholas achieved, whatever was good and true and admirable enough for any man's lifetime, Nicholas was never a man to be content with what he had.

But that's a fairytale. Fairytales deserve a happy ending. Cinderella finds her prince, beauty saves the beast, hero rescues maiden.

Real life is not so simple. The recovering and clean-handed say it's the co-dependant who makes the alcoholic. They would, wouldn't they? So much easier to bear the burden with someone else to carry the can.

So there it is. Bald as an eggshell, bland as cream.

No question that Nicholas, whatever was going on elsewhere, was always a man who punched above his weight.

Until lately, that is, when everything went to hell.

What now?

Call in the plumbers.

October 1997

Nicholas is in St Mary's Paddington of his own volition. Up to a point, that is. No one goes cold turkey for any other reason but blind panic.

The time is right, or it's not. And for Nicholas, time is running out.

One of the young women who came to stay for the weekend in Wales while I was in Romania, a doctor specializing in the disease that killed our daughter, arranged admittance.

Strangers can see what we, too close to our invalids, cannot. Greyness of skin, dullness of eye – I had grown accustomed to these things and she had not.

It helped, of course, that the young woman was flirtatious, admiring, one of those who hope for immortality in poetic print. She had no intention of allowing Nicholas to pursue the passion he declared, but she could, she told me, admire the life in the old fellow yet.

Poetic print was always my husband's way. Later she showed me his letters, proud to have inspired such passion. Her friends had read them too. All had been admiring of his style. Such a game old boy, and such a way with words.

Indeed he has.

When I arrive in time for the daily ritual of the doctor's rounds, Nicholas greets me politely but with no affection. I am not entirely sure he knows who I am.

He speaks to himself without repetition, rapidly, with a questioning curl at the end and a faint pop of the mouth.

His body twitches, limbs jerk. He doesn't seem to notice. He's wherever he is, and no one can follow.

The consultant at St. Mary's Paddington, the admirable Dr T., says they're observing him, no more.

The involuntary twitching of the limbs will improve, no question, when the alcohol is out of his system. We cannot expect miracles. Some people never recover completely. You never can tell. But those who start with plenty of brain sometimes find a way. Perhaps there'll be some left.

Dr T. is an expert in the delicate art of laser-guided surgery, the modern way of repairing the internal organs. A matter of stitching up the little veins which pop and bleed when a liver – or any other organ – is under stress. Catch a liver in time and it'll repair itself.

Dr T. had performed his magic on Peter Cook. Didn't catch it in time, I imagine, though I imagined it impolite to ask.

Life is full of unanswered questions.

Fifth day of cold turkey. Cold turkey, says Dr T. is the only way.

They'll do a scan. A few days later, he comes to find me by the patient's bedside. The news is not good. Cirrhosis has set in. The scan shows a liver so shrunk it's surprising it functions at all. Once this happens, a drinker's days are numbered. Surgery can prolong a life but cannot save it. Some of us die sooner than others. Quality of life is what matters.

How long if he gives up the bottle?

The liver is a remarkable organ. Ten years, maybe more.

And if he drinks?

A shrug. Neither you nor I can protect him from himself. If he wants to die, he will.

Nicholas, it seems to me, has no desire to die. He has, however, not yet indicated a desire to do what it takes to live. Perhaps he will.

Meanwhile, Nicholas's daily progress from drunk to sober is charted by a brisk young woman with sharpened pencils, a cheerful manner, gleaming white teeth and a clipboard.

'And how are we today?'

The scarlet eyeballs roll. 'We're fine.'

The reply seems ordinary – though not to me. Nicholas disliked the 'we' in any context, though particularly, it must be said, in marriage.

White Teeth ticks the box.

'Can you tell me the day?'

Nicholas answers politely.

Tuesday, Thursday – near enough.

'The name of the Prime Minister?'

No problem there.

White Teeth smiles.

'And finally, Mr Nicholas – where do you think you are?'

Clarity eludes him. Some days his answer is St Mary's, other days it's St Margaret's. No surprises there. This is the church in which, I'm careful to explain, my husband and I were married.

The box gets ticked.

The patient's sane.

I wait till the door clicks shut before I ask the final question.

And where, does my husband think, might one find the place in which he finds himself?

Nicholas knows the answer.

'On an ocean-going liner somewhere off the coast of Chile.'

My husband is a great dealer madder than they think. I hug the knowledge to myself. Something I know and the experts don't. It's all I have.

We're in the army now. Civilians don't count. We must do as they say or we won't get better. There are generals and there are soldiers, and there's the rest of us, ignorant and well-meaning and struggling with a situation we cannot understand.

By day, Nicholas talks incessantly. The nurses have ceased to listen. They have better things to do, more rewarding bedsides to attend. I sit by the bedside throughout the day. There's not much going on in my head except how much cream can you pack into a cinnamon cheesecake.

His mother visits. Friends pass by. Nicholas acknowledges their presence but has no interest in their lives. He has his own.

Nicholas's madness has style and texture. He uses words like a child just learning to speak, rolling them around on his tongue, savouring the taste, the shape. He speaks rapidly, without repetition, releasing the words, he says, to run round like mice.

The mice run round beneath the beds, hiding in corners, evading capture. No one else knows this, he says. No point in explaining this to the nurses. They'll jump on chairs.

There's more, he says. At night there's a rat which sleeps on his head.

Along the corridor, he believes, there are others in a similar situation to himself, imprisoned, locked up for their own protection. People mean well, but they don't understand. The other patients are more fortunate than he. They are hauling bottles of whisky up and down the outside walls in baskets under cover of darkness.

Really?

'Yes,' he says. 'But don't tell them about the rat. They'll think I'm mad.'

Nicholas is sober now. There's talk of what happens next.

It seems to me that I – we – need help. Someone who understands. Someone whom Nicholas admires enough to make him change his ways.

A.A. Gill, Adrian – restaurant critic and jack-of-all-work at *The Sunday Times* – makes no secret of the fact that he was once a hopeless drunk. He's been sober now for twenty years, attends the meetings, lives by the twelve-step code. He's a friend of many years' standing. Who better than he to persuade Nicholas to take the pledge?

The patient is still yellow as mustard with eyeballs like raspberry jam and has a problem with monsters in corners – but, I tell Adrian, he's willing to listen.

I wait at home for the telephone to ring.

How did it go?

'I went through it all,' said Adrian. 'Told him all the usual stuff. That alcoholics look just the same as everybody else. That you wouldn't recognize them if you passed them in the street. That not all of them are idiots. That some of them are clever, just as clever as he. And that not all of them are tramps living under a bridge in a box.'

What did Nicholas say?

'He said "Thank you, Dale Carnegie,"' said Adrian, and fell about with laughter.

Nicholas was never a man for self-help. There's never been a need. All his life there'd never been a time when whatever he wanted hadn't been his for the taking.

Whatever Adrian had said, Nicholas had listened. Shortly afterwards, Nicholas announces he's willing to go for rehabilitation.

He has, he says, had good reports of *PROMIS*, a rehabilitation centre that can be recommended for people such as he. It's private, of course, and expensive. But what's a little expense when a man's life is at stake?

I make enquiries. *PROMIS* is about as four-star as you can get.

I make the calls. Dr T. is willing to release him, *PROMIS* is willing to accept him. Six months, they say, is the minimum it takes an addict to come clean.

The price, of course, is immaterial, but a couple of weeks in rehab cost about the same as a respectable advance on a new novel.

It's a family business which includes the doctor's wife and son.

Rehab is big business; the price is high because addicts need constant supervision. Patients share a room, make their own beds, mop their own floors, provide their own therapy. A snip at three and a half thousand pounds a week, payable a fortnight in advance.

Nicholas is cheerful when he rings in after a week. There are crack dealers at the bottom of the garden, drink available just down the road.

A few hours later, the telephone rings again.

'Dear lady,' says a silky female voice. 'You need help for your own addiction. We call it co-dependency. You'll be welcome to join our group. We meet on Wednesdays.'

I tell the voice I'm in denial. I'll let them know when I've recovered.

Actually, I am in trouble myself. With Nicholas safely posted into rehab, my body has given up the struggle. I am paralysed and cannot move. I telephone for help. A cheerful locum prescribes a drug to loosen the muscles and bedrest for a week.

I have time to consider the future. What's to be done? What will happen now? Nicholas, in his kindlier moments, would sometimes say he wouldn't have made it as far as he had if I hadn't been there. Dear lady, you're right. I am an enabler and I'm in denial.

Eight days into the treatment, Nicholas decides the place is a prison inhabited by madmen and run by lunatics.

He returns in triumph in a taxi.

'I promised the driver I'd double the fare. Can you pay? An excellent fellow. We stopped at the pub on the way.'

Eight days. Not much to show for five hundred pounds a day, payable two weeks in advance.

I explain the problem to Dr T.

He listens quietly.

Your husband's made his choice. He has to live with it. You don't.

*****

The year of the millennium, Prince Charles plays host at Highgrove. Nicholas is among those who enjoy royal favour. I was never included in the shooting-parties Nicholas joined at Birkhall every year since the Prince had accepted to serve as patron of the John Muir Trust. The old Queen Mother enjoyed the company of her grandson's guests, young men who talked of fishing and stalking and were happy to leave their wives at home. Wives don't rate in royal circles. Never did and never will.

But I *was* once included in an invitation to lunch at the royal estate in Gloucestershire. Nicholas and I have long since agreed to differ on the usefulness of royalty. No matter. The invitation is too good to miss.

Nicholas is seated at the top of the table, one stop down from the royal ear, while I am placed well below the salt. On either side of me, equerries come and go at the master's bidding. Lacking neighbours on either side, I eat in silence. The menu is written out in copperplate. Lamb from the royal pasture, mint from the royal garden, cream from the royal dairy, raspberries from the royal garden. I have time to reflect too, on the remarkable number of servants and the fleet of four-wheel vehicles visible through the window lined up in the yard.

We are well into dessert when Camilla's sister Annabel arrives. Nicholas greets her with enthusiasm, and she him. Camilla and Annabel's parents were neighbours and friends of Nicholas's mother. The two girls grew up together with his sisters. There is much to talk about at the top of the table, many connections to be made.

Down at the quiet end, the only one of the new arrivals I know is Annabel's husband Simon Elliot, though he would have no reason to remember me. His parents employed my very own beloved Nanny before benevolent providence delivered her to my mother's door. I knew a lot about young Simon when Nanny first arrived. Nanny was particularly strong on potty-training. This kind of information can be very cheering when you're seated below the salt.

Coffee is served in the drawing-room with a view of the garden.

'I don't suppose anyone's interested,' said His Royal Highness, placing a hand on a leather-bound folder. 'One dabbles a little, if anyone might like to see one's work.'

We'd all just love to see the royal watercolours.

One of us, a flamboyant Italian contessa who has arrived with a case of her own château-bottled olive oil by way of a calling-card, is clearly hoping for a glimpse of rather more than the royal artworks. These idyllic scenes of the Swiss mountains under snow are extremely skilful, the equal of anything in the Royal

Academy's summer show. Somewhat poignantly, the work lacks any suggestion of a human presence.

We admire the paintings, the cooking, the decor and the dogs.

There is much to admire at Highgrove.

The garden is particularly admirable. Actually, I have to admit it's more than admirable, it's spectacular. The wildflower meadow has just been featured in a television documentary fronted by the Prince.

Miriam was brought in to oversee the planting of the meadow by her friend Molly Salisbury. Wildflowers are a must-have among the gardening elite. The commission, I am aware, had involved many urgent consultations with the royal gardener on whether or not to plug. Plugging is what you do when all that comes up is nettles and docks.

I would sometimes, when working at Ashton on whatever it was that Miriam wanted me to illustrate, enquire how work was coming along in the royal meadow.

'Disastrous,' she'd sigh.

Disaster meant a raid on Ashton's several acres of kitchen garden where, instead of the usual beds of lettuce, carrots and cabbage, wildflowers grew in neatly weeded rows, all three times the size of their sisters in the wild.

'Lack of competition,' said Miriam by way of explanation, never a woman for length when brevity would do. While most of the harvest was cropped commercially for seed, some of the plants were potted up for overwintering in the greenhouse. The following spring, the plugs were popped in among the grasses in Ashton's meadow, surfacing in waves of yellow and pink, violet and blue, drifts of forget-me-not and speedwell, ragged robin and corncockle.

The royal meadow is in full perfection, not a nettle or dock in sight. And HRH admits to having himself with his own hands planted the little cushions of purple-flowered thyme between the hand-hewed slabs of golden Cotswold stone.

I sneak a look at the royal fingernails.

Pink and neat and beautifully manicured. No question but HRH is just as much of a dandy as Edward Windsor, dear David, as his duchess liked to call him. The Prince has a look of his equally love-struck great-uncle. There's a fastidiousness of dress, the handkerchief in the breast pocket which echoes rather than matches the pattern of the tie, shimmering brogues, natty shirting, a glimpse of cashmere about the ankle. There is, too, the quizzical glance, the habit of modest self-deprecation which seems to serve to deflect criticism, a way of starting sentences with a negative which avoids any chance of disagreement.

The House of Windsor never had much time for wives, I say to Nicholas as we drive away into the sunset. Still doesn't.

*****

It's August 2000 and Nicholas has seen no need to change his ways.

We are on our own now. What will tell us if things go wrong? Watch for the bleeding. There are degrees of danger, says Dr T. Brown and cooked – proceed to hospital without delay. Black and raw – call the ambulance right now. Red and streaky – take the risk and wait till morning.

There's an unpredictability about our days, these long days we spend in Wales together. I don't know how long they will last, these days of unpredictability, or why we've been given them or what they're for.

Nicholas is a writer. Write what you remember of your childhood, I say to him on the mornings when he's angry. Write of who you are and where you come from.

Some days he sleeps all day. Some days he makes plans for the future. He wants to leave this life behind and return to Paris to paint. He was seventeen in Paris, had not yet slept with a girl, and he was happy.

Some days the anger boils. I tell myself it's the liver talking, but the things he says are hurtful. I listen, but I block them out.

I have no choice. There was never a choice. This was always how it would be, this was the price of who he was and is.

No time to wait for an ambulance. I pack the car with what we need for the journey – bucket and towels, though this may be rather too much information for the squeamish – and drive him to safety. Or so I think.

We are refused entry to the ambulance-only driveway. I park in front of the entrance in a place strictly forbidden for anyone to park, and we make our way unsteadily across the marble hallway towards Reception.

Reception finishes her phone call, replaces the receiver and begins to organize her paperwork.

I clank the bucket. Bodily fluids swish.

'Take the lift,' says Reception. 'First floor, turn left. Look for Admissions.'

Admissions gives us number 234. The flip-chart says 92. I knock at the window which protects Admissions from Patients.

I say we're fine to wait, but I shall certainly need a mop.

Admissions glances at the contents of the bucket and takes the point.

When I finally leave the hospital with Nicholas safely delivered to the white-coats, I have acquired a parking ticket. I resist the urge to tip the contents of the bucket over the parking-attendant's shoes.

Don't tell anyone where I am, said Nicholas.

This was not easy.

Nicholas's latest book, *The Field of the Star*, an emotional account of a pilgrimage to Santiago de Compostella taken in stages from Le Puis in central France across the Pyrenees to the far west corner of Galicia, was well reviewed in hardback, and the paperback had just been published.

The story of the walk had turned into a lament for the loss of Francesca, ill at the time of the pilgrimage. At the time, I had been less than grateful for his absence. Francesca was more charitable. And probably, as is often the way with daughters and their fathers, wiser than a wife.

'He has to do what he needs to do,' she said. 'That's his way.'

Today, with Nicholas only just admitted to hospital, one of the Sundays rings his publisher to suggest he write an article on the satire movement of the 1960s – mentioning, of course, the publication of the paperback.

The request was triggered by a story on Peter Cook and *Private Eye.* The illustration, a photograph taken at the *Eye* in the early days, shows Nicholas with Booker, Ingrams, Rushton. The four stare confidently at the camera, clear-eyed, serious – and all so young. I return the call, reach the editor's answerphone, and lie. Nicholas is away in Africa, working on a new book.

Reality is, he's away with the fairies.

The drink and its consequences makes him less than amiable, less than kind, very much less than grateful. Anger surfaces. Do this, go there, fetch this, fetch that.

Dr T., stitching neatly when the need arises, observes the anger, shows signs of losing patience.

Released from hospital, we travel back to Wales by train. Four hours by rail and one by car. The final part is a gentle ramble through green hills and rain-soaked valleys till we reach Brynmerheryn, the wild and beautiful place we now call home.

It's cold in the house when we arrive. The walls are thick and there's been no one there for weeks. I light fires, make tea. Meanwhile, Nicholas moves slowly up the stairs, folds his bony limbs between the sheets and falls asleep.

Relieved, I leave him to his slumbers. I'll sleep next door. Tonight we'll both find rest. These are hard times. The pattern of our nights is always troubled. I wake at the slightest stirring, rising swiftly out of sleep.

Something's wrong.

Nicholas has fallen from bed to floor, stick-thin limbs bent double. Despairing of my strength, I can neither lift nor bring him comfort. I push pillows under his body, cradle his head.

Words tumble quick-fire from his lips; nothing he says makes sense. His body jerks, muscles knotted, limbs twitch here and there as if attached to string.

An hour before dawn, I telephone for help.

The hospital switchboard answers. I have a special number for emergencies like this. Dr T. returns my call himself – rare good fortune at such a time.

'Tell me what you see.'

This is how it is and this is how we are.

'Is there bleeding?'

'Of course.' Bleeding has become as natural as breathing.

'What do you need to know?'

'Whether to call an ambulance or wait and hope.'

A pause. Still calm, the voice resumes: 'Call an ambulance right now. Or watch and wait. The choice is yours.'

I hesitate, then find my voice.

'What do you advise?'

'Call an ambulance and he may live. If you wait, he'll die.'

I wait. Then say, 'I have no choice.'

Silence returns. I listen till the voice resumes, this time so low I can scarcely hear the words: 'Myself, I might not be so kind.'

I dial again to summon an ambulance.

Ten miles from here to the hospital.

Two men, uncurious and strong, arrange the crooked limbs, blanket the body, lower the bundle on a stretcher down the stairs.

As they pass, one glances up.

'Is he usually like this?'

'Not usually,' I say.

And laugh. I know it's not funny, but the question seems absurd.

*****

The World Cup comes round at four-yearly intervals – I note the date because we are back in St Mary's and Nicholas has just tossed the television through the plate-glass window of the General Admissions Ward.

The jagged hole has been repaired with a square of board, reducing the light but keeping out the wind. The television itself hangs there for days, its wires and innards dangling in the void.

This new crisis is just one of many. So many I've lost count.

Sometimes the drama escalates, as now, into serious damage to inanimate things, though never, it must be said, to anything living.

When I visit the next day, Nicholas has been placed in solitary confinement in a side-ward. A bed is the only furniture. There's no chair, nothing which might cause damage.

The staff are observing him, no treatment prescribed.

The pattern is familiar. His body twitches and he can't control his limbs.

This time he knows exactly who I am – not always the way when disaster strikes – but has no notion where or who he is.

He thinks he's in a space capsule. No. He thinks that people from another planet are coming to kill him.

He chased a nurse, says the nursing supervisor, punching numbers into her computer.

I return to the invalid and ask him why.

Nicholas looks at me, working out what answer he should give.

'He was a Scotsman in a kilt. He had a knife.' And then, more thoughtfully, 'And anyway, she was rather pretty.'

The staff continue to observe.

His limbs still twitch. There's a violence there, an uncontrollability.

I tell the nurses it seems to me like epilepsy.

Someone checks his notes.

'We'll ask the doctor on his rounds.'

We wait all day before the doctor comes.

The doctor orders a scan. We must be patient. The queue for the scanner is two days long.

We wait again.

The word comes down; he's not an epileptic. My husband, says the doctor, is as normal as the next man.

The doctor's judgement's flawed.

Something tells me hope stops here.

This is a *via sin salida*, a road with no way out.

Early the following morning, the telephone rings at our borrowed flat in London.

'We're sorry to tell you your husband's gone.'

Gone? Gone where?

'We don't know. We thought you might.'

He has no money, no clothes except what the hospital has supplied. No shoes except the cardboard slippers.

As soon as I replace the telephone, it rings again.

Nicholas has arrived without money or shoes by taxi at a dress shop in the Hollywood Road. Fortunately, they're friends. They understand. But right now they need him out.

I recognize the note of panic.

They have settled him in the office at the back. He's sitting on the sofa among the dresses. Silk and tweed, all clean and fresh. He's wearing smart brown brogues under the hospital gown, an overcoat around his shoulders. And he reeks of drink.

How did you escape?

Animal cunning, he says with pride. I created a diversion.

Was it a small hill?

When he was in the army, his speciality was taking small hills.

'Of course.'

Shall we go now?

'I have something to do. I won't be a moment.'

I know what it is. I wait in the car.

Dr T. is on the phone. There's a new problem. A cancerous growth, small but visible on the scan. This is normal when the liver is under stress. There might even be something to be gained if the diagnosis is correct. Alcoholics are not usually placed on the liver-transplant list. A touch of cancer might prove itself a blessing.

This is the first time we have talked of transplants.

What are the options?

'Cancer of the liver,' says Dr T., 'is not a good way to go.'

Crown of Lamb with Honey Mint Sauce

The Highgrove way with lamb from the Duchy of Cornwall is very simple, very English. Get your butcher to do all the hard work for you.

SERVES 6 TO 8

1 crown roast of lamb, with all the trimmings
Few sprigs thyme, chopped
Handful parsley, chopped
Pepper and salt

Honey mint sauce
1 big handful mint leaves
250ml boiling water
1 tablespoon honey
250ml cider vinegar

Roast for 15 minutes per 500g if you like your lamb rare, allow another 5 minutes per 500g if you like it well done. Leave to rest for 20 minutes before carving into cutlets. While the lamb rests, crisp the trimmings from the middle in a dry frying pan till well browned.

Meanwhile, make the mint sauce. Chop the mint leaves small, cover them with the boiling water and leave to infuse for 20 minutes or so, then stir in the honey and vinegar.

Serve the cutlets with the crisp trimmings, honey mint sauce, plain-boiled new potatoes and a tender vegetable – young peas or beans or carrots, or all three.

CHAPTER FOURTEEN

Dancing with Diaghilev

'All professions are conspiracies against the laity.'

GEORGE BERNARD SHAW, *The Doctor's Dilemma* (1906)

VALENTINE'S DAY 2001, FOURTH DAY OF THE BLEEPER. NICHOLAS has been accepted onto the transplant list. We have been provided with a bleeper to alert us to the arrival of a suitable liver.

Once the bleeper bleeps, we ring a special number and come straight to the transplant ward without delay.

How long will it be? However long it takes. There are blameless recipients on the list who take priority. The distinction is subtle, but it's there.

I ask the brisk young woman who supplied us with the bleeper why she went into the liver-transplant business. She's a nurse, very soothing, highly qualified.

'It's emotional. You can keep your hearts and kidneys. But the liver, love at first sight.'

I tell her I, too, love liver. With bacon and onions. I know it's not funny and she doesn't laugh.

Before a patient can be accepted on the liver list, preparations have to be completed to ensure the recipient is capable of surviving the aftermath. Since a man who needs a transplant is not likely to be in the best of health, everything has to be done to ensure that nothing goes wrong.

Meanwhile, the mind is dictated by the body. When the liver abandons its function and feeds poison into the brain, madness happens. Nicholas is indeed mad. When handed a zimmer frame to give him a little stability in his life, he picks it up and puts it on his head.

And all the while, the desperate hope is that the call won't come through too late. And as we wait, day by day, the state of mind which responds to the function of the body can be determined by whether or not he can sign his name. A tiny scrawl tells us that things are bad. Enemas do the trick. Colonic irrigation as performed for cosmetic reasons by ladies who wish to lose their lunch does the same for madmen who need to lose their madness. Sometimes the madness would return three or four times a day, sometimes more, sometimes less.

The specialist had mentioned the treatment quite casually in passing.

Once you're home, he said, you're on your own. No nurse, even should the National Health permit, would be prepared to perform such a service, at least not as often as you'll require to keep his sanity.

And now the call has come. Nicholas is calm, and so am I. We're ready now, as ready as anyone will ever be.

*****

Wind back the clock to the year before the transplant.

We are in Wales. Inside the house, madness rules. Outside, spring and sunshine and the trees in the woodland newly planted behind the house are coming into leaf.

Nicholas is a man for the old infuriator, as David Towill called red wine, with a whisky chaser if that's what pops into his head.

I don't count the empties. I never have. What's the point? And anyway, who would believe me? No one who knew Nicholas, even close friends throughout his life, would ever have known how much he drinks. In public places – never mind if he's chairing a meeting – he simply falls asleep. Neatly, without fuss, like a hibernating hedgehog.

He never complains that the drink makes him feel anything but well. No more, that is, than a lover would complain of an over-demanding mistress. There's anger there, though he's subtle enough to hide it. As for the morning, the moment of reckoning for any hard drinker, it's hard to tell when the hangover steps out and morning shot of liquor cracks back in.

This sunny spring morning, I observe through my study window that Nicholas is tinkering with the car.

I return to my work. I have an article to finish. I have disconnected the vehicle's battery so that the car won't start. I hope to avoid what happened yesterday. Yesterday Nicholas drove himself to our little market town to buy newspapers and bounced off a line of parked cars, removing their side-mirrors one by one, like popping peas.

'Fortunately,' he said, 'I'd just been to the bank, so I tucked £20 notes behind everyone's windscreen wipers. Nobody complained.'

An expensive outing. But at least we're not in court.

There's tolerance for eccentricity hereabouts, a tradition for song and storytelling which honours poets and writers and those who want to change the world.

Nicholas fits into the accepted pattern of not-quite-as-other-men. He is fondly spoken of not only for who he is and what he's achieved but for the entertainment offered by his exploits.

There was the day he set fire to the woodland and the fire brigade had to be called and everyone brought sandwiches and coffee for a ringside seat at the blaze.

And the day he tipped the ride-on mower into the garden's dewponds and had to be hauled out, covered in lily pads and frogspawn, with the neighbour's tractor.

Today, a sunny day in the year Nicholas celebrates his sixty-third birthday, is the day he drives down the public highway on the ride-on mower. What the law would describe as being in control of an unlicensed vehicle while not in full possession of his wits.

He needed to drive a vehicle down the road in order to reach a telephone and contact the newspapers to denounce the Lord Chancellor for appropriating his credit cards.

Summoned to limit the damage, I arrive to find my husband talking persuasively to the news desk at a national newspaper. News desk has discovered that the Lord Chancellor is indeed the caller's brother-in-law and, there being nothing else of interest happening in the capital, thinks the story has legs.

I'm afraid my husband's not himself,' I explain into the void, dropping the telephone back on the cradle.

There's a grain of truth in the story. The credit cards are indeed in my sister's safe. The reasons for this are complicated and I have no desire for complications. But for the record, the credit cards are in my brother-in-law's safe because Nicholas, in the temporary absence of his wife, had broken a window to gain entrance to the London flat.

Easier and more convenient, he explained to the policeman called by a neighbour to handle a break-in, than unlocking the door with a key. The flat belongs to my sister, Charlie comes over to sort things out. With a large hole in the window, there is a need to lock up valuables elsewhere. Since Nicholas has developed a habit of dropping the cards in the street, I have taken the opportunity to leave them exactly where they are.

The result, of course, is a man without a credit card and an urgent need to visit the off-licence.

The day had not begun well. First thing in the morning, Nicholas had decided to put an axe through the telephone line to the house, breaking his link with the outside world and mine as well. Hence the need for the ride on the motor-mower, though what he hoped to achieve by denouncing his brother-in-law for stealing his credit cards is hard to fathom.

The mower is now defunct. The axe, left casually embedded in my study door, remains a worry.

'He's no danger to anyone but you,' a neighbour assures me. Psychiatrist as well as doctor, her opinion is to be respected. 'You'll be safe enough by day but well advised to sleep elsewhere.'

Farming communities understand such problems. For the next few months, till news came through that Nicholas had made it on to the transplant list, I moved my night hours to a spare bedroom in the farmhouse down the road, grateful for sanctuary, the kindness of neighbours.

*****

Today, the call comes through at last. I deliver the patient to the transplant ward, leave him to the white-coats and make my way to the upper floors to argue with the insurance company which provides Nicholas with a single room when the need arises.

The need has arisen rather often of recent years and the insurance company and I are growing weary of the battle.

The Royal Free, one of only three hospitals in the land where liver transplants are on offer, houses private patients in single rooms at the top of the building. Solitary confinement mitigates the problems that beset the public wards – lack of doctors, indifference of nurses, absence of cleaners, presence of bugs – but it doesn't solve them. You catch things in hospital. The less time anyone spends there the better.

Liver transplants are available only on the National Health; the aftermath is also on the National Health. The insurance company needs to check its policies. Transplants are a grey area, says the supervisor. Indeed they are. If the patient has himself transferred, the insurer agrees to cover the cost but he'll have to pay for his drugs. In hospital and out. Since the cost of post-operative drugs is a thousand pounds a month, I think it wise to reconsider.

When I return to the transplant floor to give Nicholas the news, his voice floats down the corridor: 'As I was saying to the Prince of Wales – '

The hospital vicar has just administered the last rites – a service available to those who ask for it – and Nicholas is feeling cheerful enough to pull rank. The vicar is looking doubtful. He's performed the same duty under similar circumstances to other lunatics who also think they're on intimate terms with royalty.

I assure the vicar that Nicholas's friendship with the Prince is real. He has indeed known the heir to the throne, man and boy, for forty years.

I do not add that his relationship with royalty has been somewhat on and off over the years. Off, that is, when Nicholas managed to wing a fourteen-pointer, a stag reserved for the royals, while under the influence of the royal hip flask. No matter. At moments like this, a man needs all the friends in high places he can muster.

I accompany Nicholas on his trolley to the operating-theatre. At the door, the theatre sister tells me to go back home and wait.

If you're worried, she says, ring this number and somebody will answer. The operation is lengthy – six hours at least – but the success rate is high. The surgeons don't like their patients to drop the ball and bugger up the batting-average. Reassuring, I think, and do as she says.

I have an interview to do, a profile to coincide with a new cookbook. Mediterranean dishes, memories of our life in Spain. I fail to cancel the appointment, thinking I will be calm enough to talk, that a subject I understand will take my mind away from what I don't. And anyway, I need the company.

I overestimate my ability to concentrate on cookery. When the article is published, it's in the medical rather than the lifestyle section of the paper.

Meanwhile, my hand sits beside the phone all day. News of life comes more slowly than news of death. Surely they will ring and tell me, won't they, if the news is bad?

Eight hours later, the call comes through. The operation is complete. Nicholas is out of surgery and tucked up safely in intensive care. It won't be long before he emerges from the anaesthetic. The operation required sixty pints of blood. I should write the number down or I won't believe it later.

Stuck in the traffic on my return to hospital to greet the patient as he wakens from his ordeal, my mobile rings. Fearful of bad news, I pull over to pick up the call.

Chris Brasher is on the line. He needs Nicholas to attend a meeting of the John Muir Trust in Edinburgh next week. He has a project and Nicholas is the man to ram it through.

I explain that Nicholas is just released from surgery. Brasher is unmoved. He wouldn't let a little thing like that get in the way of anything important and doesn't expect any less of his friend.

Just pass on the message, says Chris, as soon as the man comes out.

'It's a liver transplant,' I say. 'I'm not sure he'll be ready.'

'Lucky bastard,' says Brasher. 'I could do with one myself.'

'Scrub up. Wear these,' says the nurse, handing me boots and coveralls, hat and mask. 'When you're ready, come to the door and press the button.'

The body in the bed is propped against a back-rest, bare-chested, speckled with multi-coloured wires attached to skin by suction. Machinery bleeps and burps.

I halt at the door, unwilling to disturb my husband's rest.

The eyelids, closed from a distance, flip open.

Nicholas smiles. His face is calm, unlined, a man awakened after a sound night's sleep.

'Hello, sweetheart,' he says. 'I wondered where you'd gone.' Then adds, 'Ask me where I've been. I've had a busy day.'

In trouble or when the liver talks, he makes a life for himself inside his head. Sometimes he travels far, tracking impala across the plains of Africa, watching lions sleeping in the sun. On less ambitious outings, he takes lunch with a friend – old or new, it matters little. Some days he simply wanders from room to room, searching for a book or reading a poem or writing a chapter of a new novel. He's willing to share his dreams. The dreams have become a doorway through which I too can pass.

You've had a busy day, I say. Where have you been?

Excitedly: 'You'll never guess.'

So tell me.

Smiling proudly: 'I've been dancing with Diaghilev.'

Really? Were you any good?

Cautiously: 'Not bad.'

Were you wearing a tutu?

Irritably: 'No. Tights, of course.'

In the exhibition of Pre-Columbian Mexican Art at the Royal Academy in London, a colossal sculpture towers over the final gallery. The figure, a gigantic god, is shown with the chest peeled open to reveal the liver, the seat of the soul.

If the new liver talks ballet, what else am I to think but that my non-balletic husband has acquired a ballet dancer's soul? My enquiries, as discreet as I can make them, are met with caution. A young woman on a bicycle is all anyone will say.

It fits. A gentle soul, a dancer. Long may it last.

No chance. The liver takes on the colour of its new home. No more ballet talk. Nicholas is cunning, a soldier plotting his escape.

Hospital time is not like real time. Time for bedmaking, time for blanket-bathing, time for medication. The drugs must be taken every day for ever. For ever is not exactly what is meant. Liver-transplant patients are on borrowed time. Two years is the minimum that can be counted a success, ten the maximum anyone has lived.

The surgeons like the showy end of the business said Dr T. Anyone can pop a tonsil, but hearts and livers are make or break.

Three weeks after the transplant, the patient is free to leave.

It's borderline, but still. The record says the patient has home and partner. And here she is.

Social Services will be in touch. There's counselling. And if the patient needs support, there's advice to be had from the transplant patients' club.

How many in the club?

A dozen or so. Depends.

Do they meet every day?

Once a week at most. What we're giving you, explains the surgeon, is quality of life.

Quality of life, for Nicholas, includes access to the bottle. I cannot imagine that a man with a new liver can ever drink again.

I ask the question because I need Nicholas to hear the answer.

Can a man with a liver transplant drink?

A smile. 'Of course. He has a nice new liver.' Then, noticing the horror on my face, 'We wouldn't advise it. But drink in moderation, well, we find that patients who do survive rather longer than those who don't.'

'Champagne!' cries Nicholas, though never a man for the fizz. More of a man for the claret, with a whisky chaser for good measure.

*****

April 2003 and Nicholas is drowning the new liver. And I, as usual, cannot stop him. And anyway, we're back on hospital duty.

There is a problem with the surgery. What can anyone expect? The body's in a mess. No need for details. I'm a civilian, not a doctor. You'll have to take my word.

Another week of hospital repairs, says the surgeon. Nothing structural, just stitchings and patchings, sides-to-middles, darnings.

As I cross the road outside the hospital to buy the morning papers – Nicholas has an insatiable appetite for newspapers – I notice a young man swinging by on crutches. The young man's leg has been amputated above the knee, the empty trouser leg casually tucked up with a nappy pin – a sign, perhaps, of wife and baby. I watch the young man pass. He looks muscular and cheerful. A soldier, no doubt. A casualty of war.

Nicholas hates the state he's in, sees himself as a casualty of a different war. He listens carefully when I make excuses for his absence to his friends. 'Don't make me out a cripple. It's not as if I'm selling matches on the street.'

In Spain when we first moved there and casualties of war were as common as fleas on a cat – and just as little regarded – those who had lost limbs or were otherwise disabled sold matches on the street. They were old and poor and people bought the matches as a more graceful way of giving charity. Small goods – shoelaces, single cigarettes, pencils, matches – were displayed in a box slung round the neck to leave the arms free for the crutches.

Those who were also blind had the right to sell lottery tickets for *El Gordo*, the Fat One. The system was a little baffling. Each ticket was divided into ten parts. You could buy a tenth of a ticket, or, if you were rich or had some reason to think yourself lucky, you bought the whole thing. A whole ticket would make you a millionaire, *gordo*, fat-cat. Tap-tap-tap went the white stick through the pavement cafés till the seller halted and called out his numbers. If someone had sold a winning ticket, word spread like wildfire and the seller expected a percentage of the win.

Nicholas had long since won the lottery of life. He had every reason to live, no reason at all to die.

*****

I have just signed a contract for a new book on a subject which suits me well, the regional cooking of Spain and Portugal. There are gaps to be filled, travels to be completed before I can begin to write.

Nicholas is not well enough to be left alone for the time the journey takes. It'll be just like old times; we'll make the trip together. The plan is ridiculously ambitious.

We'll start with Easter week in Seville – something we'd always planned to do and never managed – and then drive on up the coast of Portugal and into the mountains, a wild and beautiful region which neither of us have ever visited. We will be able to rest for a week in northern Spain, where Priscilla has an apartment in the little town of Llanes on the coast. We'll finish the journey on a long sweep south through the wine-growing region of Rioja and the ravines of Aragon. For centuries, the Aragonese held the line against the Moors, and Cantabria was the heartland of Christian resistance in the days of the caliphates. Borderlands keep the print of their history long after it's disappeared elsewhere.

We fly into Madrid. Nicholas is cheerful. This is a place he loves. In a truckers' pull-in on the motorway round Granada, buried among the olive groves, his appetite returns. We eat thick slabs of yellow bread topped with slivers of home-cured serrano ham from the owner's own pigs, home-cured olives and chunks of fresh pork, satisfyingly chewy, cooked with unskinned new garlic, olive oil and wine.

The sights and scents of this land are soothing. I am beginning to feel at home. On the way past Malaga we pass the sprawling airport. La Consula is lost in the haze. Bill and Annie Davies are long gone and the house sold to the city of Malaga, who mean to turn it into a museum.

We have friends who are living in a pretty hacienda in the hills behind Algeciras, where the children spent their schooldays. The friends live in Spain all through the year, and know more than I do about the state of domestic cooking in Andalusia these days.

There are things I need to ask. I want, above all, to check on what were once Gypsy crops sold in the market at Eastertime – whether the snails and wild asparagus and thistle buds are still gathered from the fields. At a *venta* once surrounded by rice paddies, they still serve *arroz con tagarninas*, rice cooked with thistle leaves, wild asparagus scrambled with eggs, snails cooked as they were in the *venta* in Pelayo.

Meanwhile elsewhere, much has changed. These days, what was a narrow bumpy cart track pitted with pot-holes has been transformed into a broad highway, a link between Seville and the tourist developments of the coast. I notice as we drive that the tiny snails no bigger than a fingernail we used to gather with sticks from their summer quarters on dried thistle stalks are sold at motorway roundabouts by traders from Morocco.

Thirty years ago there was no road across what was once the king's hunting-forest, the Coto Doñana, the delta of the Guadalquivir, a vast expanse of pine scrub, sand and reedbeds. Rocio, the sanctuary at its heart sacred to Our Lady of the Dew and the destination for the Whitsun pilgrimage, could be reached only on horseback or on foot, a week-long journey from either direction. Nowadays, a double highway runs on through the marshland, a destination for birdwatchers with life lists. In my early years as a painter, I had spent many tranquil days among the dunes, sketching vultures and spoonbills, flamingoes and herons.

There is accommodation for tourists where there was nothing before but wilderness. Nicholas has friends who come here every year for the birdwatching. We are to be their guests in the old orange pickers' dwellings, Los Menines. I remember the dwellings as low-slung, reed-roofed earth-floored shacks among the green of the citrus trees. They have been replaced – or converted, it's hard to tell – as luxury bungalows with prices to match. The last time we were here, we travelled in a mule cart and carried our food supplies in a sack.

Nicholas sleeps long and late through the morning. The journey has tired him. He is not well enough to leave the safety of the bungalows for the city. His body needs rest. He coughs at night, has no resistance.

I leave him to the care of our host and a morning's birdwatching close to the bungalows, and drive to Seville with our hostess. Outside the city gates, we lock the car and walk. Within the walls, shops and offices are shuttered, cafés closed, the streets deserted.

The celebrations of Holy Week have a pagan undertow. At dusk on Holy Thursday, as the sun drops over the slow-moving waters of the Guadalquivir, sombre processions move out of the shadows. The *Macarena* and the *Gran Poder* – sorrowing Mother and all-powerful Son – are rivals for possession of the streets. The *Macarena* protects the poor and the *Poder* the rich, a division accepted without rancour. 'I'm sure the *Gran Poder* wears silk,' mutters a black-clad widow clutching the hand of a curly-topped grandchild.

Accompanying the statues are the *pasos*, carved images of the events of Holy Week, huge and heavy and crusted with gold. The heavier the images, the greater the glory to those who carry them. The bearers move forward inch by inch, visible only as shuffling shoes. Beside the floats walk black-robed penitents, hooded and carrying candles.

As midnight approaches, the processions turn inwards, moving through the narrow streets of the old city towards the cathedral at its heart. The crowd is suddenly younger, more unruly, pressed together thick as thieves. In the streets where the holiest of the images will pass, not a rat could find a hole. Crossroads become bottlenecks where the towering tableaux sway and falter. The watching crowds are silent, leaning forward, gasping as gilded wood scrapes stone. The crowd anticipates disaster, hungers for it, longs for blood – and, if a fight breaks out, sometimes gets it.

Nicholas is waiting for us in the darkness when we return. The journey continues along the course we have plotted. Nicholas cannot eat, though the red wine flows. He sleeps by day and is wakeful by night. I wake uneasy and sleep without rest.

On our return to London, we risk return to Wales. Nicholas is happy there, as happy as he'll ever be. Spring moves into summer. Another midnight dash to hospital. And another and another. I am wearying now, weary of the fear, weary of hospitals and the pain Nicholas endures without complaint, weary of what has become as inevitable as sunrise or nightfall.

Crisis follows crisis. Sometimes these happen in Wales, sometimes in London. Sometimes things go better, sometimes worse, sometimes it looks as if the body has given up for good.

*****

Six months have passed since the Spanish trip. I have escaped hospital duty in London for a weekend in the country with

Venetia, my old friend from the days at *Private Eye*. There's safety in old friends who don't question my need to flee the narrow world I live in, however briefly.

Venetia has invited guests for dinner. A welcome diversion, I think.

Not much is happening in my head except the need to talk. To find some way to understand what's happening in the world which consumes all my waking hours. Nevertheless, I'm careful what I say. People tire of disaster talk.

One of the guests at the gathering is a heart surgeon, the other a general practitioner. I ask the question quite casually, the opportunity too good to miss.

'Does either of you know anything about the Brompton cocktail?'

The two men glance at each other.

Then the heart man says: 'Of course. Very old-fashioned.'

Pause. 'Why do you ask?'

I explain the circumstances. No hope. Intravenous bleeding with no further interventions possible. We have time to gather the family, time to say all the things we have to say. The patient's aware.

'Are you sure?'

'My sister-in-law was there. I'm sure.'

Another pause. The country doctor breaks the silence.

He laughs, then says: 'A nice cup of tea and pop the bromide in the IVF?'

Absolutely.

Except that it didn't quite work out like that. Nicholas recovered.

After a tender all-night vigil with his family, he was out of the wood. Not quite gambolling through the trees, but certainly on his feet. When son Caspar arrived from New York – summoned in haste and not for the first time – he found his father zimmer-framing down the corridor, wearing a pink blanket over his hospital gown, looking for a better room with a wider view.

Green Asparagus with Ham and Eggs

Asparagus grows wild on Mediterranean hillsides. The shoots appear in spring beneath a prickly tangle of fern; the wild variety have a strong grassy flavour and dryish stalks. Thin spears of cultivated asparagus will do.

SERVES 4 TO 6

500g slender green asparagus
4 tablespoons olive oil
75g diced serrano ham (scraps is fine)
6 large eggs, forked to blend
Salt and freshly ground pepper

Break the asparagus into short lengths, discarding any woody ends. Heat the olive oil in an earthenware *cazuela* or frying-pan and fry the asparagus till it softens – 2–3 minutes, don't let it brown.

Stir in the diced ham and fry for another minute. Stir in the eggs, season with salt and pepper, and turn everything over a gentle heat till the mixture forms soft curds – another 2–3 minutes. Remove while still juicy and soft. Serve as a starter or *tapa* with thick slabs of bread, a bowl of cracked green olives and another of freshly toasted almonds dusted with chilli flakes.

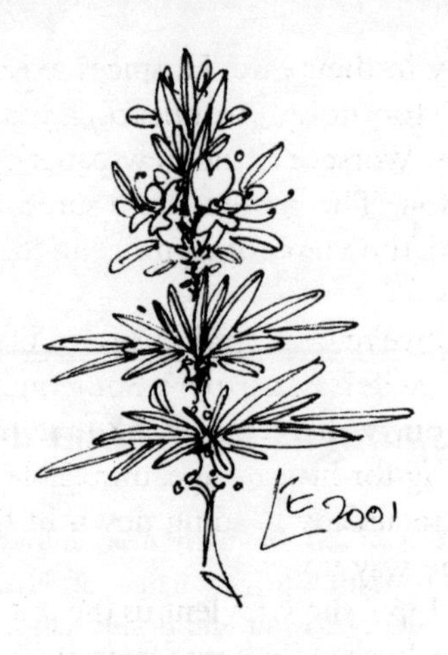

CHAPTER FIFTEEN

The End Game

'Perhaps your egg will remember what it never saw and you'll find your home.'

Oliver Postgate (creator of *Bagpuss*) on *Desert Island Discs*, BBC Radio 4, 2008, encouraging a cartoon bird to fly over the hills to visit the lake where it was born

SUMMER MOVES INTO WINTER. THE CANCER HAS RETURNED. Chemotherapy is no longer an option. Second opinions are sought. Appointments are not available for months. We have no more months to wait.

******

Another six months have passed. It's April 2004, and the hospice which took Nicholas in a week ago, released him back into the community, as they say in police reports, without charge.

He was unhappy in their care. Hospices exist to mitigate the hardship of dying. Too noisy, too uncaring, four to a room, no privacy, no laughter. Worst of all, no newspapers. There are many waiting for admission. The gardens are beautiful, magnolia trees shade the courtyard, the view is magnificent, there's a chapel for the use of residents.

We're alive until we're dead, and this is no life.

Do you have a wife? A partner? Someone who will take responsibility for your welfare? You do? You're free to go.

So he did. Calling for his carriage, unreliable transport at the best of times, we are already heading down in the lift when we meet visitors on the way up.

Nicholas's sister Lip – she who lent us the due-for-demolition basement – and her husband emerge from the open doors.

'Oh dear, you're on your way home. Isn't there anything we can do?'

If I had a fivepenny piece for the times I've heard that question, I'd not be driving a clapped-out banger.

'Follow us home,' I answer crisply. 'The car is unreliable. There's a chance we'll break down on the bridge.'

Mercifully, we make it home without mishap.

Home is a garden flat in the Fulham Road belonging to old friends who live in the house above, owners of the dress shop to which Nicholas escaped on his bid for freedom.

Bids for freedom are no longer an option.

For Nicholas, half a life is better than no life at all. For me, there are moments when I'm not so sure. But then the choice has never been mine.

We are in London for as long as it takes. Kindness sustains the life we lead. Sometimes kindness is all there is. It's not everyone who'll give shelter to the likes of us. We can't solve anything with money. Our bills have always been paid from income, and although I continue to work, Nicholas can't. But here, in this little basement, we're grateful for shelter.

The hospital to which we are now attached, full of new mothers and bustling nurses, is a hundred paces down the road.

For us, the journey takes an hour. The pedestrian traffic lights which control the traffic change with charitable swiftness, so that people in trouble may cross the road without delay.

Last night was restless. By morning it seems as if body and brain are no longer linked. We cannot move from bed to chair, still less from room to room. Anxious for us both, I telephone Community Nursing to ask them if we might be allotted a visit. They're not sure there's an opening. They'll ring us back.

There is morphine to cope with pain. Morphine masks what it cannot cure. It also masks the surface ills that beset the bedridden. I am worried that we cannot cope. We have somehow managed to fall into the gap between hospital and hospice. We are registered with a doctor 300 miles away in Wales. No one wants to claim us. We belong to no one.

Community Nursing returns my call. There's support available for cancer patients from Macmillan nurses. It's Friday today. They can do nothing over the weekend. There's an opening available next Tuesday.

We live from night to day to day to night. Visitors pass through. When Nicholas sleeps, I leave the house, grateful for a chance to walk the streets, though not for long.

A visit from the grandchildren – five and four and two – relieves our solitude. Today the air is warm. Not yet summer but one of those bright days which happen in springtime, pink with blossom, noisy with birdsong.

The children climb steep steps to grass. Over the wall they find two small friends, invite them over for a game. Hide and seek, grandmother's footsteps. Their mother, my daughter, fills a paddling-pool.

The children play, then stop mid-game, turning small faces towards the adults gathered round the table in the shade. They are puzzled, a little anxious. The man in the chair with a blanket round his shoulders, flesh of their flesh who not so long ago had swung them in his arms, is now a stranger. Something's wrong. Children know when things are wrong. Death frightens the young. And the rest of us too, whatever our age.

One child speaks for us all.

'Ooh,' he says. 'You don't look good.'

Nicholas drinks fortified milk shakes coloured and flavoured with artificial additives from a cardboard carton with a straw. No other food is possible. The cartons are very expensive to purchase over the counter at the chemist, have to be ordered specially, and can be obtained only from the National Health on prescription.

The Macmillan nurse, brisk and courteous, keeps her appointment, inspects our quarters, speaks of her role. She has lists and names and special telephone numbers which make things happen. She is a facilitator. She enables the patient to reach help, mediates when mediation is required. She is a trained nurse, very knowledgeable, knows what's available in the borough. And no, she doesn't nurse. Not even a sticking-plaster. She can report the need for medication. She doesn't medicate.

Despairing of help, I point out all the things that are amiss: the rawness, the wounds which will not heal, the troubles which beset a man who cannot leave his bed. Lists are made. What good are lists?

Community Nursing is on the line. Arrangements can be made to place the patient on the list for an appointment at the nearest surgery. The surgery is obliged to deliver an emergency service to those who live outside the borough if called upon to do so. We will, however, have to register at the surgery in person. I explain our situation. We cannot move from bed to chair. We need a wheelchair to reach the surgery. And even so, we cannot move a wheelchair to the street. And even if we reach the street, the patient is unlikely to survive the journey.

Community Nursing is on the line again. Home visits are possible only if the patient is disabled and cannot attend the surgery himself. How disabled do we need to be? On a score of one to ten, I'd say we rate a nine. Perhaps, I suggest, the Macmillan nurse who doesn't nurse will vouch for the degree of disabledness so far achieved.

Community Nursing will ring me back. I settle the patient between clean sheets and make my way to the chemist to find out what comforts can be purchased without prescription. Hospitals are equipped to deal with things that we are not. Chemists don't carry stocks of what we need. They have to order things from elsewhere. I order anyway. Despair is not an option.

Community Nursing rings again. The situation is unusual but the doctor has agreed to visit. *Clap hands children, and Tinkerbell* – scrap that thought, it's not appropriate. Few of my thoughts could be called appropriate. Lighten the load, wind back the clock, find a place I'd rather be.

Miriam used to say of her fellow creatures – ourselves and all others with which we share the planet – are conscious of what's around us all the time. We travel along three parallel roads, moving from one to another at will. Sometimes our minds choose one path, sometimes we wander along another, but this doesn't mean the other two aren't there. For brevity's sake, she said, these are shopping, poetry and sex. 'And you, my dear,' she said with disapproval, 'prefer to spend your time on shopping.'

She's right.

Shopping, the everyday tasks we undertake to make things work, is how I earn my living. I write of ordinary things. 'The mastic tree weeps silver tears when hacked with a knife; the tears when dried can be used to flavour liquor. The powdered root of an orchid, a substance called salep, when cooked in broth or stirred with boiling milk, is twice as fortifying as meat. When you pour boiling water on the dried stamens of the saffron crocus, the little threads unfold like silk and colour rice. When bruised, coriander leaves smell like the warning-scent emitted by ladybirds and the little green beetles which lay their eggs in fruit. Avocadoes don't ripen on the branch, they must be harvested before they can begin to soften. Never add yoghurt to boiling soup or the protein will harden and the emulsion will be spoilt.' You see how easy it is? How easy it is to forget, to drown out the din in the minutiae of craft?

Sex, hmm, not much, throughout my time. Not that I never strayed. There were times throughout the seven years of my husband's travails when my eye had wandered. Let's not speak of that right now. Later, perhaps, when this hard thing is done.

Poetry, these days, is not for us. Not now, when skies are blue and birds sing and meadow grass smells sweet. When your mind troubles you, said Sydney Smith, wise old Reverend Smith who saw things as they are, keep away from poets. Light blazing fires, read amusing books, be as much as possible in the open air, do good by all means. But keep away from poets.

Nicholas escapes his ruined body in his head. We'll write things down, I say. Your children and your grandchildren will want to know the things that shaped you. Listen, he says, and I will tell you how it was for me when I was seventeen. I saw a girl, he says, in a restaurant in the countryside near Milan. A woman whose name I never knew. She was dark-haired, red-lipped, bright-eyed and laughing among a group with children. The group laughed with her and glanced in my direction. She followed me when I left and kissed me on the mouth with passion. 'How beautiful you are,' she said, and then was gone.

The days are long, the nights are longer. Tonight the moon is full. Spring is a time to live. Old people die in winter, when the sun is low and the moon is on the wane. But Nicholas is not yet old enough to die. Not now. Not these days, these wonderful days when things that go wrong with a body can be fixed.

Professor Gazzard, consultant in HIV and Aids at Chelsea and Westminster Hospital in central London, has Nicholas under his care. We had to admit ourselves in a hurry in the middle of the night, rolling down the road on our National Health commode. Casualty checks his records. No diagnosis necessary. Drugs are administered to stop the bleeding. The professor arrives the following morning. Nicholas has managed to parlay himself into a private room.The patient needs rest. He must have whatever he wants. No hurry to go home.

After the professor has discharged the patient, he writes a letter: 'I'm sorry to hear of the death of your husband. He seemed such a gallant gentleman.'

I show the letter to the gallant gentleman.

Nicholas is not amused.

'I don't know why you find it funny. Your sense of humour is not the same as mine. It never was.'

Next day, I telephone the professor's secretary to set the record straight. She notes the information: patient not yet deceased. Then adds, 'The professor must have been impressed. He's a busy man. He rarely has time for letters.'

To test a patient for failure of the liver, ask him to hold his arms at right angles to the body and tip the hands upwards towards the shoulders. If the slope is less than forty-five degrees, the body is in trouble. If you suspect the brain is not functioning as it should, ask the patient to sign his name. If the writing is unusually cramped and small, this is a sign the message is not being transferred from brain to hand.

The doctor pays a visit. She is pretty, young and brisk. Things begin to happen. Wounds are inspected, dressings applied. We are to receive twice-weekly visits from the district nurse. More if required. There is a need for a bed of the right height to enable the nurse to change the patient's dressings, change the bedclothes, assist in bathing. One of the special hospital beds, large and heavy, with a mattress which responds to movement. The need is urgent enough to bring delivery next day.

Day moves into night and back to day. There are two men at the door. They have brought the hospital bed. They inspect the premises without enthusiasm. There are twin beds in the room already, no space for a third. Their instructions are to instal. They have no instructions to remove. Their terms of employment forbid them to perform any service other than is stipulated in the contract.

Perhaps, I suggest, if we tell no one and keep it to ourselves, we might be able to shift one of the twin beds elsewhere.

They shake their heads.

I look at them and laugh.

I am laughing, I explain, because the situation is ridiculous. The district nurse will not agree to nurse without the proper bed. I am unable to move the twin bed which blocks their path without their help. Perhaps they might retire and reconsider. They reconsider. Common sense prevails.

The district nurse appears, the doctor returns, the patient is transferred to safety. Of a sort. What next? Morphine on a drip. The patient sleeps. Day turns into night.

The doorbell rings. We have earned the services of a nurse to see us through the hours of night. The carer, says the doctor, needs to sleep. The nurse explains how used she is to deathbeds. It won't be long. She'll wake me when it happens so I can say goodbye. I close my eyes and wait. See, says the nurse, these are the signs. See here and here and here, her expertise unquestioned.

I'm here, I say, you're not alone, we never were alone. And other things, the gentlest things I know. He sleeps and sleeps and sleeps until the hand in mine is cold.

We never promised to be perfect. Steadfast and true, as best we could. To care for each other in sickness and in health, that too. Care for the children we shared, that too as best we could. The marriage? Who can say what makes the alliance of man and woman good or bad?

I lived for forty years with a man I loved, and he with me.

Some things are clear. No one now will ever look at me and see me as I was then, in the days when I was young. No one now will share the memories we shared, remember the times and places where we lived through the days and nights when we were wed.

We shared a life, we shared a love. A love story with flaws. And as with all such stories, there's an end.

Vanilla Salep

A useful restorative much valued among the rural poor in Britain until after the Second World War, when it was supplanted by commercial preparations such as Horlicks and Ovaltine. Still widely used throughout the Middle East to thicken ice cream; you can buy salep in powdered form in Middle Eastern food stores.

SERVES 6

1 teaspoon salep
(powdered orchid root)
500ml fresh milk
2 tablespoons sugar
½ teaspoon vanilla essence

Mix the salep with a little of the milk.

Bring the rest of the milk to the boil, remove from the heat and whisk in the salep mixture. Reheat gently, whisking till it thickens, which happens immediately. Stir in the sugar and vanilla and serve warm or cool.

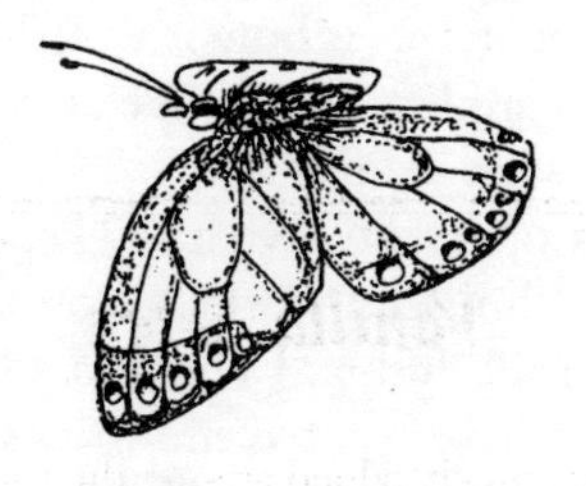

CHAPTER SIXTEEN

No Longer a Wife

> *'In troubled Water you can scarce see your Face, or see it very little, till the water be quiet and stand still. So in troubled times you can see little Truth; when times are quiet and settled, Truth appears.'*
>
> JOHN SELDEN (1584–1654)

FOR COURTESY'S SAKE AND TO KEEP THINGS TIDY, I EMAILED CAREFULLY worded news of my husband's demise to a few old friends on other continents. One of the recipients, a woman – Nicholas's first love, long before we met, American, later a professor in women's studies at Harvard – replied abruptly, rather as one might to a stranger poking their nose in someone else's business.

Thanks and so sorry, she said, but who on earth are you?

Good question.

I knew something of Nicholas's life as a young man in the years before I met him: where he was born, the years in Persia, how he acquired his love of Africa. Sometimes, as his illness progressed, he would plan a return to a place of safety, Africa, a life in Paris long before we met, even, at times, the excitement of the Hungarian border.

When a love affair is over – whatever the reason – the heart and mind keep the print. I can draw no conclusions from the life that we shared. All I can say is that this is what happened at that particular moment, this is how it was, this is how it seemed to me. Some things are left unsaid. We are free to choose what we remember and what we forget.

In the last years of his life, Nicholas kept all his records on computer – emails, thoughts, working notes. After he died and I was ready to face the future, I checked addresses, saved what I thought he might have wanted me to save – accounts of his family for his children, stories from childhood he was preparing for publication – and wiped the rest.

His diaries, the working material of his writing, I kept as he had left them, stacked neatly on a shelf. Love letters, well – none to me. No need, I was his wife. And those he wrote to others are no business of mine. In death as in life, I've no wish to know things better forgotten.

His friendships were strong. At the memorial service in Chelsea Old Church, there was considerable competition among his Cambridge friends to deliver the address which recorded who he was and what he had meant to those who mourned him.

Humphry Wakefield, owner and restorer of Chillingham Castle in Northumberland, describes Nicholas as a boxer: 'In the ring, Nicholas was a southpaw, a left-hander. Right-handers were used to fighting right-handers. And so Nicholas would carefully study the openings this offered for his famously long left arm. He always appeared to take the toughest punishment, but his combination of powerful thinking and sheer guts won him his matches and his prized boxing Blue. In the English literature faculty, Nicholas wrote and thought beautifully, winning himself a First. I remember borrowing his essay on Jane Austen and sneaking in just one Luard sentence. When I read my own essay out to my increasingly bored tutor, he suddenly stopped me: "Just read that sentence again." A bit guiltily, I did as requested. "You see, Wakefield," he said, "you really can write."'

Chris Brasher, reporting on running the New York Marathon in the *Observer* in 1979, gave a brief account of Nicholas's somewhat eccentric preparations: 'We had a marathon-mad Englishman among us .... his training consisted of one six-mile run in the early English summer followed by three months in an African desert, followed by one three-mile run before the flight to New York. The Kalahari Desert is a great place for speed training. Nick did two sessions which he swears were the equal of two of Seb Coe's world records: 800 metres chased by a lion and 1,500 metres pursued by an enraged elephant. Fear is a powerful motive.'

Denis Mollison, co-founder of the John Muir Trust with Nicholas, Nigel Hawkins and Chris Brasher, described Nicholas's methods of getting results. In 1981, the Knoydart estate, a magnificent stretch of wilderness on the west coast of Scotland, had attracted the attention of the Ministry of Defence, who wanted to use it for training. 'Nicholas happened to have dinner with Michael Heseltine the night before he became Minister of Defence and was so convincing that Heseltine's first act as minister was to cancel the MoD bid for Knoydart.'

On a sunny day in New York, a year after I am no longer a wife, I have work to do, recipes to write, a book to finish.

In Manhattan, between Fifth Avenue and 42nd Street, is the New York City Library. It's open to the public every day. Even those who have never paid their civic dues can take the elevator to the third floor and, between the hours of eleven and seven, write the books that change the world.

The desks in the reading-room, quiet and cool after the heat of the street, are crowded.

I am a mother trying to understand the death of a child. Never mind that the thing that killed her was the big disease with the little name – Stephen Fry had the wit to call it by a name which slips by unnoticed on the page.

Francesca was not yet thirty when we lost her. How do I bear her loss? It's done, is all. If consolation's what you need, don't blame yourself for what you cannot mend. It's only human to forget.

Why her, not me? If it had been me, a mother of four children already grown to adulthood, they'd say she was too young, but still, she'd had her time.

My daughter's time had just begun. In my heart and my head I see her still. Sometimes her absence is too much to bear. Not always, not often, not all the time – certainly not so that other people notice. I've no use for sympathy, no time for consolation.

No consolation? None. When it's late and the fire burns low and I'm alone, or the movie ending's sad, I remember her. That's as it should be.

Her physical presence is easy enough to recall. There are reminders all around. A certain briskness of walk, the way a young man looks at a girl as she passes in the street, a flick of a fall of hair over the curve of a young woman's cheek. Flesh, blood and bone are gone.

The spirit – who knows? Books were her passion. I can't remember a time when her nose wasn't buried in a book. She wrote clearly and well, a way to earn her living before she took the decision to change what remained of her time on the planet and took to canvas and paint.

And when she could no longer defend herself against the illness that claimed her, she loved to listen to a story – any story.

'Where have you been?' What's happening out there, beyond the dismal hospital ward where she spent her last week of her life. 'Read to me,' she'd say. And we did. Until she'd had enough of whatever it was and flesh and blood could take no more.

'The spirit is strong but the body's wrecked,' she said. 'And I want out.'

And out she went. The spirit – well, who can say?

I loved my daughter all through the sunshine of her life. For her beauty, wit and gentleness. For harshness, too. Intolerant, strong-willed – but behind it all was Friday's child, a core of kindness.

As I settle down to write, the reason I have come to this tranquil place, my mind turns to who I am and where I come from. A child left without a parent cannot help but be curious about what might have been.

'When Elisabeth married me,' said Nicholas all those years ago, 'she came across into another world and brought nobody with her.'

Although my husband's attitude to my family softened in later years, all but one of the friendships of my youth – both men and women – vanished without trace. One that survived, a friendship from my schooldays – the one who did the runner on Derby Day – came to live near me in Spain and we remain good friends.

For the rest, Nicholas's own family and friends became my closest companions throughout my marriage. Afterwards, when I no longer had to worry about my husband's wellbeing, my curiosity about my own family returned.

The day after my visit to the New York City Library, I took the train to Baltimore for an overnight stay with my mother's cousins, the Baltimore Levys, a trip organized by a cousin, Sue Casacia, my contemporary on the American side of the family.

Sue's grandfather was my grandmother Bertha Baron's first cousin. The family tree is complicated by cousinhoods: my grandfather and grandmother were second cousins and no doubt there were other keep-it-in-the-family alliances along the way.

Buddy Levy, Sue's father and my grandmother's first cousin, is my oldest surviving relative. He was born in 1920 and my mother and he were born within a year of each other.

Alvin – Buddy to family and friends – and his wife Myra live in luxurious sheltered accommodation high on a hillside overlooking the city and port, a vast converted TB clinic divided into apartments, comfortable and cosy.

Buddy looks startlingly like my grandfather.

'We came from Riga, capital of Latvia, on the Polish–Russian border,' explains Buddy as we settled down to savour the family reunion. 'We left in the 1880s because of the pogroms. When my father went back, he was given an ebony walking-stick which belonged to the family.'

Buddy's sister Anita rummages at the back of a cupboard and returns in triumph.

'See?' says Buddy, rubbing at a gleaming line of ornately intertwined brass initials running down the shaft. 'The letters are in Roman rather than Cyrillic script, which is not what you'd expect. We've never been able to find out why.'

The photograph of my cousins in their Baltimore living-room, taken in the 1930s, shows a line of serious, handsome men and women, well dressed and prosperous. Poignantly, there's a strong resemblance to my Baron grandparents.

I left my cousins the following morning, carrying a heavy suitcase full of family photographs. Curiously, too, a heavy wood-covered album devoted to the interior and exterior of Fulmer Chase. I was only a baby when my grandparents lived there, but I have a memory of a huge house surrounded by trees and grass and of being carried at night across open ground while there were explosions in the sky.

Back in Britain, I added to the story as best I could. My father's sister Janet was the last surviving member of her generation, and at well over ninety, she might not be around for long.

She must have thought me a strange child. I was very foreign and my ways were unfamiliar in the English countryside.

Aunt Jan had married a farmer. Her life was horses and farming and her children, my cousins, were good at all the things I was not. I had no idea how to saddle up a horse, still less how not to fall off an English saddle, or even how to trot by raising and lowering my bottom in what seemed to me an entirely unnatural way, let alone ride to hounds. I knew how to rope a cow and travel all day on a gaucho saddle, but I had no idea what you actually did with a horse without its trappings.

In Uruguay, horses were transport. And if you were a privileged little girl, the right-sized pony arrived at the door ready saddled. All you had to do was climb aboard and make sure you weren't scraped off when the pony decided to crop the fig tree. It was also, I remember, important to hold on to the pummel when travelling downhill and to avoid contact with ostriches. Ostriches distrusted horsemen for a very good reason. The gauchos stole their eggs and had a liking for roast ostrich if there was nothing else around. An ostrich which considers itself in peril can knock a man's head clean off his shoulders with one blow of its running-foot.

This kind of information was of no use at all in the English countryside, where no one had ever seen an ostrich or had the slightest idea how roping a cow might come in handy when chasing a fox.

What, I enquired of my aunt on an overnight visit to her little house in a village with a view of Rutland Water, could she tell me about my father's family, the Longmores and the Maitlands?

I knew the basics, of course: that my grandfather was Arthur Murray Longmore, that he had flown little string-and-balsawood reconnaissance planes in the First World War, and that he was Air Chief Marshal by the end of Second World War.

And I well remember my father's mother, Marjorie Maitland, as slender and bony, with blue eyes and a brusque manner and firm ideas on how children should behave. She let me do useful things, such as collect eggs from the hens and stir the mash that bubbled on the back of the stove. She also let me taste margarine, which pleased me greatly since it was a luxury unavailable in my mother's house, where nothing would do but butter. And she let me come into her room and sit on her bed in the morning, something my own mother never allowed.

Compared to my mother's house, with its pale walls and thick carpets, my Longmore relatives seemed to live in a welter of colour and noise. A grandfather clock rang the quarters as well as the hour. The corridors had polished oak boards with slidy Turkish carpets in beautiful deep colours, and in the ceiling just outside my bedroom there was a pull-down ladder which creaked noisily and led to the apple store in the attic. In the attic, too, was my grandfather's model railway, a cobweb network of tiny tracks with engines and carriages, stations and trees, bridges and viaducts which snaked under the eaves and buried itself in corners.

Where, I enquired of my aunt, did the Longmores come from?

'Nowhere,' she replied with vigour. 'My mother was the one with the fortune and the name. She was a Maitland of Edinburgh. Heirs to the Lauderdales.'

Right. Correct me if I'm wrong, but wasn't my grandfather born in Australia on a sheep station south of Sydney?

'That's so. He came back to Britain with his mother when he was seven. Her husband, my grandfather, went off to South Africa and that was the last anyone heard of him.'

My aunt butters her toast decisively. We drink our coffee.

I have a story in my head – a story which might well be a family skeleton, so I approach with caution.

'Are there twins in the family?'

My aunt's expression doesn't change. 'My grandmother had twins. There was a drunken bush doctor. The babies died.'

The story behind the question, I quickly explain, came from Grannan – granny-nanny – the family's old nursemaid, kept on the payroll long after the children were gone ostensibly to help with visiting grandchildren though, as was the way in those days, there was an obligation to look after elderly dependants. My grandfather's mother, Grannan had told me, had had an entanglement with a Maori chieftain which resulted in her presenting him with twins, a scandalous situation which precipitated the sale of the sheep farm and the family's return to Britain.

Never heard of it, said my aunt.

The incident of the twins, according to my grandfather's account of his early life, more or less coincided with the arrival in Sydney of a group of Maori chieftains delayed for a month or two in the city on their way to attend the Queen Empress's Jubilee in London.

The group attracted attention not only for their fine physical presence – strength and height being particularly noted – but for the magnificence of their traditional robes. Contemporary photographs show feathered headdresses, magnificent cloaks and embroidered breeches.

At my christening my father held me in his arms; my mother once showed me the photograph to prove it. And then he was gone. Life expectancy of a pilot, once qualified, was three months, two for a tail-gunner.

'When Dickie went missing, it wasn't so terrible. People you knew went missing all the time – it was normal. Everyone had responsibilities, everyone worked. Your grandfather was in the Middle East, your grandmother drove an ambulance, the boys were all at war. No one had time to worry about things that couldn't be mended.'

What would my life have been like if my father had lived?

'Like my father's, I imagine. Dick would have stayed in the RAF – no doubt become an Air Marshal.' She leaned over and touched my hand. 'Your father would have been proud of you, you know. You'd have gone places together. I don't know where, but Dickie was very adventurous. He was always up to something. I remember when he was at Eton, he had a book on telling people's fortunes from their handwriting, and he used it to set himself up in business. He had to use an address in London, he made lots of money, and he was only caught when the man whose address he was using sent him a bill and my mother opened the envelope.'

She paused for a moment. 'I know it wasn't easy for you. We thought it would all be all right. The Hildyards and the Longmores were always in and out of each other's houses. When your mother married your stepfather, we were pleased. Miles was best man at their wedding, and he made a delightful speech saying how glad he was the Hildyards would have a hand in the upbringing of Dickie's children.'

She looked at me thoughtfully.

'It didn't work out like that, of course.'

If you knew that, I say, why didn't you look out for us, your brother's children?

'Your mother wouldn't let us anywhere near you. I think my mother tried, but you were abroad. There wasn't much she could do.'

Courtesy of my aunt, I receive an invitation to an event which commemorates the loss of airmen over the North Atlantic during World War II, including my father. In early May 2007, I drive from Wales to North Berwick, a small town overlooking the mouth of the Firth of Forth some twenty miles west of Edinburgh. At the Seabird Centre, an edifice overlooking the North Sea, blue uniforms with medals, highly polished shoes, a gathering of elderly gentlemen with white moustaches and impeccable service manners awaits the unveiling. Early arrivals crowd into the bar.

Chairs are set on a rocky platform with a view of the brass plaque which commemorates the lives of members of Coastal Command. No physical evidence remains, since all were lost at sea. The dedication was made by a retired Air Chief Marshal and the RAF Chaplain General. The star of the show was Flight Lieutenant Cruickshank. 'That's our VC,' whispered my neighbour. 'He wounded the German sub first time round, so he went back to finish the job; took ninety-seven bullet wounds but still got the aircraft home.' An unexpected wave of irritation overwhelms me. Why should anyone survive if my father didn't?

An overfly by a Nimrod was promised, but the word is that all are on duty in Afghanistan. And just as none was expected, a pair of Chinook helicopters, silvery dragonflies bright against the clouds, lift over the gun-metal sea and move slowly across the headland, a tribute from the living to the dead.

I burst into tears.

Later, over sandwiches and soup, I overhear two senior airmen discussing the difficulty of retrieving memories of that time. No one had time to keep a diary, so many were lost, and since the battlefield was the sea, there was no evidence to explore, no secrets to unlock.

'There must be a million stories buried in the attic.'

I say, 'Mine, for one.'

The two men turn to look at me.

'This is probably a familiar story. My father was declared missing in 1943. My mother was left with two small children, my brother and myself. After the war, when the German records confirmed what everyone already knew, our mother wrote a letter to tell us how much our parents loved each other. She wrote of their courtship, quoted letters from my father. She kept the letter in her safe until the day she died.'

'You have it now?'

I nodded. I tell them about the manuscript, some thirty pages long and written in her distinctive spiky hand, which was addressed to my brother and myself. And yet, I explain, she never gave it to us while she was alive and took no steps to ensure we read it after her death. All this, I continue, explains why I knew so little about my father – don't even know for sure what planes he flew, the identification number of his squadron.

Such ignorance, in the present company, seems scarcely credible.

My mother, I explain, married again soon after the war and had two more children. The second marriage replaced the first. Though her new husband knew my father well, my father was rarely mentioned throughout my childhood. Since my father, an instructor at Cranwell when war broke out, had taught my stepfather to fly – he too was an airman, earning his wings under my father's tuition – this seemed, with hindsight, an odd omission. Perhaps, I add, our mother changed her mind about the letter because it was too painful. Perhaps she wanted to forget.

My listener nods. 'Don't think it's unusual. In my experience, it's more common than not. You count as an orphan – just because one parent survives doesn't mean they continue to parent the children. The children from the first marriage are the leftovers. It's unavoidable.'

He paused, then added thoughtfully, 'The girls find it harder than the boys. With boys, the loss is more natural – there's an element of competition between fathers and sons which leads to some form of natural estrangement. With a stepfather, the situation is the same, but at least it's normal – the competition is man to man. With girls, a father's instinct is to protect his daughters – that's the expectation – but with a stepfather, the instinct just doesn't crack in.'

Aunt Sadie's Apple Pie

There are eight different apple-pie recipes in my American grandmother's copy of *The Philadelphia Settlement Cook Book*, published around 1900. The almonds, an expensive luxury only available from the travelling spice merchant, make this suitable for a celebration.

SERVES 6 TO 8

Murbteig pastry
350g plain flour
50g sugar
½ teaspoon salt
250g unsalted butter
Yolks of 2 eggs
1 tablespoon brandy
4 tablespoons cold water

The filling
1 kg sharp green apples
25g unsalted butter
2 tablespoons raisins
1 tablespoon brandy
1 tablespoon blanched almonds (optional)

You will need a pie dish with hinged sides for the making of a deep pie.

Put the flour, sugar and salt into a bowl and cut in the butter with a knife. When your mixture is like fine breadcrumbs, mix all to a soft dough with the egg, the water and the brandy (the alcohol evaporates during the cooking and leaves the pastry short and crisp). Knead the pastry lightly with the tips of your fingers, adding more liquid if the mixture is too crumbly. Everything must be kept as cool as possible. The palms of the hands are too warm: using them will oil the dough and make it tough.

Put the pastry aside to rest while you peel, core and slice the apples. Fry the apples lightly in the butter. Meanwhile put the raisins to swell in the brandy for an hour or two, then mix them with the apples. Add the almonds if you are using them.

Preheat the oven to 220°C/425°F/Gas 7. Roll out ⅔ of the pastry and use this to line the pie dish. Roll out the remaining ⅓ into a circle to fit over the top. Fill the dish with the apple mixture. Damp the edges of the pastry. Lay on the lid and seal the edges by pressing them together with a fork. Decorate the lid. Make a hole for the steam to escape.

Bake for 45–55 minutes until the pastry is crisp and golden. Scatter thickly with caster sugar. Serve warm with whipped cream. Perfection after a fortifying soup.

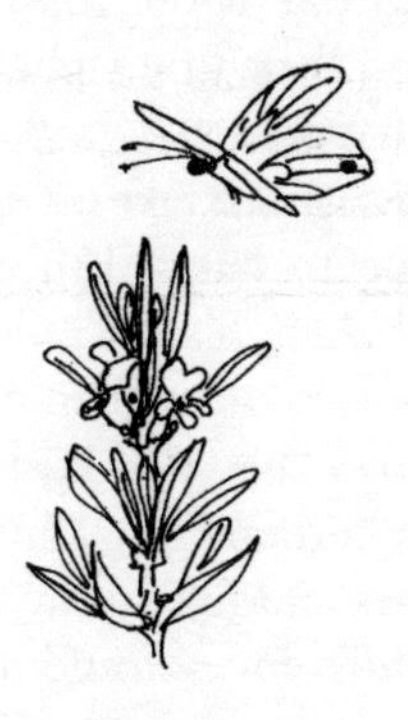

Postscript

'Wife-beating was a recognised right of man, and was practised without shame by high as well as low .... Similarly, the daughter who refused to marry the gentleman of her parents' choice was liable to be locked up, beaten and flung about the room, without any shock being inflicted on public opinion.'

GEORGE MACAULAY TREVELYAN, *History of England* (1926)

I DIDN'T HAVE AN EDUCATION, BUT I HAD THE GOOD SENSE TO MARRY one. Very different from my independent daughters and daughter-in-law, educated career makers, willing and able to make their own choices.

The battles they fight are not the ones we fought. My generation was taught to be wives and mothers, our duty was to support our man. Careers were for the unmarriageable by choice or circumstance – we couldn't hope to claim both. For that we had to break the mould. And that indeed is what we did. Mine was the generation that delivered the rights my daughters take for granted.

The Spaniards have a word for the enjoyment of maturity, *disfrutar*, enjoy the fruits. In Andalusia at feria time, it's the grandmothers who dance the fieriest rhumbas, the sexiest dance on earth. To the young as they pass by in the street, my wrinkles say I'm old. Not yet as old as the hills, but old enough to be somebody's granny. And they'd be right. Indeed I am a granny. Seven times over, as it happens.

At my age, if I were a man, I'd take a mistress. Blonde, brunette, redhead, whatever came to hand. I'm not a man. And desire doesn't make for desirable. Camilla de Martino, curvaceous blonde beauty a year or two older than me and merrily married to a much younger man, has no illusions about the options available to women of a certain age: 'Why worry? We could dress ourselves up to the nines and live in the centre of a big city, but it wouldn't make any difference, would it?'

Driving along a motorway in Tuscany with food writer Nancy Jenkins in an open sports car, we are wolf-whistled by a couple of Italian lorry drivers as they pass us in the fast lane. 'Just wait till they see our wattles,' said Nancy.

A decade or so ago, in the middle of Nicholas's philandering with Madeleine, I fell for a philanderer myself.

Golden hair, blue eyes, long-limbed and lean – one of those men you wonder about when you pass them in the street. Might even turn your head, like a man watching an unknown girl because in that single instant she's all he wants, and then walk on. There might even be a feeling of regret. A moment of wondering what it might have been like had he stopped and turned and something had happened between you.

That's not the way it is. Of course it's not. And then he turned, retraced his steps and stopped.

'We know each other, don't we?'

We'll call him Henry, a four-square English name that suits the man he is. He's married now, he wasn't then. Not that it matters. It didn't last. I told no one, and nor I trust did he.

We had met a year or two before, when I had an article to write in a sporting magazine on the state of salmon fishing on the Tweed. I arrived at the lodge – a turreted affair with many bedrooms and rented help – in time for breakfast. The gentlemen-fishermen were complaining of hangovers. Henry distributed his guests along the river bank. Two rods here, one there. The fish are running. To me he said, 'Here's your waders. Stick with me and don't fall over.'

After dinner that evening, he passed behind my chair and touched the nape of my neck. To an outside observer, the gesture would have meant nothing. There was no need for the fingertips to linger. But my skin had caught and held the print. I was astonished that so casual a physical contact could carry such a charge when every day in cities and crowded places we press against flesh and feel nothing except a flash of irritation at the touch of strangers.

Months later there was a reason for Henry to ring and suggest we meet for lunch.

We met and we talked.

He said, 'I know you're a good girl.'

How do you know?

'I found out – I like to find out these things about the women who interest me.'

Weeks later he rang me again. 'I have friends to stay for the weekend. You should come. I'll teach you to shoot.'

I had made up my mind.

Afterwards I said, 'You're a good lover. A very good lover. How do you know how it works?'

He smiled. 'It's there or it's not. You know or you don't. It's not something you can learn.'

I said, 'A shame. So much easier to say just a little to the left, up a bit, like moving the furniture.'

He smiled again, the skin tautening against my cheek: 'You'd be surprised how many women take lovers. It's only because you haven't been around, because you're a good girl, you don't know how often it happens.'

He paused. Then said, 'There's a woman in my life. I've been involved with her for months. She's married. She went back to her husband. Did I tell you?'

'No.' I had nothing to say. Then laughed and said, 'Is she a good girl too?'

'Perhaps. It doesn't matter. It's over. She lived with me for a time and then she left.'

Among the ivory-backed brushes and the silver dish with its little heap of crested cufflinks is a leather-framed photograph, a young woman with blue eyes and fair hair. The woman is lying like a discarded doll on a heap of cushions. She is dressed in a buttoned-up blue cotton dress, surrounded by toy animals, an armful imprisoned against her angular neck. Big eyes, a pouting mouth, child-woman.

I said, Is that her, the one who left you?

'Yes.'

How did it happen?

His face changed. 'It was casual at first. She was married and I was not. And then she came to me with her two young sons and said, "My husband knows about us. You know those telephone calls, when the caller rang off? That was him." '

So you took them in?

'Yes.'

Why did she change her mind? Go back to her husband?

'Women do that. You should know. You're a woman.'

What do I know? I'm not a woman who knows how to make a man do what I want.

The ending was inevitable, the parting sudden.

It had been easy for us to meet. He had given me the keys to his flat. I had meant to surprise him. The meal was the first I had cooked for us to share. I had chosen the dishes with care. The wine as well.

Henry ate quickly, without enjoyment. He had something to say: 'The girl I told you about. I saw her again last night.' A long pause. 'I'm sorry.'

The stem of the wine glass broke in my hand. It was only a small cut. It didn't hurt. But the redness of the blood and the redness of the wine shocked me.

I had no intention of weeping. Tears just happened. He handed me a handkerchief and said, 'I know you're angry. I don't know how I've hurt you. This doesn't help.'

He went to the door and held it open.

'You'd better go.'

I drove home along empty streets in the early dawn, driving slowly across the river as the mist lifted from the water and the gulls wheeled overhead. On the way home, I stopped for milky coffee at a workmen's café.

The household was still asleep. Nicholas had fallen into the habit of returning to the house whenever he pleased, came to bed without comment, slept late, had ceased to mind where I was or what I was doing. He had other things on his mind, affairs which were none of my business. We have been living parallel lives.

Later, after an hour or two at my desk, I left the house to finish my work at the library.

On my return, I found Nicholas reading the newspaper at the kitchen table. He watched me as I moved around the room, clearing the dishes, tidying the sink. There was something there which hadn't been there for months.

He said, 'I'm glad you're back. I missed you.'

'I missed you too,' I said. And it was true.

I travel to America as often as I can to keep company with my son and his family – daughter-in-law Frances and two little granddaughters. They spend the Independence Day holidays with France's folk, in a house rented by the family every year by the seaside in Maine.

The house is made of wood, a galleon in full sail against the rippling sea-grass and the darkness of the evergreens that rim the shoreline.

I'm not yet used to being one of a kind, not being one of a pair.

Sunny, windy days are followed by chilly nights. The house is full to the rafters with family. In the evening we cook up a paella with a broth made from lobster debris, steamer clams, curls of green garlic and imported chorizo packed in our New York luggage.

Beyond the deck in the early morning, an indigo ocean pulls back and forth on the midsummer tide. Along the rim, a white-gold shore curves from headland to headland in a long unbroken arc of glittering sea-wash, a rim of mother of pearl starred with little round sand dollars, tiny rooftops from the homes of long-dead sea-urchins.

My granddaughters play bucket-and-spade games with their little boy-cousin at the water's edge, digging holes and building castles, watched over by their parents and matching set of grandparents.

Close by, a pair of speckled brown sandpipers wade the shallows.

Further along, a lone fisherman casts a line. I leave my family group and walk towards the stranger.

Cautiously, I inspect the empty bucket. Fishermen are a private lot.

After a moment I say, 'What are you looking for?'

A long pause, cautious appraisal, then: 'Stripers.'

No further information offered, none requested.

I walk on.

Striped sea-bass are the shoreline's prize. The catch is monitored. I might well be an inspector, though my English accent should tell him I'm no such thing. Non-breeding fish of a certain length are permitted. You may take the fish which measure from nineteen to thirty inches, leaving the youngsters to reach a useful size and the breeding-stock to multiply.

The striper is a bony fish when young.

There's concern over diminishing fish stocks and the effect of global warming on the ocean currents.

'The storm in January changed the shoreline,' says another walker on the beach, a sturdy middle-aged woman who alters course to enquire if I'm enjoying the view.

At one end of the beach, a broad river mouth bisects the sands, creating a staging-post for the gulls. 'Black-backs. The mean kind of gull,' she adds, following my line of inspection. 'They'll attack if they're threatened.'

I ask her if the seabirds for which the nature reserve behind us was created – fairy and roseate terns – have nested successfully this year.

'I watched a flock of them only yesterday. They're here.'

Across the estuary, a patch of browning vegetation scars the headland, a line of well-grown pine trees dead on their feet in the sand.

'The storm hit right there. It felled a lot of the trees.'

'D'you think the climate's changing? Is that the general view?'

'Among some of us, for sure. For the rest – well, I walk past people's houses and they have the air conditioners going all day long and it's still the start of the summer. I feel like walking right up to the door and asking them what's in their minds.'

'But you don't?'

'It's up to them. Most folks don't see what's right in front of their noses. In the Appalachians they don't bother to dig for the coal any more, they just slice the top off the mountains and dump what they don't want in lakes. Slurry ponds, they're called. And the other day one of the walls broke and this horrible black stuff poured out and poisoned the river all the way down to Pittsburgh. Of course it's a worry. None of us want to leave our grandchildren a planet reduced to landfill.'

My feelings exactly. Chastened by the encounter, I return to my grandchildren at play in the clean pale sand.

These days, while my working life is in Wales, I sometimes find my way to London. The excuse is work commitments, but it's really so that I can catch up with the lives of my five beautiful London-based grandchildren.

Nearly fifty years on, there's been a flurry of interest around the 1960s. Veterans of the days of wine and roses – too much wine and not enough roses – have been leaving the planet in droves. Among the recently departed is Willie Donaldson, the man who had the good sense to back *Beyond the Fringe.* Not that it did him much good in the long run – or even the short run, owing to Willie's expensive tastes.

Better known in bestselling circles as prankster Henry Root, Willie is the subject of a much-praised biography by his old friend Terence Blacker.

Friendship with Willie was something of a mixed blessing. On his best behaviour he was the charming Cambridge graduate schooled at Winchester who treated ladies with perfect courtesy. On his worst behaviour he was the soft-underbelly low-life scumbag with the conscience of a sewer rat whose treatment of women was as bad as it gets.

You see the problem?

He's dead now. Of course he is. Surprising, say those who knew him, he made it as far as he did. Terrible habits, hooked on the hard stuff. Odd, considering the way he treated the women in his life, Willie was much lamented by his ladies. Terence's enthusiastic collaborators, many of them.

Many of them attend the party. This is held in a members-only theatrical club in Greek Street opposite a strip-joint that once housed The Establishment. Willie was not one of the founders of the club, though he could well have been.

Nicholas and Willie had the kind of relationship established by men who know rather too much about one another. Youthful indiscretions, whatever. Whenever they met – usually at my instigation – they circled each other much as a couple of urban foxes might when inadvertently arriving at the same dustbin.

I, on the other hand, had no reason not to enjoy Willie's company. And when I caught a glimpse of the tall, gaunt figure slouching down a Chelsea street, I'd greet him with enthusiasm and take him home to Nicholas to share his lunch. Not that either of them, it seemed to me, particularly appreciated my thoughtfulness.

I arrive at the party rather late – bedtime stories with my grandchildren overrule all other commitments – speeches are over and the gathering is settling down to some serious drinking. Those, that is, who aren't paid-up members of AA, of whom there are a surprising number. Alcoholic is the new black.

I push through the crowd, searching for familiar faces, people I might know from the days when we were all young and beautiful – or as beautiful as we would ever be.

In a crowd like this, familiar faces are likely to be familiar from the telly, and I'm too old a hand to take my chances. I find an unencumbered guest, vintage sixties, grey-haired, and ask him who he is. The London editor of *Penthouse*, says my new friend proudly. *Penthouse* Pets, remember them?

By repute, I answer politely. And what do you do now?

We have plans, says *Penthouse* wife, joining us for the conversation, for a travel-and-lifestyle magazine for swingers.

Swingers, eh? I haven't heard that word for years.

'It's for a new crowd, thirty-five-year-olds taking gap years. Believe me, they're up for anything.'

A bit like Willie, then.

'Sorry?'

Never mind.

Sarah Miles was one of Willie's women. I watch her from a distance. She's bird-boned, tiny, smooth-skinned, restless. Sarah spent two years with Willie. The woman who replaced her is Mrs Mouse. If Donaldson is to be believed, professional sex worker. Still is, says *Penthouse*, a man who knows a sex worker when he sees one.

Mrs Mouse looks very unlike a sex worker. She doesn't, I note in a moment of nostalgia for long-lost opportunities, even look like a Bluebell Girl. Grey hair carefully tinted blonde, trim, neat, skirt decorously on the knee, plain court shoes and cardie. As if she were a disapproving secretary about to take dictation.

Fenella Fielding has gone home. A pity. I was looking forward to a moment of reminiscence with the gravel-voiced diva who lived in the flat above Nicholas in Hyde Park Square. I imagine her little changed by the years.

She was, says *Penthouse*, all dressed in white and very splendid. Virginal, really. We agree there was always something virginal about Fenella. Fenella, as I remember, starred in a revue in the West End with which both Willie and Nicholas expected to make their fortune. The revue opened to disastrous reviews and that was that.

On my way to the party and knowing who might be present, I had wondered whether to remind Fenella of her brief but passionate liaison with Jeff Bernard when he was lodging in Nicholas's flat in Hyde Park Square. Since Jeff had taken up residence in the back bedroom at a time when I had a baby at the breast, the excitement, as far as I was concerned, was that the new arrangement might have included accommodating Jeff somewhere other than a bedroom sorely needed for the crib.

The liaison didn't last. Jeff had had to return to base and resort to my precious bottle of cooking brandy to drown his sorrows. He then popped his head in the gas oven and had to be rescued by Jonathan Miller, who happened to telephone Nicholas while Jeff was alone in the flat.

The situation, said Jonathan, was a cry for help since Jeff had turned off the gas in order to answer the phone. I wasn't convinced by the argument. Perhaps Jeff might have thought it was Fenella, ringing to invite him back. You see? We'd have had much to discuss.

I didn't at first recognize John Bassett, the man who brought the Cambridge Footlights Four to the Edinburgh Festival. And when I do and identify myself as Nicholas's missus – no need to give myself airs – he's anxious for appreciation.

'Have you read the book? Blacker says Jonathan Miller said I was his person from Porlock, the man who interrupted his medical career and turned him into what he is today.'

That explains it. I'd always wondered why Jonathan was who he now is.

My own memories of Jonathan go back to The Establishment. Actually, they're my *only* memories, unless you count passing each other in the foyer of a London hotel when Jonathan had just finished an interview about Peter Cook and I was on my way to do the same, hauled in, as usual, for the woman's view. And no, they didn't screen it. Not that I was indiscreet – absolutely not. Perish the thought.

What I do remember is walking down the street with Miller, Cook and Nicholas after the first London screening of Buñuel's *Viridiana* and arguing over whether the Spanish film-maker was or wasn't religious. The movie included a version of the Last Supper at which all the participants were either beggars, thieves or crooks. I maintained the film-maker was deeply religious, he just couldn't stand the Catholic Church. Jonathan said that was rubbish. He said it politely, of course. I rest my case.

I enquire why Bassett's white hair is trimmed at shoulder-length.

'I keep it like this for when I do the Queen.'

The Queen?

'I impersonate Her Majesty. The money's not great, but it pays the rent. I do a lot of supermarket openings.'

I bet you do.

Unprompted, he treats me to a sample, high-voiced and with a joke about Camilla. 'I don't do Camilla at openings. People believe I'm real.'

I explain I'm not a royalist, so I was sure I'd much prefer his version of the Queen to the Queen herself, particularly if it included jokes about Camilla.

I slip off to find the author. One should always buy the book at the publisher's party and have it signed.

Much had been made in reviews and interviews with Terence of Willie's deplorable lifestyle. Old Wykehamist and heir to a shipping fortune gone to the bad. Good money of course, though it didn't last. Willie's habits didn't come cheap. And anyway, he was easily bored. I'd noticed that myself.

Willie and Nicholas shared an uncertainty about their work as writers. I blame Professor Leavis. My experience of the great doctor and his wife Queenie – literary queen bees of Cambridge high life through the 1950s – is strictly second-hand. Buried among other autobiographical musings, Willie quotes the great doctor: 'A valid syllogism ... conveys the truth in both directions. Its conclusion refutes, or secures, its premises as much as vice versa.'

Obfuscation, or what?

Nevertheless, once you get a handle on Dr Leavis, you'll know that disobedience to any established principle leads to the conclusion that pigs can fly. Really you do.

And since everyone knows that pigs can't fly – I'm sure you get the picture – a philosophical truth which led Willie to conclude, as he put it himself, that the past can only be interpreted through the present.

In other words, what we think today changes what we think we thought yesterday. Which leads to the conclusion that all autobiography is, in Dr Leavis's judgement, a pack of lies. Which allows Willie the freedom to tell fibs. And the rest of us too, no doubt. A useful conclusion. Dr Leavis, like Mrs Mouse, is a lesson to us all.

Terence, Willie's biographer, was fresh from a round-table discussion of the book on Radio 4. Craig Brown, Willie's friend and admirer, had been poised by the telephone to join in.

'And then,' said Terence, 'they rolled on Richard Ingrams – never even rang Craig to let him know.' Outrageous, we agree, to give the saintly Ingrams his head. Richard never approved of Willie. Strong meat, Donaldson. Not a godly fellow, and that's the truth. You'd be unlikely to meet William at the heavenly gates. Unless, that is, the Almighty has a taste for jokers and a line in crack cocaine. In which case, join the group.

Later, back at my desk in Wales, a faint stench rises from somewhere around my feet. Fleur the cat has hidden a mouse. Or maybe a duckling. She's good at catching ducklings. Once caught, she loses interest. Fleur and Willie have that in common. And so, perhaps, did Nicholas.

Today, 14 September 2007, coming into autumn after a year when the summer has been as wet as anyone remembers, sunshine falls on water and woodland.

The house, beautiful Brynmerheryn on the edge of the Cambrian Mountains in wild west Wales, is nothing grand, but there's been a dwelling here for more than a thousand years. It's warm and snug in winter, airy in summer. This is shepherding country, self-sufficient and stoic, and the name of the house, hill of the seven-year-old wether, reflects, like so many others in the region, the way people live.

The sky is wide and deep over the moorland that surrounds the house. Sunbeams, dust-laden columns of golden light, fall through white clouds on to green pastures fringed with hedgerows thick with hazel and hawthorn. Rowanberries and rosehips blaze scarlet along the deep-cut lane, which links my house to the single track which leads in its turn to the main road which joins the two market towns, Tregaron and Aberystwyth, on which the community depends.

The two towns are very different.

Aberystwyth is a university centre, buzzy and cosmopolitan, with a vigorous theatre tradition. A fine new arts centre funded by Brussels overlooks the long line of the seafront, a holiday destination for Birmingham and the industrial Midlands.

Tregaron, a mere fifteen miles inland, remains heartland Wales, a market cross, Welsh-speaking to the core – two butchers, one with its own slaughterhouse, two pubs, a Spar, post office, tourist centre selling Welsh gold, garage, school, regular cattle auctions, much talk of the price of lamb and wool.

Isolated farmsteads populate the uplands. The land itself is tousled and innocent, like a child just risen from sleep, with wide swathes of uncultivatable marshland and barren hillsides steeper than even a sheep can climb.

I've lived at Brynmerheryn now for eighteen years – in this neighbourhood no more than the blink of an eye – long enough to feel myself at home. Neighbours are kind. For the ease with which we were accepted into the community, I have to thank my neighbours, the Edwardes family – particularly those of my own generation, grandparents themselves, Will and Jane.

Will, born three-quarters of a century ago in a now-ruined farmhouse just across the woodland which adjoins the house, owns the sheep which crop the pastures which surround us. From the time we arrived, Jane and Will took on the troublesome task of guiding us through what's expected of residents round here. Pitfalls are minor: don't tell a sheepfarmer how to care for his stock. Pleasures are simple: the Red Lion in Bont is a tougher bar crowd than the Black. Practical advice was welcome: which of the farms around would sell us milk and eggs or fix the vehicle when it falls apart.

Nicholas's ashes now give vigour to a pair of newly planted apple trees – as a dedicated conservationist, I assume he approves, and if he doesn't, no doubt the trees won't thrive.

Today the rain and sun have brought a crop of fungi to my lawn, among them fairy ring, a good mushroom to dry for soup. The blue tits are busy on the rowanberries and the new-cut hay is ready for my rake. Yesterday, Will and his grandson brought up the tractor and mowed my wildflower meadow, an autumn chore for which, as with fallen trees and other hazards outside the house, I depend on him for neighbourly help.

The Cambrians seem sometimes close at hand, at other times retreat to a distance. Today, each rock and gully is sharp as needles. I have spent the day raking and picking up the hillocks of feathery meadow debris – no use for sheep fodder, says Will, so next year I shall either improve the flower quota by plugging in home-grown ragged robin and corncockles, or look for another crop than meadow-grass: potatoes, oats, hemp, whatever will survive.

Creatures displaced after the mowing are a hatch of baby frogs no bigger than a thumbnail, a single newt with black skin and golden belly patches, two fat grey fieldmice with shoe-button eyes and stumpy tails, a nest of naked baby shrews and, every time I scrape the rake, more earwigs than there are fleas on a barnyard rat.

I pile the hay on the nettle patches at either end of the garden where I hope it will eventually become manure. The two gardening-ladies who come in once a month can decide what to do with the debris. Maybe it might work as a mulch. I need mulch to keep down the tangled growth round the dewponds. Dewponds, as their name suggests, are refilled from the skies: an uncertain situation in summer, infallible in winter.

Wednesday is cooking-day with photographer Clare Richardson for a series in a magazine. Autumn's gatherings provide the raw material: cepes drying on a flat basket woven from vine trimmings, sloes to put in the freezer for sloe gin, damsons from the neighbour's overladen trees, misshapen windfall apples, blackberries from the overgrown corners of the garden, blueberries from the edge of the young woodland, hazelnuts from the banks of the dewponds.

We drop everything on the long table of weathered golden oak. My workspace is a barn converted to an artist's studio by Monica Rawlins. Monica was a friend of Augustus John, who encouraged her to set up home in the house, and paint. Monica left us the house and I work in what was once her studio. I have added shelves for my library at one end, work-desk in the middle, while the debris of the household piles up everywhere else.

Clare makes her way up and down the table, photographing at random. Meanwhile I crop the little that's left in the garden: courgettes and their flowers, potatoes – nothing fancy, supermarket sprouters (next year I must earth them up so the top layer doesn't go green). Summer's heat has produced a fine crop of cut-and-come-again Mediterranean herbs. Marjoram, rosemary, sage all thrive in the stony soil.

Yesterday, thinking the weather was turning cold, I filled up the log basket and lit a fire. The scent of woodsmoke fills me with happiness. When I was a child, I relied on scent more than I did on any other sense.

My grandchildren have come to visit for the half-term holiday. My children's children, as were their parents before them, are undiluted joy. We cook together, eat together, learn together. The kitchen plot would win no prizes, but it's enough to teach a grandchild how things grow. We gather nuts and berries from the hedgerows, fungi from the woods, attend the birth of lambs and shearing of sheep.

There's an old saying round here: when you have children, plant trees; when you have grandchildren, plant oaks. Seven years ago, in the hundred-acre wood behind the house, a thousand oaks took root. Not enough to change the world. But it's a start.

STILL LIFE

KLIPFISK, CLOUDBERRIES AND LIFE AFTER KIDS

When her children flew the nest, Elisabeth Luard decided it was time to discover new worlds, beyond the family. As a prize-winning food writer, Elisabeth Luard chose to explore through her cookery. Guided by a trail of enticing aromas and flavours, Luard travels from kitchen to field to restaurant, taking us on a journey which criss-crosses the globe, from the gastronomic delights of the Bosphorus to life in the Arctic circle and the glitzy cuisine of Hollywood.

Full of the sparkling anecdotes of the people she meets, and scattered with exotic recipes picked up along the way, Elisabeth Luard provides a window into fragile, often vanishing, ways of life as she explores new countries through the kitchens, market places and traditions of the locals. Funny, uplifting and insightful, *Still Life* offers a fresh look at the world outside the family.

'Birth, death, life, nourishment, mystery, company: once again, it's all here'
THE TIMES

'Luard writes like a greedy angel'
GUARDIAN

'Elisabeth Luard is one of the greatest food writers of recent times'
ANTONY WORRALL THOMPSON, DAILY EXPRESS

ALSO AVAILABLE BY ELISABETH LUARD

FAMILY LIFE

BIRTH, DEATH AND THE WHOLE DAMN THING

A BBC Radio 4 Book of the Week

Not everyone keeps an eagle owl in the spare bedroom cupboard, plays chess for the French Foreign Legion, or goes to school on an obstinate donkey. But this was all just a day in the life of the four Luard children. For the Luards, growing up as their family travelled across Europe, life was a series of adventures. Yet no family is immune to tragedy, and in Francesca, the eldest of three daughters, we find a true heroine. Honest, perceptive and passionate, she tells her own story – until she can tell it no more.

Full of anecdotes and peppered with their favourite recipes, *Family Life* is an extraordinary story of joy, grief and, above all – love. Elisabeth Luard gives a truthful and moving mother's account of their unconventional, unforgettable tale.

'Unspeakably moving ... She deserves a medal'
THE TIMES

'Books can be good, bad or patchy, but there are some that you will never forget. Elisabeth Luard's belongs in the last category'
INDEPENDENT

'One of the most powerful accounts you will ever read of a mother's love for her child'
DAILY MAIL

B L O O M S B U R Y